# On The Ground in the 30s

Paul Taylor

# ON THE GROUND IN THE THIRTIES

**PAUL TAYLOR**
Preface by Clark Kerr

➔P

Gibbs M. Smith, Inc.
Peregrine Smith Books
Salt Lake City
1983

First Edition 1983

Copyright © 1983
Gibbs M. Smith, Inc.
Peregrine Smith Books
PO Box 667
Layton, UT 84041

Manufactured in the
United States of America

Book Design by
J. Scott Knudsen

ISBN 0-87905-142-6

**Library of Congress
Cataloging in Publication Data**

Taylor, Paul Schuster, 1895-
  On the ground in the 30s.

    Bibliography: p.
    Includes index.
    1. Agricultural laborers–California–History–20th
century–Sources. 2. Agricultural laborers–West (U.S.)–
History–20th century–Sources. 3. Agriculture–Economic
aspects–California–History–20th century–Sources.
4. Agriculture–Economic aspects–West (U.S.)–History–
20th century–Sources. 5. Depressions–1929–United
States–History–Sources. I. Title.
HD1527.C2T39  1983    338.1′09794    83-19542
ISBN 0-87905-142-6

# Contents

# PREFACE

Paul S. Taylor came to my attention because he was the only faculty member around who had the slightest interest in what then interested me. This was during the academic year 1932-33. I was then a graduate student at Stanford working for an M.A. degree. I had chosen for my thesis topic a study of the self-help cooperatives then operating in California as an effort by the unemployed to support themselves and do so with self-respect. This involved extensive field work; and it gave me a chance to get close to some of the human impacts of the Great Depression. Faculty members at Stanford were tolerant about, but totally uninterested in my thesis topic. As with so many economists at that time and even more so since, direct contact with reality was not just not at all attractive to them but actually repulsive.

I heard of a professor at Berkeley who did have an interest in and, in fact, had already made some field trips to see these cooperatives. This professor was Paul Taylor, and I went over to Berkeley to talk with him. Because of him, and also the advice of my major professor at Swarthmore, Clair Wilcox, who kept writing to me that Berkeley was a far better place to be than Stanford (and at that time it was), I transferred as soon as I could to Berkeley. This then led to assisting Paul during the cotton picker's strike in the fall of 1933, as well as with continuing studies of the self-help cooperatives.

Paul never gave me but two instructions: (1) to record what people said in their own words; and (2) to send him my notes as soon as possible. The reward was that he read these notes carefully and enjoyed them immensely.

I did not then fully realize to the extent I do now how rare a professor Paul really was. He has belonged to a very unusual breed of what might be called economic anthropologists with an interest in labor problems. These economic anthropologists made contact with reality, not through somebody else's statistics or through documents, but by talking with people and by thinking about what they heard. This small group also may be said to have included Carleton Parker (*The Casual Laborer and Other Essays*), Paul's predecessor at Berkeley; Thorstein Veblen (*The Instinct of Workmanship*); Stanley Mathewson (*Restriction of Output Among Unorganized Workers*); Elton Mayo (*The Human Problems of an Industrial Civilization*); E. Wight Bakke (*The Unemployed Worker*); and a very few others. How Paul developed this approach I have never really known.

Presumably he did not get it at Wisconsin, where the "institutionalists" were then in a dominant position, for their emphasis was upon organizations and upon documents. I have guessed, however, that it came, at least in part, from where I got my sympathy for this approach: out of a rural background that made one want to be in contact with the hard facts, made one want to be "on the ground" where things were happening.

Scholars like Paul create the too few bridges to reality; bridges that cross those broad moats with the armchair theorists in their crenalated castles on one side and the everyday life of the market places on the other. Paul recognized important new developments before there were any statistics about these developments, and he collected information with far greater depth of meaning than statistics by themselves could ever provide. Unfortunately, he never made contact with mainstream economics. This was the fault of mainstream economics and helps to explain its rigidities and its abstractions—the theorists were not interested and were not listening. Paul was always out there finding out what was really happening while others played around with their theoretical models and ran their regression analyses. He leaves behind, not another model or two or a few statistical calculations, but, rather, some totally irreplaceable accounts of historical reality; of how it actually was when history was being made.

*Clark Kerr*
*Berkeley, California*
*October 1982*

# INTRODUCTION

For me, field work on the ground began in 1927. As an economics major at the University of Wisconsin, I had found that to study labor meant to study organized labor. Seeking an outlet for my interest in research in California where I had come after World War I, I found labor in the important agricultural industry to be conspicuous but unorganized and generally unstudied. The Committee on Scientific Aspects of Human Migration of the Social Science Research Council gave me an opportunity to investigate the field. I received a grant, first for six months, later expanded to three years, to study Mexican immigration which had close links with labor on the land. Immigration from Europe had been interrupted by the 1914-18 war and Congress had barred Asians in 1924. Mexican immigration was increasing. For three years I crossed the country, searching out regions where Mexicans worked in agriculture or industry.

I learned my first lesson close to home in California. On the advice of a member of the agricultural extension service and overlooking the importance of seasonal migration, I got into my car early in February and drove to Napa Valley. There I found no Mexicans. I had come too soon. Mexican workers, landless and seasonal, would not find employment in Napa vineyards until summer. So I turned back and headed southward.

When I reached Imperial Valley on the Mexican border what I saw hit me in the face. I found myself in the midst of an agricultural society with a labor pattern the opposite of all that as a youth I had known in the Middlewest. Production was highly organized by American managers employing Mexican workers off and on to meet seasonal needs. Mexicans constituted more than one-third of the valley population. They were separated from the American population in domicile, in the schools, and in employment status. For them there was no "agricultural ladder." In 1926, a quarter of a century after Colorado river water flowed into the valley, only six Mexicans had become owners of farm land, with a total assessed value of $5,910, and improvements valued at $600. Mexicans and Americans, I concluded, "live socially in two worlds."

I then followed the Mexican migration into Colorado, Texas, Illinois, Michigan, and Pennsylvania. A Guggenheim grant enabled me to study in Jalisco, Mexico, the original home of many of the immigrants.

My academic colleagues did not uniformly endorse such prolonged absence from the classroom. My economics department chairman told the university president not to grant my request for additional time to complete the writeup of the research results. "Now is the time to get back into the center of your field," he cautioned me. "What is the center of my [labor economics] field?" I asked. "Workmen's compensation," he replied. Fortunately the president accepted my view; he gave me another semester free of teaching to write the results of my investigation for publication.

Even so, the way was not wholly clear. When one of my completed monographs came off the university press and was laid on the desk of the then president—an astronomer by profession—word came through his secretary that the president had "gone up to the ceiling and stayed there all morning." About that time the United States Department of Agriculture announced the availability of new research funds. The agriculture college dean so informed me and encouraged me to apply for funds to support my work. The next time when I saw him, however, he informed me that he had seen the president and now advised me not to apply.

University press funds met the printing costs of much faculty research including my monographs on Mexican labor. A dean of the graduate division—another astronomer—had taken a hand in making these funds available to faculty members in the budget. They were not unlimited, of course, as the continuing submission to the press of my monographs made evident. My application for more funds from the faculty publications committee brought the issue to a head. Invited to appear in person before the committee in charge of the funds, I was questioned whether publication of the first 100 typed pages presenting the history of Mexican labor in South Texas could not be eliminated without injury to my research. My response was that the past is related to the present, and that in my monograph knowledge of the past contributed to an understanding of the present Mexican migration. As a practical solution, the Social Science Research Council arranged publication by the press of another university, and I obtained funds for further publication of my research from a private benefactor.

Then came the era of the Great Depression. When it really took hold in the early thirties, Mexicans left the United States in large numbers. Relief agencies in cities frequently paid the railroad fare to ship them home to Mexico.

For those who remained and for others of various nationalities working in agriculture, farm wages dropped sharply. Labor unrest grew, especially in California. Acutely strained relations between workers and employers built up to a climax in the 1933 cotton pickers' strike in the San Joaquin Valley. It was the largest strike by agricultural laborers in the nation's history, before or since.

The New Deal administration, only recently come into office, took steps to meet the crisis by creating a commission to hold public hearings on the site of the strike as a means of ending violence and bringing peaceful settlement. Members of the commission came from academic and religious institutions.

Asked to assist the commission as a consultant, expenses paid, I brought with me a graduate student, Clark Kerr. We sought to help the commission find a compromise acceptable to strikers and growers. Together we documented the strike from oral and local press sources. The opportunity was rich because special interest had not yet sought to control publicity.

We found no academic channels available to publish our report. Seven years passed until the LaFollette Committee of the United States Senate, in the course of its investigation of "violations of free speech and the rights of labor," printed the document. It is included in this volume, together with a later article entitled "Uprisings on the Farms."

Natural disasters as well as human conflict marked the mid-thirties. Drought and depression on the Great Plains, which I had seen first-hand in North Dakota in 1934, unloosed a high tide of refugees bound for irrigated California and the West. They flooded the labor market in agriculture. Searching for employment they zigzagged up and down irrigated valleys from crop to crop and from one operation to another. Job opportunities were meager compared to the numbers desperately seeking work. Yet fresh competitive chances came to each individual with each change of season and each shift from one locality to another.

Again I was given opportunity for contemporary research. In 1935 the California Emergency Relief Administration employed me, and my University freed me, to undertake field research designed to help in shaping public action toward this human tide. My research team included, beside persons trained in economics, a photographer in the person of Dorothea Lange, later to become my wife. The aim was to include visual as well as verbal and numerical evidence in support of the expected recommendation of action to meet the problem. The culmination of this assignment was the construction of a chain of sanitary camps for migrant families working in agriculture. The Resettlement Administration of the federal government took over responsibility for the camps from the state Relief Administration, and in time with Congressional support, expanded their number across the country.

Then the Social Security Board, under Congressional mandate, asked for study of the administrative feasibility of extending social security benefits to the widely dispersed laborers in agriculture. By this time Dorothea Lange was on the payroll of the Resettlement Administration (later known as the Farm Security Administration). The head of its photography unit, Roy Stryker, arranged with Thomas Blaisdell, of Social Security, for us to travel in the field together. We each were paid about $15 a day and expenses, sufficient to enable us to cross the Far West, the Middlewest, and the South from Texas to Florida.

The fruits of these researches on contemporary problems of the thirties were habitually recorded in field reports to administrators, in government publications such as the Monthly Labor Review, in pamphlets, in Congressional hearings, and occasionally in public addresses. In this volume are two talks on the contemporary problem of people on the land, delivered before the Commonwealth Club of California. Also reprinted are two reports to the Social Security Board. Besides, I wrote articles for the *Survey Graphic*, whose editor, Paul Kellogg, had gone from New York to Dimmit County in Texas to share with me a first-hand look at Mexican immigration. Years later he gave Dorothea Lange and me the title "American Exodus" for our then forthcoming book in which we distilled the essence of our work in the thirties.

My methods of researching human problems on the land were not beyond criticism from scholars or within or outside government. Particularly it came from statisticians. My answer at the time was made in the preface to a recording of field observations made as I crossed the northern Middlewest from Nebraska to the Dakotas and Iowa, observing the effects of mechanization, drought, depression and experimentation in cooperative farming.

Land Policy Review, a government publication of that day, printed my field reports on this area under the title "Nonstatistical Notes from the Field," adding the comment on my method of work: "He is not interested in averages, he says. He is interested in people." My own answer was in these words: "I'm not interested for the moment in averages. . . . I'm looking for trends, and don't want to cancel out the very item where I think I see the future foreshadowed by history, by averaging it with another whose future had not yet struck." This was my guide to learning the fundamentals of what was happening on the ground in the thirties from South to North and from coast to coast.

For me, an academic background was laid on the eve of World War I as a student at the University of Wisconsin. In a field called economics I found three professors of special importance to me. John R. Commons, with his students, studied past and current efforts of workers to organize and to meet their problems with government help. Richard T. Ely studied the place of the legal institutions known as property and contract in solving society's social and economic problems. E.A. Ross in the economics department, under the title "sociologist," was concerned with the problems of people. All three stirred the interest of students at the ground level.

*Paul S. Taylor, 1982*

# MEXICANS NORTH OF THE RIO GRANDE

The Mexicans are here—from California to Pennsylvania, from Texas to Minnesota. They are scattered on isolated sections along our western railroads in clusters of from two to five families; they are established in colonies in the agricultural West and Southwest which form, in places, from one- to two-thirds of the local population. They have penetrated the heart of industrial America; in the Calumet steel region on the southern shore of Lake Michigan they are numbered in thousands; in eastern industrial centers by hundreds. And they have made Los Angeles the second largest Mexican city in the world.

With the stoppage of European immigration and the increased labor demands of the war, the trickle of Mexican immigrants enlarged to a stream which ran its course for a decade. In what follows, it should be understood that the statements about Mexicans refer to this whelming labor class migration, not to Mexicans, in general, nor to Mexican culture in Mexico. Variety and contradiction characterize the situations arising in different areas in the United States. There is hardly a statement I shall make, or an illustration I shall give, but that its opposite has been observed, and a whole series of gradations in between.

Traditionally the growing of cotton connoted mud, mules, and Negroes. Just so today the irrigation ditch stands for intensive agriculture, hand labor, and Mexicans. In Imperial Valley, California, they thin lettuce in the fall, and from December to March, they cut it by hand for shipment so that the cities of the East may have fresh salads in mid-winter. From the middle of May to July, Mexicans with eyes keen to judge the ripeness of melons work under the hot sun at high speed, picking at 15 cents a crate cantaloupes to be consumed by Chicago, New York, or St. Louis. By mid-July the majority of the Mexican families have left for the grape harvest in the San Joaquin Valley.

In the Salt River Valley of Arizona, irrigated from the reservoir of the famous Roosevelt Dam, long staple Pima cotton has been grown on an increasing scale for the past fifteen years. Beginning in September some thousands of Mexican families annually are shipped in from California and Texas to pick cotton until January or February. In the spring many of these families drift away; others remain for the lettuce and vegetable harvest, and the cantaloupes which ripen just at the close of the season in Imperial Valley.

In the Winter Garden of south Texas, in November and December, Mexican men, women, and children, on hands and knees, transplant Bermuda onions. With a short forked stick as a tool they make a hole, set the plant, and tamp it; they achieve incredible speed, and at from 6 to 8 cents per acre row (157 feet), with plants three inches apart, they frequently earn $2 or even more a day. From January to to March they cut spinach and carrots and tie them into bundles; in April and early May they pull onions, pile them into windrows, clip off the roots and tops with sheep shears, grade, and crate them.

In central, west, and south Texas, the westward movement of cotton has been sustained by Mexican labor. A line drawn from northwest of Corpus Christi on the Gulf, to San Antonio, thence northward through Austin to Dallas marks roughly the western fringe of the so-called black belt. West and south of this, Mexicans play the role in cotton traditionally played by Negroes. They are the tenant farmers—sharecroppers on halves if they furnish only their labor and that of their families, with larger shares for themselves if they furnish teams, tools, and seed. In this region there are white American tenants too. They are in competition with the Mexicans for farms, and in the eyes of some landlords the lower living standards of the Mexicans are an asset in the competition. Said one proprietor of seven hundred acres of cotton land:

*I would rather have Mexican tenants than either Negroes or whites. You can't tell the whites so well what to do. They think they are on an equality with you and they want to live in a house about like you do. They are always wanting better clothes and more provisions. The Mexicans have bigger families and more labor to get out a big crop. If the Mexicans learn English they don't work so well; if they get educated a little they don't make such good farm hands.*

A large part—probably the majority—of the Mexican population is migratory. It is the most mobile element in our labor supply. It moves in seasonal cycles covering hundreds, even thousands of miles.

A Mexican family I met in south Texas during the onion harvest two years ago had come to the United States in 1920. Entering at Laredo, its working members began by grubbing brush to clear land near San Antonio. Shortly they set out (with the entire family, of course) for Belton, Texas. There they secured employment in a cotton-seed-oil factory where an uncle had preceded them. When work gave out they went to Fort Worth, and from there shipped to the beet fields near Billings, Montana. The next season they worked in sugar beets near Casper, Wyoming, wintered in Denver, and worked the following season in the beet fields of Colorado. In 1927 they "came out with $15 and an old car to Raton, New Mexico." When they got there they were broke; so they went to work in a local coal mine, and stayed for a year. In the fall of 1928 they drove to Texas, picked cotton until the season closed, and followed the stream of laborers to the Winter Garden to try their luck at transplanting onions. The wanderings of individual Mexicans over a period of years may thus appear more or less erratic, but they usually follow one or another of the seasonal swirls.

The Southwest is the great reservoir of migratory Mexican labor. It winters there, or across the line in Mexico. Throughout the postwar years the pull of the labor market of Wyoming and Pennsylvania was felt on the *mesa central* of Mexico, six or eight hundred miles below the Rio Grande. On the river, El Paso, Laredo, and Nogales form a secondary tier of labor centers— gateways to the United States. Every spring from San Antonio, Fort Worth, Kansas City, Albuquerque, Phoenix, Los Angeles, and latterly from Chicago, St. Louis, Omaha, Denver, Sacramento, and in smaller numbers from a score of other cities, Mexicans are gathered up by *los enganchistas* and shipped out for a summer's work on the tracks at from 35 to 40 cents an hour in Nevada, Dakota, Kansas, Illinois, Ohio, or Pennsylvania, for with the spring the railroads resume maintenance and construction work. Skeleton section crews are augmented, and large extra gangs of fifty, sixty or more Mexican *solos* are organized for special projects. These men live in the converted boxcars so familiar to all who travel, rolling from job to job, working in places remote or near, town or desert, strumming their guitars of an evening, and singing their Mexican songs.

In May, the sugar beets of the North need thinning—and the Mexicans of the Southwest are called upon to furnish their quota of hand laborers, as the German-Russians who preceded them are no longer immigrating. For this work families—families as large as possible—are wanted. They are transported by the train load to the Arkansas and South Platte Valleys and the western slope of Colorado, to Wyoming, Idaho, Montana, Nebraska, Dakota, Iowa, Minnesota, and Michigan. When they reach the beet fields they are scattered out on the farms, each family under contract to tend its allotted fields at from $23 to $25 an acre. A single Mexican tends ten acres or more in a season; families contract two, three, or more times ten acres, depending on the number of workers (men, women, and children) there are in the family. In May and June, beets are blocked and thinned. Time presses, and hours are long, perhaps twelve per day on the average. Women and children help although the Mexican men do not work them so long or so hard as the German-Russians. In July and August there is hoeing, and in September comes topping, lasting through October and into November. The beets are loosened by a machine lifter, pulled up by the tops by hand, piled in windrows; the tops are struck off by blows with a large knife, and the beets are hauled away to dumps for weighing and thence to the factory where they are made into sugar. In the winter the tide of beet workers, like that of the railroad laborers, recedes. But an increasing number stay on, responding to the stimulation of beet farmers or of sugar companies who offer houses rent free, or opportunities to build in colony tracts. In the valley of the South Platte, in northeastern Colorado, the number of Mexican families so remaining rose in six years from 537 to 2084. Other families winter in increasing numbers in the cities of the North. Many drift into industry, particularly in Detroit.

Mexican labor off for the melon fields in the Imperial
Valley, June 1935. *Photo: Dorothea Lange.*

This old Imperial Valley farm laborer helped drive the
French from Mexico, fought against Maxmillian, and
served the crops for many years, March 1935. *Photo:
Dorothea Lange.*

The maturing cotton crop puts wheels under Mexican labor in Texas. They come down the Rio Grande in late June and July to Brownsville to chop and pick the first cotton of the season. In July and August seemingly most of the Mexicans of the state converge on Corpus Christi. Here on the flat Gulf coastal plain huge tracts of land have been planted to cotton; the young fields have been "chopped," i.e., thinned by hoeing to a proper stand of plants, by Mexicans, and now await the army of pickers which from far and near mobilizes at "Corpus." They used to come by train and by wagon; now they come by auto and truck, loaded with camp equipment. As the cotton season opens in other parts of the state, the Mexicans move on. Guided by the United States Employment Service, by the experience of other years, by correspondence with farmers, and by their own grapevine telegraph, they take to the highways by single families, groups of families, or by caravans led by *contratistas* who know enough English and have sufficient initiative and experience to take the lead in finding employment and making labor contracts for the others. The contractor weighs the cotton in the field, and as he is paid by the bale, the more pickers in his gang, the more he makes. At San Antonio the stream of pickers divides. Some work westward with the cotton to San Angelo and Sweetwater. Others make their way northward by stages to Taylor and Waco, thence west to Dallas and across west Texas even as far as Amarillo in the panhandle. By the latter part of the year the cotton of the state is harvested, and the cycle of migration is closed by the return of the Mexicans to the places they call home.

A similar flow and ebb recurs annually in California. In May the Mexicans move northward from Imperial Valley. They "follow the fruit," thinning apricots and peaches, advancing as the season advances. They are joined by those who have delayed in order to harvest the cantaloupes, and together with thousands of Mexicans from all over southern California they surge northward to practically all the valleys of the state. Most of them ascend the ridge of the Tehachapi and pour over into the great Valley of California. In cars of all makes and all ages, used Fords predominating, with the entire family inside and the washtub and lantern tied on outside, they move along the highways, stopping in the hot sun by the roadside to repair blowouts, on grades to let the engine cool, or under eucalyptus trees to camp for the night.

From June to August the Mexicans are busy thinning fruit; then picking fruit. They work in the San Joaquin Valley, around Bakersfield, Hanford, and Fresno, or they cross the Pacheco Pass to Hollister and Gilroy; they invade the Santa Clara Valley at the southern end of San Francisco Bay, and tongues of the flood pass on northward to the Napa Valley above the bay, and up the Sacramento Valley into the northern interior of the state.

In late August the grape harvest, centering in Fresno, sucks in to its vineyards Mexicans who have been dispersed in the fruit, together with fresh recruits from over the ridge to the south, some even from the states lying southeast of California. Mexicans, Japanese, Filipinos, "whites" from California, Texas, and Oklahoma, a few Indians from the mountains, Negroes, and still fewer Chinese and Hindus all enroll in the army of pickers which strips the vines. In the orchards under the fruit trees, down on the river banks, by the roadside or in the town park, in tents on the ranches of their employers, with or without tents elsewhere—sometimes as well without because of the heat—with or without water and sanitary facilities at hand, amid clouds of flies, you can see them preparing their *tortillas* and *frijoles* over open fireplaces or on portable stoves, and heating large galvanized iron tubs of water in which to do the family washing.

By the end of September, leaving a large nucleus to finish the grape harvest, the pickers begin to scatter. Many return to Los Angeles and southern California for urban employment, and for the walnut and citrus harvests; others return to Imperial Valley for the oncoming lettuce season or for cotton picking. The expansion of cotton in the San Joaquin Valley extends the season of employment in that region, and with the additional attractions of weatherproof housing and school facilities which are increasingly provided, operates to increase its year-round Mexican population. But most of the tide which moved across the Tehachapi recedes southward during the fall, and winters in southern California. In February, probably 80 percent or more of the Mexican population of the state is found there.

The American public has known that, since the war, Mexicans have been playing an important role in these hand labor operations of our modern agriculture, but it has been less generally realized that important nuclei of Mexican immigrants are found in the industrial centers of the Middlewest and the East. The largest employer of Mexican labor I came across in my field studies is located on the southern shore of Lake Michigan.

Here the Mexicans followed the immigrant European and even the migrant Negro. Most of them are still on the lowest rung of the ladder, but appreciable numbers are rising to the ranks of the semi-skilled, some drawing wages of $6 and $7 a day.[1] They show capacities seldom attributed to them by their agricultural employers. Mexicans entered the basic industries of the Chicago-Calumet region during and just after the war. With the economic slump of 1921 they almost disappeared from industrial payrolls in the North. A return movement set in strongly by 1923, stimulated by labor recruiting in the Southwest, and it is these recruits, in common with the general run of wage earners in the northern centers, who have been caught in the present unemployment. Mexicans form a large proportion of track laborers of the

Chicago-Calumet area; signs in Spanish advertising track work are general on Canal and Madison Streets, and Mexicans are conspicuous among those sauntering by, or loitering before offices, who are fair game for the "man-catchers." They form an important element in the common labor supply of the steel mills, rising in one case to 30 percent. To a lesser extent than in steel they are found in the packing industry. In considerable numbers Mexicans work in Michigan, not only in the beet fields, but in the automobile and other industries of that state. Small outpost colonies of two hundred, four hundred, or perhaps more each are scattered through the principal steel centers as far east as Ohio, Pennsylvania, New York, and New Jersey.

The story of Mexican labor in the United States might almost be told from the types of housing which characterize its settlements. I am not referring to the pathology of housing—all too often the laborers are poor, and their houses in accord with their purses; their families are large and their houses crowded— but I am speaking of the anatomy of housing.

Close along the border—not generally, but in some of the byways of south Texas, along the Rio Grande, in a place or two in Imperial Valley, one will find grass huts, which add the charm of the subtropical to an American landscape. Perhaps the house is made of mesquite, mud-plastered on the inside, its rough surface carrying the marks of the sweep of the hand of the *peon* and his wife who built it in two weeks time, ten years ago. It is roofed with grass or *tule* sewed to the rafters; the light, bark-covered timbers of the frame are bound together by strips of cactus which harden and hold like buckskin thongs. The floors are of dried mud, swept clean. Here are people migrating, and figuratively, like the turtle, carrying their distinctive culture pattern with them in the housing over their backs.

More widespread are the earth-brown adobes of El Paso Valley, New Mexico, and Arizona, almost indigenous to those parts of the Southwest, literally growing up out of the soil. Clusters of them have appeared farther north in the past few years, where the beet-workers— Mexicans from Old Mexico, and Spanish Americans from New Mexico—have erected them with their own hands in the Arkansas and South Platte Valleys of Colorado. There they stand in rows, out in the midst of the fields, mute but eloquent evidence of the penetration of Indo-Spanish into North-European culture.

Most of the housing of Mexican laborers, however, is not culturally so distinctive. Its class character is clearer, located in the poorest parts of town and crowded on small lots usually relieved by flowers in the yard. At the start, they may resort for building materials to flattened oil cans, cardboard cartons, lumber discarded in repairing boxcars, or other refuse of American economic life. Generally this is but a way station to something better. I recall one house which told plainly the story of its builder's aspirations. The first floor was patched

Mexican gang labor working a cantaloupe field in Imperial Valley, June 1938. *Photo: Dorothea Lange.*

This old adobe—said to be over a hundred years old at the time—housed four families of agricultural workers in Guadalupe, November 1939. *Photo: Division of Immigration and Housing.*

together almost entirely of short pieces of wood from what had been packing boxes; the exterior of the second room, added later, was of drop-siding; the third room, under construction, was of stucco. When the housing of immigrant Mexicans rises to the level of that of resident American wage earners, it of course attracts less attention. As a whole, the approximation of this standard proceeds very slowly, for reasons of poverty and of difference in cultural aims. But notable improvements in individual cases and even in whole communities are significant.

Where housing is provided by employers it bears an occupational stamp. The converted boxcars which shelter railway extra-gangs tell their own tale; so too the dismounted boxcar, which is being replaced along the right of way in the Southwest by rectangular concrete or hollow tile houses which accommodate several families, each allotted two rooms. On the plantation farms of south Texas the broad fields which comprise the landscape are interrupted occasionally by groups of two-room rough lumber houses, often row upon row, one like the other, twenty, thirty, sixty of them.

In the industrial centers of the Middlewest and East, the Mexicans live where the immigrants from Europe lived before them, or still live with them. Accommodations range from basement to attic, from the poorer brick tenements and backyards of the near West Side of Chicago, to rows of frame houses whose roofs cut across the vision like sawteeth, and on to the neat brick, single-family dwellings to which the more fortunate workers of all nationalities may attain in Gary or Indiana Harbor. Their housing reflects the position the Mexicans themselves hold among the other immigrants in northern industry; it is less distinctive and less isolated than that which, as members of *la raza*, they occupy in the Southwest.

The rapid influx of a large laboring class, migratory, prolific, with primitive standards of living, different in race and culture, is bound to disturb the social equilibrium. Whether this disturbance raises "problems" depends upon one's point of view.

Take for instance the schooling of rural Mexican children. Is their nonattendance a problem? The farmers want their labor, the parents their children's earnings; it costs money and effort to put them into school, and causes a lot of disturbance after they get there. If you think Mexican children should have the pressure of the American state behind their education, it is a "problem." If you do not, their nonattendance may mitigate local difficulties in getting the kind of farm labor you have a hard time finding anyone else to do. Said an Imperial Valley farm manager:

*If they were miserable or unhappy, I would say, "All right; Mr. Educator, do your damndest." But the Mexicans are a happy people, happier than we are; they don't want responsibility, they want just to float along, sing songs, smoke cigarettes. Education doesn't make they any happier; most of them continue the same sort of work at the same wages as if they had never attended school. It only makes them dissatisfied, and teaches them to read the wrong kind of literature (IWW) and listen to the wrong kind of talk.*

In the Cotton Belt of Texas, and the sugar-beet fields of the North, nonattendance generally is not treated as a problem; in California and in cities elsewhere, it is, and Mexican children are generally checked up, and, if need be, compelled to go to school.

If Mexican children do go to school, Americans of almost all points of view see their presence as a "problem." Differences of language, culture, class, race, standards of cleanliness, and rates of educational progress between the children of the Mexican laborer and those of the American farmer or townsman raise difficulties. Shall their children be educated in the same schools, or shall they be separated? If separated, shall the separation continue through four grades, eight grades, or twelve? American communities answer these questions in the light of educational and hygienic considerations, financial and administrative expediency, and racial feeling. With such a diversity of viewpoints, the resulting situations are varied, as can be imagined. They range from separation through the first grade to separation through high school; from excellent school buildings and teaching staffs to inadequate shacks inadequately equipped and staffed, while the local American schools may be operated with the aid of state money allotted to the district because of the numerical count of its Mexican children. Sometimes no school at all is provided for the Mexicans. On the other hand, notably in larger cities and in rural communities under the adult education system of California, men and women as well as children are reached by classes which are genuinely appreciated.[2]

Again, there is politics. Very few Mexican immigrants naturalize, but many men and women of Mexican blood amongst us were born in the United States and are citizens. At one extreme is political debauchery—Mexicans used as tools of American politicians—witness the elections of 1928 in Hidalgo County, Texas. At the other is Dimmit County in the same state which, to end purchase of Mexican votes by Americans, established a "white man's primary" in the name of "civic righteousness," and thus effectively eliminated the Mexican vote.

Then there are questions of social equality and race, delicate but insistent. The 1921 census of Mexico classified its population as 9.8 percent white, 59.3 percent *mestizo*, 29.2 percent Indian. The great bulk of Mexican immigrants come from the *mestizo* and Indian groups, particularly *mestizos* in whom the Indian strain predominates. There are generally sufficient social and economic grounds to explain the slow educational progress of the children of Mexican *peones* without resort to the theory of race inferiority. There are many individual instances of excellent educational progress among them. Not infrequently, Mexican young people of working-class parentage and largely Indian ancestry have made brilliant records in high schools and even colleges, at times ranking as valedictorians of their classes.

That many Americans in 1931 think in terms of race superiority and inferiority is itself, however, a fact of profound significance to the social and economic status of Mexicans in the United States who are of Indian or Indo-European origin. This attitude is exhibited in its cruder forms by signs in the windows of restaurants, billiard parlors and the like, reading, "White trade only," "Se sirve solamente a raza blanca," "Este Baño solamente para americanos." The bald statement is often made in conversations that the Mexican laborers are an "inferior race," and therefore to be separated in school, in domicile, at the soda fountain, in social affairs, and in buses (but not on trains and street cars). There is the hazing and taunting in the public schools. Later on the race line occasionally bars job promotion; the shade of brown on the cheek may determine whether a man is employed in an industrial establishment, or whether a girl is accepted as a clerk or stenographer.

The Mexicans who come to the United States are hospitable and courteous. Often they possess personal charm and magnetism. Even the *peones* are sensitive to the social ostracism to which they are subjected. They may shrink in suffering like the proud old Texas *vaquero* who said to me: *"Distinción?* I feel just like if they stick me through to the other side. *Si, señorito,* we are Christians, too; we are sons of God!"* Or, but rarely in the presence of Americans, they may burst out like a young Mexican machinist in the San Joaquin Valley of California: "The white race must be brought to its knees." For the most part, however, the Mexicans keep to themselves the more because of ostracism, instead of hurling themselves in defiance against it.

The coming of the Mexicans has provided the Southwest—Texas, New Mexico, Arizona, and California—and those portions of the Middlewest and North which raise sugar beets, with an agricultural proletariat. The vast majority are laborers, not hired men who are going to become tenants and owners. California and Texas farmers are strongly anti-Japanese, because the Japanese, with lower standards of living and working their women and children, were ambitious to lease or purchase land and become competitors. Those same farmers are not bothered because Mexican laborers have a low standard of living and work their women and children; rather the reverse; they use them and feel safe. As the wife of one farmer put it: "There is no danger from the Mexicans. They won't save enough to buy land."

The Mexican has at times been used as a strikebreaker, and not alone in agriculture. Less well known is his role as striker. He went out from the coal mines of Colorado with the IWW in 1927. In Imperial Valley in the spring of 1928 he formed a union of his own. In quaint language he appealed to the chambers of commerce for aid in establishing higher rates for cantaloupe picking:

*In accordance with the bad occasions we've had the past years, it makes us necessary of a better understanding of our business among the Mexican people residing as strangers in the United States. We want to keep on cooperating with our hand of labor, but we claim a more liberal wages, enough to cover our most urgent necessities of the actual situations, and we hereby propose to you gentlemen the points of our wishes.*

*During the year we scarcely work 185 days, of which we acquire the sum of $555.00 in which we couldn't meet our expenses of alimentation, clothing, house rent, medicine, automobile, and other small exigents....*

*As you understand, with this amount above stated, we live in the most unhonorable and miserable way, in our concept....*

The refusal of some Mexicans to work for less than the union rates was met by a semihysterical outbreak from the sheriff. No strike of any extent occurred; most of the demands were granted by the growers; the Mexicans were aroused, and a union organization was launched. In 1930 the Mexicans of Imperial Valley again participated in a strike movement in which Communist leaders sought to play a leading role until they were arrested, and several of them convicted under the California criminal syndicalism law.

In Colorado in 1928 a beet workers' union was formed which has spread into other areas. A Mexican editor hailed its advent with none of the courteous tones used in Imperial Valley:

*Some ranchers, individuals without morals and with the sentiments of dogs, only see in a Mexican a beast; they treat him as such, giving him wretched scraps to live on; miserable shacks much worse than the stables they have for their plow horses, fat hogs, and milking cows.... Although they live in a free country they are nothing but regular slave drivers who see nothing in a Mexican but a beast of burden or even less than that. (The "docility" of Mexican laborers, so frequently extolled by employers who seem to have believed them racially strike-proof, is not to be taken too literally.)*

The migration from south of the Rio Grande is predominantly rural; the Mexican laborers live, on the whole, as a class apart, maintaining a separate domicile and culture. Many factors serve to maintain the class and culture line and to prevent those contacts which might break it down. The coincidence of class, racial, and cultural differences combine to maintain a social ostracism, which in turn reinforces and stabilizes the differences upon which it is based. The earlier immigration of impoverished Europeans, who congregated in colonies in our large cities, was also largely a labor class movement. The Mexican migration differs in that its distribution is largely rural, and in that it involves strong consciousness of racial difference. Both these differences accentuate the domiciliary and social isolation of the

Mexican field worker, the father of six children in Imperial Valley, March 1935. *Photo: Dorothea Lange.*

Mexicans. They delay the *rapprochement* of the two cultures (or the disappearance of one), and retard the blurring of the class line.

American employers of Mexicans have welcomed them as laborers, and done all possible to obtain their admission as immigrants. They have often cared well for their needs. Yet very often they have been but slightly sensitive to low and irregular earnings, child labor with inferior schooling, and social discriminations to which the Mexicans have been subjected in their communities. Some employers have made genuine and effective efforts to meet the situation. In Colorado, for example, businessmen's service clubs took steps to secure the removal of discriminatory signs from the windows. Some employers, however, have contented themselves with the defense that whatever the conditions among Mexicans here, many of them are materially better off than they were in Mexico. Others have shared the view of a southwestern onion grower:

*Perhaps I'm talking to the wrong man; if you are from the North you won't understand. The Mexican is getting paid about four bits too much. He should get about $1 a day. . . . What a Mexican should be paid is just enough to live on, with maybe a dollar or two to spend. That's all he deserves. If he is paid any more he won't work so much or when we need him; he's able to wait around until we have to raise the price above what's legitimate.*

The nonemploying groups in the American community have often treated the Mexicans with less consideration than their direct employers. At best, their welcome has generally been as laborers, rather than as people.

The Mexican immigrant is usually conscious of his role in the United States, but seldom faces the probability that his migration is more permanent than he had intended. The expected return to Mexico continues to recede into the future while ties to the United States become stronger.

Revolution, poverty, and the lure of economic opportunity were common factors behind the emigration. "We left Mexico," said a Mexican in the offices of the Immigrants' Protective League of Chicago, "when things got pretty bad over there, and it was very hard to get something to eat regularly. We had heard, too, that in six months we would be able to buy a car and have a piano for my little girl who likes music." The vision of wealth often turns out to be a mirage, as it did in this case. Discouragement, sentiment, resentment against the discriminations, and a passionate patriotism all urge return to Mexico. "Mexicans," began an orator addressing his compatriots gathered at Hull House in 1928, "we are but the children of Israel who are passing through our Egypt here in the United States, doing the onerous labors, swallowing our pride, bracing up under the indignities heaped upon us here."

Other attractions to residence in the United States are

discovered. We are told, for example, that although it often is disliked by the men, "the women find out the freedom of the United States is pretty good for them." For the children there are schools and social agencies. "I like the United States," said a Mexican mother in Chicago. "If my babies are sick the Welfare takes care of them. I can go to the dispensary. The nurses and doctor come, and when there is no money we don't pay. It is better than in Mexico." Even the sting of discrimination is forgotten in the presence of friendliness and help:

*We heard of this Hull House even as far as South Chicago, and they speak of it in the railroad camps outside the city. We remember those things more than the taunts of ignorant Americans....*

But it is the young people whose attachments to the United States become the strongest anchors against return. The movement to establish Mexican schools where Mexican culture and patriotism can be inculcated is a conscious effort to resist "de-Mexicanization" of the children, who, their parents sometimes remark regretfully, learn of Washington and Lincoln instead of Hidalgo and Benito Juarez, and say "father" instead of *"mi padre."* But very few Mexicans realize until it is too late that their bonds to the mother country have become tenuous, while at the same time they have failed to establish close cultural contacts with Americans. Fleeing as so many of them did from ferment and poverty, they have obtained greater security and material benefit at the price of cutting themselves off from the cultural renaissance of their own people at home. Meanwhile they occupy in the United States a role of isolation often stigmatized with inferiority.

The epoch of Mexican mass migration to the United States is now closed. As a result of increasing political pressure for quota limitation and the desire of the Department of State to forestall such statutes which might be regarded by Latin-American countries as discriminatory, the federal government has diminished the flow of Mexican immigrants to a trickle. Without legislation, but by more stringent enforcement of old legal provisions barring the admission of illiterates, of alien contract laborers, and of persons liable to become public charges, the issuance of immigration visas to natives of Mexico by consular offices has been cut from a monthly average of 4,848 for the fiscal year 1927-28 to only 281 for the seven months ending January 31, 1931. The Department of Labor at the same time has effectively increased its efforts to return to Mexico persons illegally in the United States and to strengthen its defenses against surreptitious entry.

The uprooting and return to Mexico of persons already in the United States naturally causes personal hardship which is of course not mitigated by any legal flaws in the right to be here. Therefore it has aroused protests both from Americans (usually employers concerned primarily over the loss of laborers), and from Mexicans, who charge that the immigration officers "persecute systematically with exasperating passion," and by their methods of enforcement themselves "violate the same immigration laws." It is fairly apparent that the hardships now visited on Mexicans are in considerable measure due to the present efforts of officials, stimulated both by the imminence of quota legislation and by widespread unemployment, to undo the effects of previous weak enforcement of the immigration laws.

The economic depression in the United States has in turn caused the return to Mexico of many immigrants, just as it did in 1921. It will be recalled that when business picked up in 1922 and 1923 a new tide set in. Following this depression, however, thousands whose right hitherto to be in the United States rested upon an entry of dubious legality or clear illegality, or whose period of permitted absence from the country will have been overstayed in Mexico, will be unable to qualify for return to the United States under the new standards of law enforcement.

We may well recognize, therefore, the end of the tidal wave of immigration across our southern border. But we need not expect the Mexican population in this country to melt like the snow, as some have thought. The net balance of repatriations to Mexico of 45,000 in 1930 reported by the Department of State upon advices from Mexican sources is much less than a similar balance of 97,000 in 1921. Even if year after year such a balance should be maintained, and assuming neither births nor deaths among the Mexicans in the United States, it would require a quarter of a century (and how much longer we shall know only when the 1930 census is published), to return our Mexican population to Mexico. No such exodus is probable. The representatives of our two cultures will remain in juxtaposition in large and widespread areas of the United States, with contacts of varying types and degrees of intensity. The stamp of the Mexican migration will be visible for generations.

*Hearings Before a Subcommittee on Education and Labor; United States Senate; Seventy-Sixth Congress; Third Session; Part 54; Agricultural Labor in California*

# DOCUMENTARY HISTORY OF THE STRIKE OF THE COTTON PICKERS IN CALIFORNIA 1933

## INTRODUCTION

As the faulting of the earth exposes its strata and reveals its structure, so a social disturbance throws into bold relief the structure of society, the attitudes, reactions, and interests of its groups. In the San Joaquin Valley of California the alignment of groups, their opinions, and behavior under stress of an unfamiliar situation were exposed by the cotton pickers' strike of 1933, when thousands of agricultural workers, largely of alien race and under Communist influence, clashed with conservative American growers. The significance of the event is far more than incidental. It exhibits in full detail the essential characteristics of numerous lesser conflicts in California agriculture both before and since, in which ardent organizers agitate and lead, incensed "vigilantes" organize and act, growers, officials, and laborers each overstep the law, and citizens finally cry to the state authorities for peace, if necessary at the hands of troops. The documentation and analysis of this early impact of labor organized under radical leaders on a previously undisturbed rural community is undertaken to illuminate and record an unsettled situation, which in its basic features persists despite truces, and flares up again and again through the valleys of California as harvest after harvest rises successively to its peak.

There need be no surprise that this extended uprising of cotton workers occurred in California earlier than the unrest which had developed among southern sharecroppers. For in California the pattern of cotton culture approximates that of industrial production, and the "family-farmer" is subordinated to the large-scale "grower." More than 30 percent of all the large-scale cotton farms of the country in 1929 were located in California, all or practically all of them in the San Joaquin Valley. ("Large-scale" means annual gross income of $30,000 or more.) The concentration of big operations which this represents is all the more striking because in the same year California produced less than 2 percent of the nation's cotton. Large numbers of wage laborers are concentrated under a few employers under the predominantly "industrialized agriculture." Sharecroppers are virtually nonexistent. Thus the growth of paternalism which traditionally has moderated labor relations in the cotton belt is discouraged by the size of the labor force, and practically prevented by the dependence in California upon migrant wage workers who, with few ties to the community, come and go with the seasons.

The historical background of organized labor unrest in California lies in the rapid changes in the utilization of the valley lands of the state which have occurred during the past two generations. From cattle raising and the production of grains by rainfall farming, the basis of rural economy has steadily been shifted to irrigated agriculture, with emphasis upon production of fruits and vegetables, grapes, sugar beets, and latterly, cotton. This transition to intensive farming, with its insistent and increasing demands for great hordes of hand laborers, has given the state an agricultural proletariat, practically landless and propertyless, and exceedingly mobile. It accounts in large measure for the waves of immigrant laborers—Japanese, Hindustani, Mexican, and Filipino—which have swept successively into California and found employment there. Cotton, of recent appearance in the central valley of the state, has added southwestern whites and Negroes to the diversity of nationalities already at work in the fields. But the Chinese had practically abandoned agriculture before cotton became important in the San Joaquin Valley, neither Japanese nor Filipinos pick cotton, and Hindustani pickers have long been numerically inconsequential. Of the 15,000 or more pickers engaged in the harvest of 1933, probably 75 percent or more were Mexicans and the balance were southwestern whites and Negroes, with many more of the former than of the latter.

California agriculture has not been entirely free of labor disturbances in the past. The Wheatland hop riots of 1913 focused the attention of the entire state and called forth the notable investigation by Carleton Parker at the request of the governor of the state. During the war, especially, strikes broke out in the citrus belt and elsewhere, some of them, like the Wheatland strike, led by the IWW. Sporadic refusals of small groups to work under certain conditions have often occurred, but generally these have exhibited little or no semblance of organization, and should hardly be dignified by the term "strike."

In 1928, there sprang from a Mexican mutual benefit society a labor organization among the Mexicans of Imperial Valley, which became involved in a sort of "strike." The following year leaders from the Trade Union Unity League, sponsored by Communists, sought to conduct another strike of Mexican laborers in the valley. As a result, a number of the leaders were tried for criminal syndicalism and some were convicted.

During the first years of depression, strike activities in agriculture remained at a low ebb. Outbreaks among agricultural laborers were confined chiefly to violence and threats by white laborers against Filipino competitors.

In late 1932 a strike occurred among the orchard pruners of Vacaville, and the spring of 1933 ushered in a whole series of strikes, many of them under Communist leadership, which effected most of the important harvests of California. They began in the pea harvest in the Santa Clara Valley and in the berry crops near El Monte, east of Los Angeles, continued in the sugar beet, apricot, peach, lettuce, and grape harvest, and reached a climax in the cotton harvest.[1] The cotton pickers' strike centered on Kern, Kings, and Tulare counties, in the southern San Joaquin Valley where more than half of the cotton acreage of the state was awaiting harvest. It directly involved over 10,000 pickers, held up harvesting for more than three weeks, and threatened, with longer duration, to spread to areas where the harvest was late and thus tie up practically the entire crop of the state.

## THE STRIKE INTERRUPTS THE HARVEST

The opening cotton bolls in Kern County were the signal for picking to begin. Crews of pickers were mobilized, ready to enter the fields at a word from the grower. On many farms this word was given, and the first bales came from the gins at the end of September. Suddenly picking slowed down, then practically ceased, as pickers responded to the October 4 strike call of the Cannery and Agricultural Workers' Industrial Union, and to the activity of the strike pickets.

The shock of the first cessation of work traveled almost instantly through the elements of the population immediately concerned with cotton—the pickers, the growers and the Labor Bureau, the ginners and finance companies, chambers of commerce and the Farm Bureau. It involved immediately the local officers of the law and soon the merchants, ministers, American Legion, and even the PTA. Metropolitan papers carried the news, emotions, and tragedy of the clash to the public of the state. Sympathizers with the pickers became interested, sent aid, and investigated. Soon the health, relief, conciliation, and highway patrol agencies of the state were actively involved under orders of the governor, and the national guard awaited his call. Even the federal government was affected through participation of the National Labor Board of the NRA, the presence of a federal conciliator, and the use of federal relief funds. Even the international aspects of a situation involving thousands of alien laborers was thrown into relief by the killing at the hands of armed growers of an honorary consular representative of Mexico, and by the investigations and activities of a Mexican consul.

The drama of the strike as it unfolded can be well and succinctly told in the very form in which it played upon the emotions of the public by using the headlines carried by valley, metropolitan, and Communist press. These reveal the main events, the widening clash of interest, the increasing involvement of different elements in the community, and the charged and unconcealed feelings of the participants. A chronological panorama is therefore presented in these terms to give perspective on events and attitudes before embarking upon more detailed analysis and documentation of the attitudes and activities of principal groups.

September 21. Cotton picking price is raised in San Joaquin. Schedule is set at 60 cents for each 100 pounds at Fresno conference. *(Bakersfield Californian)*

Thus was announced the action of several hundred assembled growers who raised the picking rate above the 40-cent rate of the preceding year, but rejected the $1 rate demanded by the pickers' union. *The San Francisco Western Worker* (Communist) thereupon announced that battle would be joined:

September 25. Cotton pickers prepared to strike.

The first blow fell in Kern County, where the harvest begins, and the strike quickly spread over the valley. Picketing, arrests, underestimation by growers of the strength of the strike, and assertions of their determination to stand pat, featured the early headlines:

October 2. Cotton workers' strike hits Wasco area. Arvin agitators fail in efforts to halt picking. (*Californian*)

October 3. Eleven arrested Kern cotton strike. Few workers leave fields. (*Californian*)

October 4. Valley cotton pickers' strike is commenced. (*Tulare Advance-Register*)

Kings growers to stand pat on cotton pay. Corcoran meeting agrees to stick to 60-cent scale; not worried over strike. (*Hanford Journal*)

Strike agitators are thwarted in cotton districts. (*Californian*)

Evictions of strikers from the growers' camps and activities of pickets, including the appearance of mass picketing, were announced:

October 5. Growers evict cotton strikers in Kern area. (*Fresno Bee*)

Thirty-five families are ousted in cotton strike. (*Advance-Register*)

Agitators intimidate Kern cotton pickers. (*Californian*)

October 6. Picket caravans active locally. (*Advance-Register*)

The growers formed "protective associations" and armed themselves. They sought to disperse strikers, and to resist picketing. Violence or anything that appeared like an overt act breaching the peace was featured:

October 6. Growers form group to buck cotton strike. (*Journal*)

Valley cotton men organize; fight strikers' wage demands. Protective league for valley now being planned. Kern growers meet at Wasco. (*Visalia Times-Delta*)

Growers to protect Kern pickers. (*Californian*)

October 7. Ranchers arm as precaution. Strike trouble spreading. (*Bee*)

Cotton pickers become violent in cotton areas. Assault and damage to car asserted in allegations against twenty-five suspects. Battle against agitators in many districts planned by growers, citizens. (*Californian*)

Woodville farmers break up meeting of striking pickers. (*Advance-Register*)

Offers of mediation by state labor officials were spurned by the growers, who continued to organize, sent their own parading caravan into the Kern cotton district, centered their attack on "reds and agitators" and clashed with the strikers. The Corcoran camp of the evicted strikers, so anathema to the growers, sprang into being and became one of the dramatic features of the strike. *The Western Worker* featured the Communist effort to drive a wedge between the large and small growers:

October 8. Growers reject mediator offer to stop strike. Won't deal with "radicals." Can take care of own problems, officials told. (*Journal*)

October 9. Four thousand growers to protect labor. Organization perfected by farmers. Cotton areas visited by five-mile parade. (*Californian*)

Growers organize to smash strike. (*Bee*)

Growers plan to drive out agitators. (*Times-Delta*)

Small farmers with strikers. (*Western Worker*)

October 10. Farmers form strong unit to halt picketing. Over 700 cotton growers sign as members. Plan vigilante set-up. Present wage upheld. Assert unrest caused by work of professional agitators. (*Tulare Times*)

Four more arrested. Three thousand cotton pickers camp near Corcoran. (*Journal*)

Report three slain, several beaten in Arvin Strike riot. Hugh Jewett seriously injured. Many hurt in grim battle. (*Californian*)

Violence again flares up in cotton strike; new clash at Woodville. (*Advance-Register*)

[Gov.] Rolph not to send troops into valley. (*Times*)

Then came the Pixley tragedy, federal intervention, appeal by the Mexican consul to disarm the growers, and the arrest of growers and strike leaders:

October 11. Three strikers dead, twenty wounded in Pixley, Arvin riots. Eleven growers in murder net. (*Journal*)

Strikers threaten Visalia Jail. (*Californian*)

Rolph to send troops here if he is asked to. (*Advance-Register*)

October 12. U.S. takes action to end strike. Chief federal mediator. Department of Justice agents on visit. (*Californian*)

Mexican consul asks Gov. Rolph to take guns from farmers. (*Advance-Register*)

Pat Chambers [Strike leader] nabbed on riot charge after Visalia strike investigation. Valley quiet after Tuesday uprising. (*Times-Delta*)

Strikers face starvation. Hatred, misery spread through trouble area as new outbreaks loom. (*San Francisco Chronicle*)

October 13. Kings sheriff to take charge of Corcoran strikers camp. (*Advance-Register*)

Mexican consul to probe Arvin riot death. (*Advance-Register*)

Three more strike leaders arrested at Corcoran. (*Journal*)

Chambers admits Communist record as agitator. (*Journal*)

Deputies sworn in as ranchers make threats. (*Times-Delta*)

Strong efforts to accomplish mediation failed when the strikers refused even at the urging of the Mexican consul to resume work pending investigation. Announcements of the end of the strike proved premature. The consul alleged that the growers who killed the consular representative at Pixley were being "whitewashed" by the authorities. "Mass funerals" were held for the dead strikers and the Communist press cried out against the armed growers. Federal relief found its way to the strikers:

October 14. Strike is due to end as growers agree to mediate. (*Bee*)
Mexican consul Bravo urges national return to picking. (*Times-Delta*)
Consul gets death threat. Raps whitewash of growers. (*Chronicle*)
Huge crowd attends rites for two men slain at Pixley. (*Advance-Register*)
Governor says strikers to be provided food. (*Times*)
October 15. Cotton strike ends, picking begins Monday. All agree to mediation to settle charges. (*Journal*)
Martial law faces cotton strike area. (*Chronicle*)
October 16. Strikers refuse to return to work. Idleness in cotton fields continues in face of arbitration. (*Times-Delta*)
Pickers refuse to resume work. Reject U.S. food. Milk sent by U.S. left to sour by hungry men. (*Bee*)
Tense feeling in valley masked by ominous Sunday calm. (*Chronicle*)
Fifteen thousand cotton strikers defy thugs. (*Western Worker*)

Confusion and contradiction characterized the reports of a kaleidoscopic situation in which there were more premature announcements of peace. An investigating board, appointed by the governor, appeared on the scene. Its members were Archbishop Edward J. Hanna, Dr. Tully C. Knoles, and Professor Ira B. Cross.

October 17. Workers return to fields. Five hundred and fifteen bales ginned in Kern as farm strike is broken. (*Californian*)
Pickers remain on strike. Demand $1 wage, U.S. relief, Chambers' release. Huge caravan pickets cotton ranchers. (*Journal*)
October 18. Strike virtually ended. (*Californian*)
Creel [NRA administrator] arrives by airplane to settle cotton strike. (*Advance-Register*)
Striker's infant dies in Hanford of malnutrition. (*Advance-Register*)
Corcoran group say camp health menace. Want closing order. (*Journal*)
Five pickets arrested on Tulare Ranch. (*Advance-Register*)
October 19. Arbitration board meets today to iron out strike troubles. Cotton picking price in valley is best in United States. (*Advance-Register*)
Kern ginning jumps to 724 bales. (*Californian*)
Radical leaders and students take hand in local cotton strike situation. "Cocky" strikers defy officers. (*Times-Delta*)

As the governor's fact-finding committee began its hearing, each side plead its cause, and an outraged rural community made dire threats against radicals and recalcitrant aliens. Even before the governor's committee could make its report, the growers sought to repudiate it. The state director of industrial relations immediately came to the valley and made a vain effort to settle the strike along the lines desired by the growers, probably acceptable to the strikers, but unacceptable to the federal government:

October 20. Growers, pickers tell board of financial plight. Mediators hear same plight from both sides. *(Bee)*

Grand Jury indicts 8 ranchers and 16 strikers; Chambers, strike leader, charged with syndicalism. *(Pixley Enterprise)*

Strikers face deportation. "Bull Pen" looms for Communists and aliens. *(Corcoran News)*

October 21. Cotton strike in deadlock. Cross' peace plea fails. *(Bee)*

Growers refuse mediation. Growers' committee explains objections [to] fact-finding committee. *(Times-Delta)*

Food is offered workers to quit [work], sheriff charges. *(Journal)*

Merritt [manager of Tagus Ranch] flays Chambers as Communist in strike hearing. *(Advance-Register)*

October 22. Reardon [director of industrial relations] here. Devises plan to end cotton pickers' strike. *(Times)*

Federal credit group enters strike parleys. Credit Administration has millions in loans in valley. *(Journal)*

Move to close schools to aid cotton picking.

Strike headquarters reeks with Communist literature. *(Times)*

The fact-finding committee made its recommendation of a 15-cent wage increase. The growers reluctantly accepted it; the strikers delayed during four tense days, then finally returned to work at the 75-cent rate. Even before the end of the cotton strike fears were voiced of Communist strikes to come in the citrus harvest, and threats were heard of secret organizations against strikers, and of enforced repatriation of Mexican pickers:

October 23. 75-cent rate fixed by commission. *(Times-Delta)*

Kern cotton growers wire U.S. for help. Declaring they have lost faith in state officers, ranchers demand federal mediators. *(San Francisco Examiner)*

Rolph manoeuvre fails; strike solid.

Evidence shows police, growers planned Pixley massacre. *(Western Worker)*

October 24. Troops asked to quell strikers. Pickets invade cotton fields, clash with workers. Bloodshed feared at Corcoran as mob of 1,000 threatens officers; eleven nabbed. Growers refuse 75-cent wage. *(Journal)*

Militia may invade strike zone. One hundred highway police sent into Corcoran area to halt riots. *(Californian)*

Growers ask government to reduce relief. Legion will investigate communism. *(Times)*

October 25. Rolph moves to force 75-cent wage. Pickers won't get aid,

no loans to farmers if new wage ignored. (*Times*)
Cotton men accept 75-cent rate. (*Californian*)
Officers seize autos. Pickets have to walk.
Night raiders take [working] families from ranch.
Texas Negroes are invited to harvest crop. (*Times*)
October 26. Mailed fist ends strike, but riots seen in Corcoran.
(*Chronicle*)
Strikers turn down 75-cent offer. Stick to 80-cent wage and other demands. (*Times*)
Valley strikers defy U.S. (*Chronicle*)
Strike in Kern vanishing. Cotton gins busy. (*Californian*)
Corcoran strikers defy officers; refuse either to pick cotton or evacuate camp. Sheriff Buckner broadcasts message and is booed by strikers. State patrol will not participate in attempt to force evacuations; officers temporize. (*Times-Delta*)
Southland fears "reds" will launch strike in citrus area. (*Times*)
October 27. Strike crisis believed over. Union fighting for recognition. Cotton strike spreads into Merced area. (*Times*)
Five thousand pickers busy in Kern cotton fields. (*Californian*)
Strikers make daring attack on government. Say officers working for [cotton] finance companies, gin interests, use force against strikers. (*Journal*)
Girl's plea ends strike in state's cotton area. Thousands of pickers will return to their jobs today at wages fixed in meet. (*Examiner*)
Repatriation of Mexicans now looming. (*Times*)
October 27. Ku Klux crosses flame in warning to valley strikers. (*Chronicle*)[2]

As the strikers finally returned to work, the angry growers vented their wrath on officials for their part in the strike, just as the strikers had done; and a handful of students on the picket line gave occasion to attack the state university for "teaching radicalism." The Communist press hailed the outcome as a victory, demanded release of arrested strikers, and cried for infliction of the death penalty on the Pixley growers. A threat of extensive importation of pickers from Los Angeles increased tension:

October 28. Strikers break camp at Corcoran. Families set out for cotton fields. (*Times-Delta*)
Cotton growers ask "shake-up" as strike aftermath. (*Examiner*)
U[niversity of] C[alifornia] probe of student action in cotton strike asked. (*Oakland Tribune*)
November 6. Cotton pickers win 25 percent raise. Workers agree to accept 25 percent if the growers hire union pickers. Many farmers signing up, while those in Corcoran region can't get pickers.
Two million dollar raise in wages. Rolph admits victory won by Communist leadership. Strong Communist party and fighting union will guarantee victory. (*Western Worker*)

Four thousand Mexicans [imported from Los Angeles] invade valley in strike peril. *(Chronicle)*

In the aftermath of the cotton strike came the trials of the strike leader charged with criminal syndicalism, and of the growers charged with murder of the strikers. Then the rumble of strike fears in other areas, and the shift of the scene of conflict to the citrus belt and to Imperial Valley, as new harvests came ready:

November 11. Communists back of cotton strike, [district attorney] Haight says in talk at Porterville.

Strikers freed after entering pleas of guilty. *(Times-Delta)*

November 13. Demand release of cotton strikers. *(Western Worker)*

November 18. Citrus belt strike threatened. Agitators stir up new trouble in citrus belt. County growers meet with officials here. Groves to be patrolled. *(Times-Delta)*

November 20. Only Communists lead, cotton pickers learn. *(Western Worker)*

November 27. Pat Chambers on trial; send your protests to Visalia at once. Cotton strike leader faces growers' court. Police and machine guns guard court to keep workers out. Sheriff conspires with [Governor] Rolph to frame leader. *(Western Worker)*

December 4. Chambers trial procedure shows growers' plan to frame-up leader. Visalia court keeps workers off jury panel. *(Western Worker)*

December 6. Chambers jury fails to agree. *(Times-Delta)*

January 4, 1934. Tulare seeks to oust ex-leaders of cotton strike. Mayor rejects union demand for relief; says city not hotbed for radicals. *(Bee)*

January 8. Death penalty for killers of cotton strikers demanded. Attempt whitewash. *(Western Worker)*

As the new year began, the noise of conflict was coming from Imperial Valley where vigilantes abducted an attorney of the American Civil Liberties Union, and a California congressman demanded investigation of Communist activities in California agriculture. The accused ranchers of Pixley were found not guilty and the criminal syndicalism charges against Pat Chambers were dismissed. But amid the closing of old cases came news of the spread of the Imperial Valley strike from lettuce to peas, and the rumble of more conflict to come in the San Joaquin Valley, as farmers there were "organizing quietly into vigilante committees, determined to prevent a recurrence of agricultural strikes," and Communists "planned to call a strike in Imperial County as soon as cantaloupes and other melons were ripe; to move from there into vegetable fields, and to continue with harvests until the cotton harvest next fall."

January 13. Imperial Valley police fight strikers. Both sides toss bombs when attack is made on Brawley quarters. *(San Francisco News)*

Jails filled in Imperial Valley row. Meeting of strike leaders in valley dispersed by bombs. *(Tribune)*

January 24. Wirin kidnapped by vigilantes. Striking cotton pickers convicted [of disturbing peace at Arvin]. *(News)*

February 1. Pixley ranchers "not guilty." Applause greets verdict returned after three hours. Defendants weep as verdict is read before Judge Lamberson. (*Times-Delta*)
February 7. Valley striker is freed of charges [Chambers criminal syndicalism case dismissed]. (*Examiner*)
February 10. Labor agitators ready for action [in San Joaquin Valley harvests]. (*Berkeley Gazette*)
February 11. Valley farm vigilantes set for red war. San Joaquin ranchers organized secretly to resist onslaughts of harvest foes. Special investigators in field to uncover plots for labor riots. Imperial pea harvest halts. Agitators scare 4,000 men from fields. (*Chronicle*)

### THE UNION ATTACK

The strike of the California cotton pickers did not come unannounced. Indeed, as early as May, strikers in the berry crop at El Monte had warned a labor agent of the valley growers that "You'll have to better [in the matter of wages] in the San Joaquin."

The Cannery and Agricultural Workers' Industrial Union which was organizing the series of strikes among migratory agricultural laborers grew out of a strike in lettuce workers in the Imperial Valley in January 1930. As one of the results of its early activities, eight leaders were convicted of criminal syndicalism by a local court.[3] For the next three years the union was comparatively inactive among the masses of laborers. However, it was developing an organization through Communist channels, affiliated as it was with the (communist) Trade Union Unity League. Headquarters of the union were established in New York, but principal strike activities were confined mainly to California.[4]

Western district headquarters were maintained at San Jose. In a statement before the governor's fact-finding committee, the district secretary described union organization and membership requirements as follows:

*All workers in the agricultural industry who agree to abide by the principle of the union are eligible for membership. To date, the union membership in the state of California numbers twenty thousand [see comment below], including in its ranks workers of every color, creed, nationality, or political belief. It is an economic organization which has as its main principle the organization of the agricultural worker for the purpose of bettering his living and working conditions.*

*The district of the union is divided into sections and subsections; these, in turn, are divided into locals. The local is the basic organization of the union and no decisions of policy are valid without majority approval by the entire membership.*

*There are only two paid functionaries of the union. One, the district organizer who receives $5 per week. Two, the district secretary,* *who receives $7.50 per week. The district organizer and secretary are elected at district-wide conventions. Section organizers are elected at section conventions, and local presidents and secretaries are elected directly by each local.*

*The union recognizes and maintains the unalienable [sic] right of the workers to ORGANIZE, STRIKE, AND PICKET, and urges this method to better living and working conditions, when other methods fail.*

### DUES

|            | Dues per month | Initiations | Membership books |
|------------|----------------|-------------|------------------|
| Employed   | 25¢            | 25¢         | 5¢               |
| Unemployed | 5¢             | 10¢         | 5¢               |

*Forty percent of this fund is retained by the local of the union, 30 percent by the section and 30 percent by the district. A small per capita fee is paid to the national office.*

The claim to a membership of 20,000 is, of course, not to be accepted at more than a fraction of its face value. Indeed, the *Western Worker* itself, at almost the same date, October 16, claimed only 4,000 members among the strikers where the union strength was greatest, and on November 20 asserted that "The membership is around 7,000 and constantly increasing as a result of the victory." Because of fluctuating conditions affecting low-paid migratory laborers, and the fact that many are members only nominally, it is impossible for the outsider to determine the exact membership as one might the membership of a stable urban trade union. Dues-paying, steady membership, however, is probably even less an index of potential power to sway large numbers of migratory agricultural laborers than it is of power to influence the actions of urban industrial workers.

At the close of 1932 and in early 1933, the emphasis of Communist activity in California was shifted, at least insofar as it involved public agitation of masses of people. As numbers of unemployed were drawn back into employment, as relief became more adequate under federal direction, and as prices and wages stiffened, "hunger marches" and protest meetings declined, and strike activity in the field of agriculture, long neglected by the American Federation of Labor, assumed increasing importance.[5]

As the cotton pickers gathered in the San Joaquin Valley in preparation for the 1933 harvest, the union established nineteen locals in the southern cotton district.[6] Demands, among which a wage of $1 per hundred pounds for picking was prominent, were prepared and approved by a large conference of delegates elected by these locals. Additional demands were: Abolition of the contract system—gangs working under contractors instead of directly for farmers; hiring to be done through the union; no discrimination among pickers. (*Western Worker*, September 25)

The growers assembled later at Fresno on September 19, somewhere between 300 and 500, to fix the picking wage in their usual fashion. Pat Chambers, chairman of the strike committee of the union, was permitted to read, but not to discuss the resolution of the union asking for a rate of $1. Immediately he departed, and the meeting deliberated. A prominent grower summarized the issue:

*I had advocated 75 cents, but was in a minority of one. Some growers wanted the wage set at 50 cents. Growers objected to the 75-cent wage saying that if we set 75 cents, they would strike for 85 cents, and so on; it was, therefore, better to stand on 60 cents. I thought that at 75 cents there would not be so much cause for striking. The wage was set at 60 cents.*[7]

*(Interview)*

Probably sensing a possibility that revision might become necessary, as well as intending to maintain unity of action among growers, it was decided that no change should be made in the rate without convocation of another growers' meeting.

The reaction of pickers to the growers' decision was, of course, not uniform. But dissatisfied elements among them naturally appealed to the union in their midst, which skillfully organized, spread, directed, and fanned the discontent. A strike leader described the beginning of the process:

*Word spread that there was something the agricultural workers could do to better their condition and that was to strike, to struggle. Individual workers came in to the union headquarters at Tulare, established at the time of the Tagus Ranch strike, and delegations came in from the ranches and we advised them to organize, which they did. . . . Incensed, the workers gathered and waited for the picking to start. They organized locals in tents, in hovels, and in holes in the walls. Strikers who had taken part at the Tagus Ranch had experience and formed the nucleus. The strike cry began to ring through the valley—"Not a pound for less than $1 a hundred." (Speech)*

The tactics of the Communist leaders have been worked out carefully in the light not only of their own experiences, but those of the American Federation of Labor unions and the Industrial Workers of the World as well. Following the 1933 strikes in California agriculture, a manual of tactics for conducting agricultural strikes was prepared which described the modus operandi in ample detail. It provided instructions:

*(1) for intimate survey of the territory preceding a strike, including establishment of contacts with workers, small growers, and even large growers or their agents; (2) for setting the strike demands, which should be very few, and vital to the workers (in contradistinction to demands the leaders may think the workers ought to make); and for calling*

*the strike at exactly the time "when the boss needs the workers most";
(3) for organizing small meetings, then committees, in order to draw
in workers, especially in the places from which large ranchers will draw
their workers; (4) for calling a wage conference with broad representa-
tion, but "not so broad that it exposes itself to the police and growers";
(5) for organizing the central strike committee, and for developing leadership among the workers; (6) for organizing auxiliary activities, such
as relief, finance, legal defense in cooperation with organizations such
as International Labor Defense, negotiation, publicity through both
strike bulletins and releases to the newspapers "answering the slanders
against the strike, and presenting the workers' side of the struggle";
(7) for enlisting maximum active strike participation of even women,
youth, and children, the first in relief, and all on the picket lines, with
children taught to play "workers and growers" instead of "cops and
robbers"; (8) for organizing and equipping union headquarters, to be
open "where possible," with "reserve strike headquarters where comrades can gather in case the open headquarters are attacked"; (9) for
organizing picketing and defense "against vigilante attacks"; (10) for
making the settlement, taking into consideration the mood of not only the "vanguard of the workers," but also that of its "most backward
sections"; (11) for avoiding jeopardy of the success of the strike, or loss
of confidence in Communist leadership, by premature issuance of
leaflets, by excessive promises of the leaders, by exposure to seizure
at a single time of all equipment or all leaders, by correction or immediate removal of leaders who show signs of discouragement; (12) for
avoiding disruption by continual advance warnings to the strikers of
the guises in which it might come; (13) for bringing the Cannery and
Agricultural Workers' Industrial Union, the Trade Union Unity League,
Communist Party, and Young Communists League to the favorable
attention of the strikers, the two first by appealing to them as
authorities on strike tactics, the latter two by utilizing "every incident
in the strike to prove that the government is on the side of the bosses
and that we must have also a party that will bring the government
on the side of the workers."*

As the union proceeded with its campaign to organize and solidify
the ranks of the pickers, its visible strike tactics unfolded. Mass
meetings were held for the workers congregated on farms, on vacant
lots of towns, and in "Mexican towns across the tracks"; union
"literature" and membership cards were liberally distributed. In this
campaign the union was favored by the late maturity of the crop, which
was retarded about two weeks. The situation might have been materially different had work engaged the pickers immediately upon arrival
in the cotton area. But waiting in idleness, union meetings became the
center of attention, and the coming strike the chief topic of
conversation.

In addition to meetings with speakers, mass demonstrations were staged upon appropriate occasions during the strike in order to enlist active participation by the pickers and stir their enthusiasm. The shooting of strikers at Pixley furnished opportunity for a meeting of protest in Visalia:

*Strikers from all parts of the county formed a caravan of cars and drove from Tulare to Visalia before noon. As the caravan entered the county seat, it consisted of thirty cars and trucks loaded with striking workers, accompanied by an escort of state traffic patrolmen in cars and on motorcycles.*

*Assembling at the main entrance to the courthouse, approximately 600 workers heard their leader, Pat Chambers, assert that the strikers would hold county officials responsible for the slaying of the two members of their union.* (Tulare Times, *October 11)*

The meeting approved a four-point demand which included "Death penalty for slayers of the two workers killed at Pixley."

Although Communists disapprove of organized religion, they welcome "impressive ceremony" upon suitable occasion, such as granting a charter to a union local. They are quick to recognize that a funeral of slain strikers, even when performed with religious rites, offers good, if somewhat incongruous, opportunity for a demonstration. So it was when the Pixley victims were buried at Tulare:

*With a huge crowd in attendance, last rites for Delfino D'Avila, 55, and Dolores Hernandez, 50, victims of the Pixley cotton striking rioting last Tuesday, were observed at the St. Aloysius Catholic Church here under the auspices of the Cannery and Agricultural Workers' Industrial Union.*

*Estimates of the crowd ranged from 1,200 to 4,000, with experienced observers setting it at a little over 1,500.*

*Assembling in the city park adjacent to the Southern Pacific tracks, strikers formed an orderly line of approximately a thousand persons and marched down Kern Street to the church. The members were segregated into groups representing various local chapters of the union, with captains in charge of each corps.*

*Banners and placards evenly distributed along the ranks of the marchers advertised the policies and demands of the strikers, while marchers from each district carried a placard giving their location.*

*"We demand the release of Pat Chambers," said one poster. A broad banner borne by two men revealed: "The Mexican Consul represents Mexican bosses." A third observed, "Rolph sends aid to Pixley—24 Special Deputies, 12 Patrolmen—we want food."*

*The crowd filed into the church until all available space had been exhausted. All seats and most of the main aisle were filled, yet they accommodated but a minor portion of the crowd; outside were hundreds of others, waiting patiently the conclusion of the long ceremony.* (Tulare Times, *October 14)*

A mass protest and appeal directed at the Kern County Board

of Supervisors illustrates another type of demonstration, of which there were a number during the strike:

*Approximately one thousand men, women, and children, bearing banners claiming that they were striking cotton pickers, assembled at the courthouse grounds early this morning in an orderly manner and after marching down the street to the south end of the building, took up a position near the old city jail platform near the city hall, where various speakers addressed the throng.*

*The strikers sent deputations of men and women, some of the latter with children, to attend a meeting of the board of supervisors.*

*This deputation walked quietly into the board room and took seats in the spectators gallery while the board was holding a road hearing.*

*Two men of the delegation presented a petition to the supervisors for the board's consideration. In substance it was as follows:*

*"We, the Cannery and Agricultural Workers' Industrial Union, demand: (1) The release of Ladislado Guerro. (2) Relief for striking cotton workers. (3) That armed guards and thugs be kept out of strike areas. (4) Hot lunches and clothing for our school children. (5) No evictions from cotton ranches. (6) The right to assemble. (7) Sanitary camps."*

*Seven striking cotton field workers addressed the supervisors after presenting the petition. Thomas E. Ferry, one of the spokesmen, said that their pickets had been instructed to carry and use no weapons—that they were not armed even with pen knives. He contended that many farmers, to the contrary, were armed with rifles and shotguns.*

*Mrs. R.E. Walker made a plea for warm lunches for their children in the schools. Chairman Perry Brite said he understood all schools furnished warm lunches. Mrs. Walker said this was so providing the child had 10 cents with which to pay for his lunch. She said she did not have the money herself and the children needed food.*

*Carl Walker, of the deputation, said the Los Angeles Welfare Department had ordered him up here to get to work picking cotton. He said he couldn't earn enough money picking cotton to support his sick wife and children.*

*The idea which the strikers expressed was to keep peace and "provide relief for the kids."*

*Chairman Perry Brite and Supervisor Stanley Abel said the board would do its utmost to keep peace and maintain order and that no citizens properly belonging to this county will be allowed to starve.*

*The meeting was a very quiet one and perfectly orderly . . . .*

*Guerro, referred to in the demand of the deputation attending the board, was being held for investigation by the United States immigration officers, it was reported, with some question as to his entry into the United States involved.* (Bakersfield Californian, *October 9)*

The excitement of the parades, the fiery talks, the cheering, appealed to the Mexicans particulary, and race discrimination, poor housing, and low pay, especially the latter, were rallying cries which appealed to a class of workers with adequate personal experience to vivify the charges hurled by Communist leaders, and rendered exposition of the theories of Karl Marx superfluous.

Furthermore, the union was not entirely strange to most of the assembled pickers; the Communist leaders already had gained prestige in earlier strikes, in which some of the pickers had even participated. Though the union never had organized the pickers before, it had organized many of the same people when engaged in other harvests, for members of its inner corps, most if not all of whom were Communists, had followed the laborers as they migrated from crop to crop, and from region to region. Indeed, from among these people with past training in strike activity, Mexicans, Negroes, and whites, was formed the nucleus of local organizations and subordinate leadership. Emphasizing the importance of these junior leaders, a Communist leader said, "Only because we developed leadership from the rank and file were we able to conduct and win the cotton strike. Leaders arose from the ranks—they were not sent from Moscow." Thus the groundwork for the cotton strike was laid in a score of places scattered from the El Monte berry fields to Tagus Ranch and the vineyards of Lodi.

Although the original Communist leaders were white Americans, unable to speak Spanish, this proved no great barrier in establishing effective contact with the Mexicans. Most of the latter understood a little English, and plenty of young Mexicans, raised in this country and possessing a fair knowledge of English, were ready to serve as lieutenants and interpreters. And with ample time hanging on the hands of most of the strikers, the additional time required to translate speeches was no serious drawback. As for the race differences between white leaders, and Mexican and Negro led, both the latter groups welcomed cordially the unaccustomed vigorous championship of their cause by members of the dominant race. A Communist leader described the welding of the races under stress of common strike experiences:

*Mexicans, Negroes, and whites picked together [they had done this before without unionization], lived, cooked, were beaten, and went to jail together. Southern [white] workers would say to Negroes, "Comrade, would you do this? Comrade, you're elected to that committee." (Interview)*

Unlike the organizers of the union, few members or even minor leaders were Communists. They were manual workers, not professional organizers. However, with the common immediate aim of winning the strike the two types functioned together effectively. Special efforts were made by the Communists to instill in the mass of workers a sense of their own importance and leadership.

An incident at the Corcoran camp illustrates the rank and file spirit of the strikers, the spirit of unbreakable collective leadership.When the bosses set up a loudspeaker in front of the camp to intimidate the strikers, they asked for the leaders to step out and meet the bosses. "We are all leaders," came back the spontaneous shout. (*Western Worker*, November 20)

This incident is to be understood, of course, as an evidence of esprit rather than as a statement of literal fact. A Kings County official laid counteremphasis on the undoubtedly powerful influence of the central group of leaders:

*Those strikers at the Corcoran camp tried to tell me they didn't have any leaders, that they were all equal and were all leaders. But when I went down to tell them that the camp would be condemned if it wasn't sanitary, they found a leader quick enough to talk to me. They had leaders all right who gave them orders just what to do. (Interview)*

With the leadership and organization described, the union began the stoppage. As cotton picking started in Kern County, union "agitators" entered the fields. On October 2, the *Bakersfield Californian* brought in the first strike reports:

*That between 750 and 1,000 cotton pickers in the Wasco area of the county are on strike for higher picking wages was reported here today. Motorists traveling down the highways noted pickets bearing the legend on wrapping paper, "This field under strike." Approximately thirty pickets were observed.*

Agitation failed in the Arvin and Weed Patch districts, but Pat Chambers predicted optimistically that 5,000 pickers would be on strike the following day. On the third, the strike spread to the Shafter and McFarland districts; in the latter, 15 percent of the pickers were reported on strike, but at Arvin, again "picking was proceeding as usual." Among those who continued to work during this strike were newcomers from the Southwest. As a white union leader said: "I don't know whether they come from Oklahoma or not, but that's what we calls 'em. They'd work for ten cents a day and think they were getting good money." (Interview)

Outwardly, the growers did not appear seriously worried as yet, and generally both growers and peace officers minimized the effectiveness of the strike:

*Cotton men said today the striking was not sufficiently serious to cause them undue worry over harvesting the crop as the labor supply is plentiful in the county. They [growers] did not care whether the cotton was picked immediately or not. They said they could leave it standing on the stalks till next spring if necessary and lose only a few points in price due to standing. (*Californian, *October 2, 3)*

*Cotton growers are not particularly concerned over the threat of the strike. (*Journal, *October 4)*

*Claims of strike agitators at Tulare that 3,000 pickers were out on strike in the Corcoran district got a laugh from local officers who said that only about 200 were out to date. (*Journal, *October 5)*

The following day the *Corcoran News* estimated 2,000 pickers on strike.

Union leaders tended to maximize the extent of the stoppage, just as growers tended to minimize it:

*Valley strike headquarters ... claimed practically complete walkouts in most localities, while grower spokesmen claimed the strike was slipping in these same localities.* (Times, October 5)

Obviously, each party had sufficient motive to shade estimates in its own favor.

In fact, the extent of the walkout rapidly increased after October 4, the date set by the union for general cessation of picking. It continued to grow in Kern, Kings, and Tulare counties under the spur of union strike activity until final settlement, except when growers, by advancing wages above 60 cents, induced pickers to resume work. This was done most extensively in Kern County toward the close of the strike.

At no time did the strike spread to include the farms of Fresno, Madera, and Merced counties, although numerous threats and a few belated walkouts occurred. (*Times*, October 13; *Times-Delta*, October 26)

An index of the effectiveness of the strike is the record of ginnings. Ten gins in Kern, Tulare, and Kings counties which had ginned 57.4 percent of the season's total the year before by the end of October, had ginned only 19.1 percent by the same date in 1933. A late season in 1933 was only partially responsible for the great retardation; undoubtedly the strike was the principal cause.

The increasing success of the strike made its conduct of picketing activities the most conspicuous of union tactics. Picketing scores of thousands of acres of cotton presents new aspects of an old problem. It is only partially comparable to picketing a factory in an industrial center, or a coal mine which has a restricted location; even peach orchards or pea fields involve production in a comparatively confined area. But the cotton strike extended 100 miles from south of Bakersfield almost to Fresno with a varying width up to thirty and even forty miles, and included over 2,000 cotton-raising farms in three counties.

The endeavor to prevent "scabbing" over such a wide area was new to both strikers and leaders. Picketing was even newer to the growers and local law officers, who had had little or no experience with strikes, than it was to the strike leaders. This inexperience lent itself to mistakes and excesses on the part of all three parties.

Picketing followed the initial walkout immediately and continued intermittently and with varying intensity in different regions during the entire strike. On October 5 the *Visalia Times-Delta* reported the first picketing in the vicinity in "the Parkwood district where a crowd of forty men, most of them Mexicans, were parading up and down the road and shouting to cotton pickers on a ranch there to join the strike."

"Auto caravans of pickets were visiting cotton ranches in the Tulare vicinity" on October 6. Picketing continued simultaneously in Kern County where:

> Two hundred strikers who paraded from the Arvin and Weed Patch districts yesterday were halted by guards and prevented from entering the Kern Lake zone... a second parade... was started by strike sympathizers in the McFarland district. (Californian, October 5, 6)

These early excursions were followed by many during the ensuing weeks.

In order to enlist active participation by a large number of strikers for its moral and educational effect upon them, as well as to enhance to effectiveness of the demonstration upon working pickers, mass picketing methods were employed. Distances to be covered and numbers of pickets to be used compelled use of automobiles and trucks, and the presence of "scabs" working on rows far from any road necessitated employment of unusual methods to attract their attention.

Caravans of cars and trucks filled with men, women, and often children of striking families were formed at camps or union headquarters and dispatched to fields and districts where picking was reported. Leaders endeavored to establish picket lines early in the morning before work started, as more likely to prove effective by intercepting pickers en route to the field than lines formed after workers reached the fields. Secrecy of destination was sought in order to evade accompanying officers and the vigilance of growers who might offer resistance of various forms or withdraw pickers from the field temporarily upon the approach of pickets. But usually the caravan moved along its intended route flanked by highway patrolmen, peace officers, growers, newspaper men, and even spectators. Sometimes the caravan divided to reach different destinations or to throw watchers off the scent. Sometimes it was secretly assembled either in an inconspicuous part of town or at the point where the line was finally to be maintained that day. The pickets conducted their demonstration while driving slowly past the fields, or by dismounting to parade on foot or simply to stand along the highway. When pickers were working close to the highway, the strikers would first talk to them, encouraging them to join the strike. If such persuasion was of no avail or if pickers were distant from the road, shouting and bugle blasts were resorted to. Placards and banners against "scabbing" were also used.

As strikes wear on, feelings on all sides become increasingly charged, and strike leaders endeavor to raise morale of the strikers to the highest pitch in order to maintain their resistance unbroken. A union leaflet on October 12, for example, urged vigorous picketing to take advantage of the increasing concern of the growers over loss of their crops:

> Comrade Strikers. The weather is threatening. The growers are becoming desperate. We must Mobilize All of Our Forces to Keep the

*Fields Clean. Do not let stool pigeons or anyone else call off the picket lines. There must not be A Scab in the Field. Mobilize more picket lines to cover your whole territory and call the workers out of the ranches. We have the legal right to organize, strike, and picket. (Reprinted in* Times Delta, *October 13)*

With such feelings, which characteristically prevail during a strike, it is obvious that the courtesies of a social gathering are not to be expected from pickets who see workers in the field undermining the cause for which they, the pickets, are sacrificing, and in the benefits of which all workers—strikers and nonstrikers alike—will share if the cause is successful. Employment of abusive language, insulting catcalls, gestures suggesting what the pickets would like to do to the "scabs," were frequent occurrences. Workers were sometimes warned that "We can't get you now, but some day you'll have to come to town, and we'll get you then." Sometimes more vigorous threats were employed. According to the *Bakersfield Californian* (October 26):

*A truck load of pickers en route to work in the Rosedale district was halted by strikers and threatened with death, members of the group said, if they went to work.*

Strike leaders declared that they urged peaceful picketing only, and abstinence from all violence of any nature at all times:

*Each picket line, each local, received iron-clad instructions from the union against violence. We understand that one gun found in the possession of a striker will be the signal for the growers and authorities to massacre defenseless strikers. ("Brief history of the San Joaquin Valley cotton strike," document presented by the union to governor's fact-finding committee.)*

The unionist in charge of picket lines of the McFarland local described before the fact-finding committee the instructions given to pickets:

*I instruct my men if any of them are armed to remove them before going on duty, obey the law and do not trespass, do not block traffic and comply with the law in every respect. In warm weather the pickets are not allowed to wear their jackets. I have ordered them to cooperate with the officers in every way. (Hearings)*

Picketing led even to violence on several occasions, however, the responsibility resting sometimes clearly on the shoulders of the pickets, at other times less clearly so. The Arvin riot, which resulted in the death of one striker, started with picketing activity; its details are stated in the section on law enforcement.

The willingness of Communist leaders not only to let pickets trespass, but even to organize them to do it under circumstances favorable to success, is indicated in what purports to be the manual of tactics, printed in the appendix to this study.[8] The resolution states that picket lines:

*. . . should be of two general characters; guerrilla picket line, and*

*mass picket line. Both must be utilized together and to supplement one another. In other words, even while the mass picket lines are parading up and down the highway and calling upon the workers to strike, the guerrilla picket lines must find other entrances to the ranches and help take the workers off.*

This resolution was passed after the cotton strike, it is true. However, pickets actually trespassed upon the fields where pickers were at work in several notable instances during the cotton strike. For example,

*At the Hansen Ranch, it is reported, "Women picketers who ran into fields cried to pickers to 'come on out, quit work; we'll feed you. If you don't, we'll poison all of you.' " (Journal, October 25)*

The principal occasion upon which trespass occurred followed the lull in picketing while the governor's fact-finding committee was preparing its report. Interestingly it took place upon the ranch of a large grower who has succeeded in maintaining a force of pickers at work during the strike, but who assumed a much more moderate attitude at the hearings than most of his colleagues.

*Striking Kings County cotton pickers today won out in a hand-to-hand battle with pickers on the Guiberson Ranch, three miles east of Corcoran, and serious trouble threatened as bands of strikers, estimated at 500 to 800, moved in trucks and automobiles toward the Progress Land Company ranch where a large crew of pickers was busy at work, late this afternoon.*

*Kings County officers, unarmed, were unable to hold the strikers in check.*

*Leaving the Corcoran strike camp this morning, the strikers went to the Peterson Ranch and drove pickers from the field.*

*Arriving at the Guiberson Ranch later in the day, they met opposition and a hand-to-hand fight followed with both sides sustaining bruised heads and faces. Pickers gave up the fight when several cotton picking sacks were slit. Considerable cotton acreage was reported trampled down.*

*Continuing to the Hubbard Ranch, the strikers stayed out of the field but served notice on the pickers to be out of the field when they came back, or they would drag them out. (Times-Delta, October 23)*

The next day, as an aftermath, it was reported that:

*Protection was sought of Corcoran police yesterday by a worker from the J.W. Guiberson Ranch near Corcoran, where fighting between cotton pickers and picketers occurred yesterday.*

*Upon the man's request, he was placed in the city jail. His identity was not revealed by police. The man told officers that picketers had threatened his life after he had engaged in the affray on the ranch, and assertedly knocked one of the woman pickets down. (Times, October 24)*

On the same day picketing in another locality, accompanied by extensive trespassing, developed into a near riot when officers, using tear gas, curbed the activities of the pickets. Strikers were reported to be deliberately planning and executing violent activity against working pickers in the following instance:

*Night riders, bands of strikers, were reported active in Tulare County during the night. One band, it was learned here, removed two families of pickers from the Overton Ranch near Goshen, loading them bodily into trucks and taking them away.* (Times, October 25)

*Unconfirmed reports reached Pixley that strikers forcibly caused a crew of cotton pickets to stop work near McFarland.* (Advance-Register, October 5)

The various acts of the strikers to enlist the support of the majority of pickers—persuasion and appeal, covert and open threats, and occasional trespass and violence—succeeded. To measure the effectiveness of each of these elements is of course impossible. Local newspapers, officers, and growers emphasized the element of fear:

*At Woodville, very little picking was reported Thursday morning, with pickers said to be remaining out of the field through fear they might be manhandled by picketers as one picker was Tuesday.* (Advance-Register, October 12)

*In the Arvin, Magunden, and Weed Patch districts it was reported many pickers, intimidated by agitators, had left the cotton fields.* (Californian, October 5)

*With picking almost at a standstill, pickets were on the rampage all day. Eighty-five workers were intimidated by pickets into deserting the B.A. Overland Ranch in Kings County. The quitting workers admitted they were frightened.* (Chronicle, October 25)

After the strike at least one physical clash took place between those who had struck, and those who had continued to work:

*Strikers and strikebreakers sought to settle their dispute by individual combat when the Hanford Mexican colony staged a dance at Armory Hall this Saturday night. Several men were injured in half a dozen fights that broke out during the evening.* (Times, October 29)

The role of strikers' concentration camps in discouraging from picking those who otherwise might do so, the pressure exerted by growers to keep pickers from joining the strike who might wish to do so, and efforts to stiffen resistance of all growers and citizens who might be disposed to make concessions to the strikers, are discussed elsewhere.

A cherished part of the Communist strategy was the endeavor to drive a wedge between small growers and laborers on the one hand and large growers and finance and power companies on the other. Even before the cotton strike they had attempted to stimulate organization among the smaller farmers to defend themselves, by striking or otherwise, against those whom they regarded as opposed to their interests:

*The small farmers likewise face a desperate future. Their fight will force them to more and more unite with the workers, against the real exploiters, the finance, gin, and power companies.* In the same manner *as the workers organizing in union, they are having to organize into the United Farmers League, are taking up the strike weapon against the exorbitant power rates and foreclosures.* (Western Worker, November 20)

This league, sponsored by the Communists, issued a statement after the strike urging its members to "Support the pickers' union by signing this union hiring contract." *(Western Worker,* November 13)

Some small growers did exhibit active sympathy with the strikers' demands; doubtless more would have done so if such expressions had not been obliged to face the strong pressure of widespread grower and community opinion. But practically no growers, small or large, went so far as to pay the $1 per hundred pounds demanded by the pickers: union representatives submitted to the governor's committee but one such written offer. A small grower who spoke sympathetically of the pickers before the committee said, "We will be glad to pay more than 60 cents to the poor slave who has to do the work. Under present conditions we cannot do it." In the closing days of the strike a number of growers, small and large, raised the rate to 75 cents.

## THE GROWERS' RESISTANCE

The initial attitude of the growers, who expected a strike, but not one which would cause great difficulty, was reported to be relatively mild; at least they would attempt no general lockout.

*No retaliatory measure will be used by the growers in case the strike should materialize, but any workers will be accepted who are willing to go to work for the 60-cent scale.* (Journal, *October 4)*

However, when the strike became general the attitude changed. Growers and other elements in the community interested in combatting the strike, such as gin and finance men, immediately organized local groups, which were loosely federated and known as protective associations.

The character of these organizations, which appeared throughout the strike-affected area, and their effect on the mind and emotions of the public appear from the accounts of their activities. Only a few of these groups are described here. The *Bakersfield Californian* (October 6) gave the following survey of concerted action by growers in Kern County:

*Growers to protect Kern cotton pickers. Crops, workers will be guarded; arms to be used if necessary.*

*Protection for Kern County's $3,300,000 cotton crop—as well as for a reported 80 percent of cotton pickers ready and willing to work at prices the growers can afford to pay, provided they are not intimidated by alleged radicals and Communists, will be afforded here within the next twenty-four hours, the Executive Committee of the Agricultural Protective Association announced today:*

*"Acting with great rapidity the protective association is organiz-ing the county today—and within a few hours will be prepared to offer growers 'adequate armed protection.' "*

*As cotton picking throughout the county has been reported paralyzed to a great extent and there is no legal recourse for the growers of the county, citizens are banding together today, with assistance solicited from the Kern County Chamber of Commerce, the Bakersfield Chamber of Commerce, and the Farm Bureau.*

*The executive committee said:*

*"These organizations have been solicited by land owners and pro-ducers to join in this movement of a citizens committee to prevent out-side radicals and Communists from dominating and ruining a great industry.*

*Within twenty-four hours we will have a countywide organiza-tion for the protection of growers and their families, as well as their property. These people have been threatened and are taking steps to protect themselves against potential hurt and damage.*

*Ample funds will be provided for those employed by the asso-ciation.*

*More than 80 percent of the cotton pickers in the county want to work for the wage scale the growers are able to pay. This wage scale is as high as any paid for cotton picking in the United States.*

*Many of the pickers, however, have been intimidated by radicals and are afraid to go into the fields and pick cotton because of numerous threats made against them.*

*A survey made of the county showed today that very little cot-ton is being picked.*

*Growers have been advised that they have the right, under the trespass law of this state, to protect their property from invasion and use force if necessary in so doing."*

The growers' organizations were partly open in character, and partly secret. Public mass meetings of growers, and even parades were held. The Kern County committee to resist the strike, which was formed with the approval and support of a large meeting of growers at Wasco, was composed of the directors of the Kern County Farm Bureau, the Executive Committee of the Kern County Chamber of Commerce, and representatives of other organizations. Nonsecret committees were ac-tive at Corcoran, but a semisecret organization was also formed, called the Farmers' Protective Association:

*Growers declined to divulge the names of leaders of the associa-tion, intimating they feared the men's property might be molested in the event they were known. (Bee, October 10. L.D. Ellett acknowledged membership before the governor's fact-finding committee.)*

The characteristic program of the growers' groups included five main points, which will be described in some detail:

(1) *Wide publication of the fact that the growers were "standing*

*pat"* on the wage offer of 60 cents, with insistence that this "is the maximum the farmer can afford to pay on the 1933 crop and that the wage scale is satisfactory to regular cotton pickers, practically all of whom would now be at work were it not for the alleged 'professional' agitators," and the general maintenance of a solid resistance among the growers before the pickers and the public. (*Times,* October 10; *Journal,* October 4)

Undoubtedly, many pickers were willing to work, and regretted the intrusion of the strike. For example, a growers' agent stated that pickers would come to him with the request to "send us to some corner of the valley where there is no trouble"; that one Mexican picker who had joined in a strikers' demonstration appeared the next morning to request a gasoline advance to move to the west side of the valley to pick, sensing no serious incongruity, and naively explaining his presence in the demonstration by saying, "They viva'd and we viva'd'; and that the Corcoran camp guard prevented unauthorized exits of workers as well as entrances. Particularly resented by growers was a statement before the strike actually began, attributed to a deputy labor commissioner, who said, "Your people are on strike, and you don't know it." But in view of the great effectiveness of the strike, and the likelihood that many workers joining it would naturally explain their action to their employers by some excuse such as fear, the growers' estimate of 80 percent willing to work can be accepted only far below face value.

(2) *Eviction of striking pickers from camps of the growers.* When refusals to work began, many hundreds of pickers were ordered either to go to work at 60 cents or to vacate the quarters provided by the growers. (*Bee,* October 5; *Corcoran News,* October 6) In some instances the eviction orders were actually enforced by groups of growers. For example:

*At these [union] meetings, the pickers were instructed to remain in the cotton camps after striking, being informed that the growers would find it impossible to evict them for several weeks, if they went to courts for redress.*

### FARMERS TAKE INITIATIVE

*On Wednesday afternoon, late, about seventy-five growers of the Corcoran district assembled at Peterson Farms and gave the occupants of the cotton camp five minutes to get their sacks and start for the field. Those who did not wish to work were instructed to leave the camp immediately. The proposition of the growers was received with derision, and within a few minutes several trucks were backed up to the cabins and farmers began loading belongings of Mexican cotton pickers on the trucks. These meager possessions were dumped off on the highway a short distance from Peterson Farms headquarters, and the occupants of the camp ordered to leave forthwith, which they did peacefully. But for a few who wished to work, the camp was comple-*

*ly deserted by 7 o'clock. The camp at Peterson Farms was made up of a total of approximately 150 Mexicans, ages ranging from babes in arms to one old man ninety-seven years of age. Guards were placed about the camp to prevent the return of the Mexicans during the night.* (Corcoran News, *October 6)*

The eviction at the Peterson Ranch was carried out "with the approval of the officers." (*Journal,* October 5) A district attorney stated the officials' view in an interview after the strike:

*I don't know whether the growers had a legal right to evict the strikers or not, but the logic of the situation was all in their favor. Maybe, legally they should have been given thirty-days notice. This talk of serving three-day notices is all wrong. I think the sheriff's logic was good, that the shelter, fuel, lights, and water furnished to the pickers by the growers is part of their pay for picking cotton. So, if they refuse to pick, they shouldn't get this pay any more than money. The sheriff and I told the growers not to worry about the pickers' rights anyway. The growers had all the logic on their side. If it isn't the law, it ought to be.* (Interview)

The next day it was reported that, "The strikers from Peterson Ranch were still camped along the highway yesterday after being evicted, but are expected to leave today after their water supply is cut off." (*Journal,* October 7) The Corcoran growers' committee appealed to the state highway patrol to "keep the strikers moving once they are evicted." (*Bee,* October 8) At the Hansen Ranch,

*some twenty-five ranchers began moving their belongings out onto the highway. In cases where striking pickers preferred to move their own belongings, they were permitted to do so, but where they refused to move, their belongings were loaded upon trucks and moved out. There was no trouble, the evacuation being accomplished good naturedly, some of the Mexican workers even assisting the ranchers in moving.* (Journal, *October 6)*

An eviction in Kern County was reported as follows:

*Late this afternoon . . . the situation had cleared somewhat when armed pickers numbering almost 200 men, heeded a growers' ultimatum to go to work or leave their campground. The campground, located 2½ miles south of Wasco, was visited by an army of between 200 and 300 armed farmers who demanded evacuation. . . .*

*Reports stated that about 100 of the pickers went back to work, heavily guarded by farmers and deputized citizens. The balance began moving out of the district.*

*Trouble flamed early in the day when a delegation of unarmed farmers visited the campground, urging the strikers to go back to work and offering free transportation between the camp and cotton fields for workers who would pick at 60 cents a hundred pounds.*

*Growers reported the strikers "became ugly," holding out with their demand for $1 a hundred.*

*Within a few minutes after the farmers left to begin recruiting their forces, approximately 150 additional strikers were reported to have assembled at the campground.*

*With reports of the "misunderstanding"—as one Wasco man termed it, a gathering of almost 400 growers assembled in Shafter, then transferred its meeting place to Wasco.*

*Following a hurried conference, the majority of the growers visited the campground with the ultimatum, recruited scores of pickers, and permitted the balance of the strikers to leave the area.* (Californian, *October 10*)

A minor clash occurred at a Kings County ranch when,

*approximately fifty strikers and agitators drove to the ranch for the purpose of assisting striking cotton pickers move out of the cotton camp cabins. May [the rancher] and his men met them at the highway and warned them to stay off the ranch, most of them obeying the warning. Lopez, however, broke through the guards and was going toward the cabins when he was arrested by Mr. May. The man did not specify who it was he intended to kill, but shouted, "I'm going to kill someone," it was reported by members of the growers' committee.* (Journal, *October 7. Lopez was released a few days later.*)

Some complaint of the manner of eviction was made to Enrique Bravo, Mexican consul from Monterey, by his nationals:

*Bravo said that Mexican workers had complained to him that they had been evicted from the Peterson, Hansen, and May ranches at the point of guns, and that at the Peterson Ranch particularly their belongings had been dumped unceremoniously into the highway and the water supply cut off and no other adequate supply within fourteen miles. He said they had complained that the usual three-day notice had not been given.* (Journal, *October 12*)

The strike leaders at Corcoran "instructed occupants of various cotton camps to vacate peaceably as soon as they were ordered to do so." (*Corcoran News*, October 6) Throughout the strike area, eviction from the growers' camps was carried out practically without physical encounters, although upon some occasions the growers made a show of force to ensure evacuation. On other occasions strikers were requested courteously to leave more or less at their own convenience.

The growers felt wholly justified, morally, in evicting those who would not work at 60 cents, and used the tactic in an effort to eliminate "agitators" and to deter pickers from striking. Kern Lake growers, for example, issued eviction notices, then declared a picking holiday, and expressed the opinion that "many of their workers will resume work as soon as the strike agitators are evicted." (*Bee*, October 6) But the extent of the strike was greatly underestimated by growers, who expected to fill the places of the strikers with other workers in the valley as had customarily been done in other years when sporadic disaffection had arisen. Growers and their sympathizers resented suggestions that wholesale eviction was a mistake, but a large grower of more moderate opinions stated:

*The growers thought that if the pickers wouldn't work, then there was no reason for them to stay and use water and fuel, and they wanted to have the places vacated for others to come in. They didn't know how unusual the strike would be, and thought others would come in from other places in the valley. As it turned out, it would have been just as well not to have evacuated them. I told the growers at the time that it was better to let the Mexicans stay; then when the strike is over, they would be right here. (Interview)*

In general, the evictions were tactically unsuccessful and proved to be a boomerang, as they forced the strikers into concentration camps easily dominated by the union.

(3) *The endeavor to "rid" the valley of "outside radicals and Communists."* The fact that most of the principal strike leaders were Communists greatly inflamed the already heated feelings of the growers, and was seized upon to arouse the public. The *Sacramento Bee* on the third day of the strike queried editorially why such people should be tolerated:

People getting weary of Communist agitators

*People of California of all classes are in favor of decent working conditions and salaries for all categories of employees.*

*This state has been one of the leaders in the enactment of statutes for the protection of those who toil; for abolishing the sweat shop; for providing minimum wages for women; for preventing the exploitation of children in the shops and in the factories.*

*Public opinion strongly supports the idea of a fair day's pay for a fair day's work. And every legitimate and honest effort directed toward that end is praiseworthy.*

*But our people are getting exceedingly weary of the activities of professional Communist leaders, mostly from New York, who are motivated by no honest desire to improve working conditions, but rather propose to feather their own nests while promoting the cause of social anarchy and red revolution.*

*And they are getting very tired of the spectacle of these unprincipled agitators, most of them of alien origin and strangers to California, actually forbidding those who want to work from working on threat of physical violence.*

*They do not work themselves except in stirring up strife and disorder.*

*They look to their dupes to supply them with food, clothing, shelter, and spending money. They loaf between working seasons and then descend upon the scene like vultures who have smelled carrion from afar.*

*Why should they have such wide tolerance?*

Growers' leaders promptly published their intention to rid the valley of the leaders of the strike. Forrest Frick, of Arvin, announced that the Kern County committee "will seek to drive agitators out of the county." *(Bee,* October 6) L.D. Ellett, chairman of the committee of fourteen named at a Corcoran meeting of cotton producers and businessmen, stated an even broader objective: "We are going to rid Kings County of all the strikers and strike agitators." *(Journal,* October 7) Whether or not the means to be used in the elimination of strike agitators were to be solely "legal" means was a question which later produced tensely dramatic charges and denials at the hearings before the governor's fact-finding committee. The record states:

*Kearney [an independent farmer]: Two weeks back last night, I was invited to the meeting in Corcoran of the growers. When we got to town the meeting was at the Legion Hall, but it was not big enough and we went to the ball park. Mr. Ellett, the manager of the Ellett gin, said he did not want them to think it was a gin meeting, but that it was a growers' meeting. He said the time had come when the growers would have to take the law into their own hands, since they could not get any protection. . . . Their conversation was that we had to use force to get rid of these pickers, so that we could get new pickers. I jumped up and someone in the crowd shouted "Put him out." I said, "Gentlemen, I am strictly an American and I do not believe in mob law. You are getting into deep water." I refused to sign the petition to take the law into our own hands. I did not read the petition. It went around to seven or eight, and it got back to the banker, Mr. Guiberson. Mr. Guiberson said, "I could not sign that because it said 'eliminate.'" (The petition as revised and signed read: "We the undersigned pledge our support to the farmers of the Corcoran territory in protecting the workers on their ranches and legally eliminating the leaders of the strike agitation and join this organization for this purpose.") About that time two or three got up and hollered, "Let's go across the track and clean them out now." Mr. Ellett did not object. . . . There was a shorthand report taken of what was said. . . .*

*Abel [growers' attorney]: Did you say you heard him say that force would have to be used to get rid of the leaders of the pickers? Kearney: Yes.*

Later Mr. Ellett took the stand to deny he had said that the growers had to take the law into their own hands. He resented the imputation of lawlessness to the Corcoran meeting, asserting that it "was attended by the whole neighborhood, and if there was a bunch of outlaws and cut throats there, they were our own best people." He added by way of explanation:

*We wanted protection.*

*Cross: How were you going to get it?*

*Ellett: We asked the sheriff for more deputies, but they had no money.*

Events on the side of the growers moved swiftly. On the third day of the strike, a crowd of seventy-five growers formally ordered the strikers assembled at Woodville to disperse and either go to work at 60 cents or to leave California. After a physical encounter, in which neither side used firearms, a grower read aloud to the strikers the following proclamation:

*Porterville, California, October 7, 1933. Notice to Public at Large: We the undersigned the agricultural producers and businessmen operating in the Porterville, Cutter, Woodville, and Tipton sections of Tulare County, State of California, do hereby, by this agreement declare ourselves to be in a frame of mind to protect ourselves from present strike agitators and strikers, and do hereby incorporate ourselves into an agricultural protective association with full intention legally to disburse [sic] all strike agitators and strikers from our locality. Our motto: Strikers work peacefully or leave the State of California. (Note: We have been informed by a source believed to be reliable that the word "legally" was inserted after the proclamation had been read to the strikers.)*

Strike leaders and strikers were ordered generally to work or leave California—an assumption of authority to do what neither they nor the constituted authorities had power to do legally. Specifically, the "leaders of the ranchers said they had forced J.H. Bowen, a speaker at the strikers' meeting, to promise he would leave the country before 9 A.M. today." (*Bee,* October 8) Emphatic public appeal was also made in at least one town that the agitators be "driven from town."

The intent of organized farmers then, to get rid of strike leaders, and even of strikers, is sufficiently clear from these declarations. (Note: In April 1934, Filipino and Japanese strikers near Florin actually were forced by officers to evacuate the community en masse.)

(4) *Resistance to picketing, and insistence upon "protection" of pickers willing to work at 60 cents from the activity of strikers' pickets.* To a very minor extent, especially in Kern County, growers in outlying sections expressed some apprehension for the personal safety of themselves and their families. After the strike a prominent grower and gin representative of Corcoran was said to be in fear of the vengeance of ex-strikers, and a bullet did strike the house of one of the farmers tried for the Pixley killings. But apprehension of growers for their own safety was exceptional; their concern over disturbance of pickers willing to work, however, was acute and general.

The sheriffs generally were reluctant to appoint numerous deputies, so growers were warned to defend their own property and advised of their rights under the law of trespass to use force in so doing. Defense of property referred only slightly to infliction of physical damage to farm crops, buildings, etc.; practically it meant prevention of successful picketing. The Farmers' Protective Association of Corcoran, for example, planned as a chief objective "to prevent any untoward efforts at picketing or intimidating laborers now working or who wish to resume work in the cotton fields." *(Times, October 10)* As an initial gesture, demonstrations of growers were arranged to counteract those of the strikers:

*Although caravans of growers were reported visiting various districts of (Tulare) County ostentatiously to break up picketing activities or meetings of strikers, no clashes were reported....*

*In Kern County, a long parade of growers toured the county yesterday as a gesture of defiance to strikers. Leaders said 4,000 farmers had organized to assure protection to all pickers and to warn agitators that interference with willing labor will not be permitted.... The caravan of farmers met with a similar parade of strikers and strike sympathizers in Bakersfield...but no clash occurred.* (Times, October 10)

When parades and meetings of growers and sympathetic citizens proved unavailing to halt the spread of the strike, sterner measures were taken. Promptly farmers in various parts of the strike area took steps to "resist with gunfire attempts of strikers to prevent harvesting of their crops" *(Advance-Register,* October 7):

*Interest in Kern County centered in the Kern Lake district, where roads from the Golden State Highway into the cotton picking district are privately owned and were being guarded against strikers.*

*Two private guards and two deputy sheriffs watched over the entrance to the district and prevented strike agitators from going into the area.* (Bee, October 5)

*Fifty strikers attempted to rush the gates of the Kern County Land Company at Kern Lake yesterday but were repulsed by guards, and strikebreaking pickers were kept on the job.* (Californian, October 12)

*[An] observer said that the ten pickers being guarded by the farmers on the John Allen Ranch were men who wanted to work, and that sixteen farmers with guns barred the roads when a caravan of 500 strikers came to pull them out of the field.* (Times, October 10)

The clashes of armed growers and strikers which resulted in bloodshed at Arvin and Pixley are described later.

The growers in their attempt to stop picketing were on the alert to prevent strikers from exceeding what were considered to be their rights and to keep them from invading private property to pull pickers from the fields. Thus a group of growers, thinking to protect their pickers, participated in the Arvin riot ending with a fatal shooting, and other armed ranchers continually stood guard over their property determined to resist the pickets. Deputy Sheriff Hill reported on October 13:

*Ranchers told our patrolmen that beginning today... they would blow to hell every striker who so much as laid a hand on the fences of their property... Armed ranchers are standing guard over their property throughout the strike area, and unless a constant watch is kept, violence will break out.* (Times-Delta, October 13)

A cooperative intelligence service was quickly developed by the growers:

*Pixley farmers, meanwhile, were reported to have developed a system designed to render picketing ineffective. By telephone they were declared to be informing each other when a picketing caravan was on its way. Farmers in the path of the caravan are reported to call in their crew, leaving nobody in sight when the caravan arrives. (Bee, October 17)*

This method was extensively employed, as a concealment of pickers in the level fields was practically impossible. Said a large rancher:

*We tried to figure how we could place the pickers in the fields to keep them away from the pickets but we couldn't. There are county roads around every section and we found we couldn't hide the pickers. (Interview)*

Strikers charged that an even more drastic method was employed by one of the Pixley ranchers who was tried for murder:

*Four pickers, Billy Hoff, Jessie Silva, Ramon Sanoya, and J.R. Hudson, signed a statement declaring that Kruger told his pickers that the first one to start to leave the ranch to join the cotton strikers wouldn't get off the place. (Times-Delta, October 13)*

John Curry, McFarland picket leader, described antipicketing activities before the governor's committee:

*Curry: The first trouble we had on the picket line was when a farmer by the name of Jess Lake drove out with one of the finance company men. I do not know his name. He drew a gun on P.C. Stewart and J.E. Maston.*

*Cross: Were they picketing?*

*Curry: Yes, they were picketing off of the pavement but not on the property. They were on the shoulder of the road, on the right of way. This man came up to Stewart first and drew his gun and said "Drop that sign." The word "picket" was on the sign. He laid it down in front of his gun and said he had a right to be there. . . . I could hear Maston but not Stewart as he spoke in a low tone. . . . On the eleventh of this month the man who had charge of that picket line sent a picket out, heard a shot, the man came back shot. Some were hit with guns by passing autos. . . . At the time the first trouble occurred a man drove his car zigzag along the highway, on the shoulder so that the picket had to get on the right of way to avoid being hit.*

*Cross: Who did this?*

*Curry: A farmer . . . within the last two days a farmer came on the highway with a Winchester. The officers saw him and never requested him to get off the highway with his Winchester.*

*Cross: Did you see them?*

*Curry: No, but I can get witnesses. On the same day that this man was arrested an equipment car owned by the power company did*

*the same zigzagging to run the picket lines into the ditches.*
*Cross: What is the reason for the zigzag?*
*Curry: To drive the picket over on the farmer's land so the farmer could shoot him.*

Other direct means employed to break the strike were attempts to jail strike leaders, to dissolve concentration camps, to starve out strikers by refusing relief, to discourage the strikers by threats of incarceration in "bull pens" and of deportation of striking aliens, to disrupt the strikers' ranks and secure repudiation of Communist leadership.

(5) *Efforts to increase the numbers of pickers at work.* Some harvesting continued in every part of the area affected by the strike. Growers and their families who picked their own cotton were not disturbed by strike pickets. But a good many year-round hands and seasonal laborers continued at work, and just as the pickers sought to diminish their number, so the growers sought to increase it. During the cotton strike proposals were made to introduce laborers from four sources:

(a) After the strike had been in progress about two weeks it was reported that "One rancher of the Tulare district planned to put twenty-five Tule River Reservation Indians to work in his fields today." *(Bee,* October 17) But little if any actual use of these inexperienced Indians was made.

(b) At the close of the first week of the strike, and again, after the recommendation of the governor's committee had been accepted by the growers, but before acceptance by the strikers, threats of importation of Texas Negroes were made:

*Chairman L.D. Ellett of the Corcoran Cotton Growers' Committee announced that unless striking pickers return to work in that district soon, pickers will be brought in from Texas, where he declared the cotton harvest is almost completed.* (Bee, October 10)

*Importation of thousands of Texas cotton pickers to break a San Joaquin Valley cotton pickers strike was planned by growers today, L.D. Ellett, Corcoran grower, revealed.*

*Ellett said an advertisement was carried in today's Dallas News, Dallas, Texas, inviting Negroes to California. He declined to say who placed the advertisement.* (Times, October 25)

*Ellett said that San Joaquin Valley ranchers have inserted advertisements in newspapers in Texas seeking to hire at least 8,000 Negro cotton pickers to come to California.* (San Francisco Call-Bulletin, October 25)

(c) Proposals were also made to bring additional pickers from Los Angeles. The first rumor appeared early in the strike:

*The Hoover Ranch, which is rumored to have connections with the former president, and is located between Shafter and Wasco, is reported to have imported 300 men from Los Angeles. The "Shafter*

*Local" [union] is reinforcing Wasco and the shouting slogan is: "No
scabs can pass us. We are out to win even if we have to build a human
fence around scab ranches."* (Californian, *October 7)*

Later, at the same time that talk of importing Texas Negroes
was rife, while acceptance by the union of the recommendation of the
governor's committee was awaited, further proposals to bring pickers
from Los Angeles were advanced. George Creel, who had opposed such
a move while negotiations were in progress, now was sympathetic:

*L.D. Ellett, chairman of the Kings County growers' group, told
the* Journal *last night that George Creel, member of the Federal Labor
Board and NRA administrator for the West, and Frank McDonald,
state labor commissioner, had promised the growers "all the labor you
need," and that the growers had signed requisitions for 5,000.* (Journal,
*October 28)*

As rumors of incomplete acceptance by the strikers persisted
even after the union authorized return to work, the threat of importation was made more definite:

*An exodus of 4,000 Mexican unemployed to the San Joaquin cot-
ton fields started today. The jobless were transported on rail and
highways to supply valley planters with pickers, Superintendent of
Charity Earl Jensen announced. All have been on local charity relief
rolls.*

*The "immigration" began today when the first consignment,
trucks laden with Mexican families, left for the valley.*

*Jensen said the workers were recruited from the relief rolls at the
specific request of J.H. Fallin, assistant director of farm labor service.*
(Times-Delta, *November 3)*

The *Western Worker* uncritically repeated the story, declaring
that "4,000 Mexicans were cut off the relief rolls in Los Angeles County
to force them to scab." (November 13) But the Mexicans were still "on
their way" on November 6:

*... a new tenseness was injected into the cotton field situation
today when it was learned that 4,000 Los Angeles Mexicans were on
their way into the Valley to break a threatened strike in the Pixley
district....* (Chronicle)

Very few, if any, of these laborers ever arrived north of the
Tehachepi mountains. An official of the state employment service
estimated that no more than 300 Los Angeles Mexicans arrived in the
valley, and a peace officer of Kern County was of the opinion that
almost none at all picked cotton in his county. A large supply of pickers
was available locally, and it was unnecessary for the growers to carry
out the threat.

(d) A number of local school children were attracted into the cotton fields, and it was suggested that the schools be closed to increase
this help:

*With several hundred school children in the fields Saturday pick-*

*ing cotton, an informal movement to urge declaration of a school holiday for a short period to assist in the cotton harvest was gaining momentum here today.*

*Children were picking on a number of ranches, while on two west of Tulare there were several crews of twenty or more students taking advantage of the opportunity to assist the farmers and at the same time earn a few extra dollars spending money.*

*Meanwhile businessmen and growers gathered in groups today and discussed the situation, urging that a general meeting be called at which time a formal request would be made to citizens and students for a school holiday in order that all who could would be enabled to reap part of the $6,000 per day paid out in labor in this district for cotton picking.*

*It was pointed out by one grower that schools frequently remain closed during the critical period of the harvest season in many sections of the state and that with nearly 60 percent of the necessary pickers in the field, the additional help from students and townsfolk would enable the farmer to save his crop without the aid of radicals who have invaded the district.* (Times, *October 22)*

The proposal of a school holiday, advanced just as the governor's committee was issuing its report, evoked a number of protests, of which the following is illustrative:

*Declaring 12,000 school children are being worked to break the cotton pickers' strike in San Joaquin Valley, Lincoln Steffens and his wife Ella Winter, authors, and Noel Sullivan, San Francisco capitalist, appealed to President Roosevelt today against this use of child labor.* (San Francisco News, *October 25)*

The estimate of numbers actually employed is greatly exaggerated, although it might have been possible to employ a good many had the schools been closed for that purpose.

(6) *Not only importation of strikebreakers and use of local school children were talked of,* but also threats of deportation of both leaders and strikers were employed in an endeavor to break the ranks of the strikers. This tactic, too, had been employed before when Mexicans struck against California growers. In Imperial Valley in 1928, for instance, it was threatened but not carried out. During the pea pickers' strike in Alameda County in April 1933, the following sign was posted in Spanish:

*Notice! Any person not a citizen of the United States of America who joins the "laborers' union" of strikers exposes himself to deportation to his own country. For U.S. Immigration, K. Watson. (Translation)*

It is extremely unlikely that any officer of the Immigration Service had anything to do with the notice.

While the cotton strike was in progress reports of activity of immigration officers in the valley were published frequently. A mild intimation which probably in fact referred simply to the normal activities of the service, but doubtless was intended to affect the morale of the strikers, appeared early:

*Not in line with the strike situation itself but in keeping with the governmental program which calls for a close check upon aliens, the immigration department is known to be actively making investigations concerning the right of a number of foreigners to be in this country. Inquiry developed that there is a close operation between this department and the sheriff's office, that at least one deportation is imminent and that the inquiry runs to points generally throughout the county.* (Californian, *October 12)*

The following editorial appeared on the front page of a valley newspaper:

*Practically all of the striking cotton pickers are Mexicans, so this article is addressed to people of that nationality.*

*First of all, many of you are visitors in this country, here only through our sufferance.*

*You have been fools, many of you, trying to reach a goal that is not possible for you to reach, the right to dictate to American employers what they shall pay, whether they can pay it or not.*

*With cotton at the price it is today, and the wage demanded by you Mexican cotton pickers, cotton growing in the San Joaquin Valley would be a thing of the past. Because YOU killed the goose that laid the golden egg!*

*If the cotton grower is finally required to pay $1.00 per hundred for picking his cotton, it is a sure and certain thing that he will not pay it to you striking Mexicans, who not only refuse to go to work at the scale of wages set but will not go to work and leave the matter to a board of arbitration of which the government of the United States will be a party.*

*What fools many of you have been in the strike! Most of you want to work and all of you should be at work. In fact many of you will have to go to work very soon or go back to your own country. . . .*

*If the strike continues, it is more than likely that every last one of you will be gathered into one huge bull pen and given the opportunity of proving your right to be in this country. And, what will a bull pen mean to you? Many of you don't know how the United States government can run a concentration camp. First of all, every last one of you will be deloused. That does not mean that any of you need it, but it will be the first step to prevent typhus. Then comes vaccination for smallpox, innoculation for diptheria, and what not. The ordeal will be sufficiently rigorous to prevent the outbreak of any disease.*

*Do you want to face the bull pen? Do you want to be deported to Mexico?*

*That is what you face, and don't fool yourselves about it!*

*Your leaders told you that they could get you a dollar a hundred for picking. They HAVE NOT—and they WILL NOT, because the grower has not the money with which to pay. They will tell you now that you will not be deported. Perhaps they will be mistaken about that, too.* (Corcoran News, October 20)

Tulare County officials requested that the federal government deport strikers receiving relief and the sheriff threatened deportation if the strikers did not return to work pending the recommendations of the fact-finding committee:

On the same day the *Tulare Advance-Register* published similar threats:

*The wartime "bull pen" may be invoked by the United States government to break the cotton pickers' strike in central California, it was learned today.*

*Indications that overstrained federal patience and refusal of strike agitators to accept government mediation might result in a general rounding up of undesirables and their confinement under federal guard in a wartime internment camp was plainly apparent as strikers and cotton growers deadlocked over mediation plans.*

*Deportation of undesirables, Communists, and agitators found not to be citizens also loomed as a possibility as federal lines tightened. That government interference was imminent was indicated by county officials, Sheriff Hill declared.*

*"The federal government is very liable to throw some of these people into a bull pen and ship them out of the area if they remain recalcitrant to the plea of conciliator Edward Fitzgerald that they return to work until the fact-finding commission has studied the situation and determined an equitable wage.*

*They have nothing to lose by returning to work, and if they refuse they are defying not the county government, but the federal government,"* the sheriff said significantly. (Advance-Register, *October 20*)

Three days later Tulare County officials definitely requested federal authorities to deport strikers who were aliens receiving relief:

*Deportation of Mexican cotton strikers in this county was sought today in a telegram sent to the commissioner of immigration, Washington, D.C., by District Attorney Walter C. Haight, Alfred J. Elliott, chairman of the board of supervisors, and James R. Fauver, foreman of the Tulare County Grand Jury, in a final effort to solve a problem which Sheriff R.L. Hill said might result in slaughter within the next three days.*

*The telegram follows:*

*"We appeal to and urgently request you to at once take all the necessary steps to deport all those aliens, the majority of whom are Mexicans, now in this county who have become public charges, who are a menace to public peace and health, who are now and will continue to be a heavy and impossible charge on the resources of the county and who are subject to deportation under the treaties between the United States and their respective countries."* (Times-Delta, *October 23*)

The deportation threat had little effect. It was not carried out and little regard was paid to it by the Mexicans themselves.

Individual leaders, as well as the Mexicans in general, were warned of deportation. As early as October 9 it was reported:

*Word comes from Los Angeles that the immigration department is sending deputies into the field to investigate some of the leadership which has manifested itself among the unemployed, the report being that a number of them are in this country contrary to the immigration laws.* (Californian, *October 9)*

The threat was carried out to the extent of arresting at least one "white" leader of the Corcoran camp:

*Leroy Gardiner, alias Leroy Gordon, arrested twice in the last two weeks by local authorities in connection with strike outbreaks in the Corcoran district, was in further trouble last evening, when he was arrested on a federal warrant by Federal Immigration Inspector A.J. Borstadt of Fresno. Inspector Borstadt said that Gardiner admitted he was born in Canada and is still a British subject. He is being held for violation of a federal law which says that a man may be held if it is proven "that he is a member of, or affiliated with an organization, association, society or group that believes in, advises, advocates, or teaches the overthrow by force or violence of the United States or of all forms of law."*

*Mr. Borstadt said that he expects warrants for Mexican arrests in the Corcoran area.* (Journal, *October 28)*

Special attention was given to deportability of strike leaders, and at least one was deported. The threat of deportation, however, had little or no effect on the morale of the strikers. The growers, of course, did not really want wholesale deportation of their laborers, and virtually none took place.

Curiously, the Mexican strikers used the threat of repatriation against the growers, when officers threatened to evict them from the Corcoran camp. Some of the leaders sent a telegram to former President Calles, as follows:

*We, 5,000 compatriots in Corcoran, California, district request your quick personal guarantee for we are disposed to migrate en masse to our own country because of force by business and local authorities.*

*These committees have told us to abandon our camp at 3 P.M. because of unsanitary conditions despite the fact it is in better condition than others in the valley. Compatriots in the valley complain of conditions and ask that a representative other than Consul Bravo be sent to investigate the matter here.*

But the Mexicans were no more anxious to return to Mexico than the growers were to have them. The Mexican government took no action on the telegram, and the Mexicans made no move toward voluntary repatriation.

(7) *Efforts were also made on behalf of the growers, and through*

*the Mexican consul,* to undermine the confidence of the strikers in their Communist leaders, to induce the formation of separate unions on the basis of nationality groups, and to invite direct dealings between strikers' representatives and growers, which would ignore the Communist-dominated leadership.

The effort to discredit the leaders in the eyes of the strikers was directed toward exposing them as Communists and racketeers with ulterior motive. A Corcoran grower-ginner appealed to the Mexican government to protect its countrymen from radical leaders:

*Ellett sent a telegram to the Mexican government informing it that Mexican workmen were being terrorized and controlled by American radicals, suggesting that that government call the situation to the attention of the American government.... In reply, it was learned, he received a curt note informing him that the Mexican government was watching the situation through its own representatives.* (Chronicle, October 22)

The tactic of the Communists to meet the charge of radical leadership was to inform the strikers and the public about it themselves and if possible, in advance. Two Communist leaders said publicly:

*The "red" issue was sent in to demoralize the camp. It is always a red herring whenever workers are engaged in a struggle to better conditons. Yes, Communists did organize the union.... (Speech) Communists get at the head of the union because they are elected.*

*The fight of the starving cotton pickers is a fight against starvation wages and the recognition of their union. The workers will not be misled by charges of communism.*

*In every strike the charge of agitator has been made by those serving the interests of the bosses in order to continue exploitation of the worker. I have been called an agitator. I have been agitating against starvation wages.*

*The Communists are the only ones who are fighting in the interest of the workers. No other political party has by its action shown it is for the workers. (Pat Chambers, quoted in* Times-Delta, *October 13)*

The attack against Communist leaders was based not only on their radicalism, but also on charges of racketeering and discrimination. An editorial declared:

*Promotion of so-called agricultural workers' "union" in California within the past two months and consequent "strikers" launched in various localities give evidence of a new type of racket which is being vigorously promoted within our borders.*

*A variety of attempts similar to the local cotton "strike," all organized in the same manner and bearing the earmarks of the same group of racketeers directing them, have been launched at opportune times in various parts of the state....*

*It is sufficient to state that a membership of some 4,000 pickers is claimed, with an initiation fee of 50 cents a head, and would total*

Pat Chambers (left) with his aides on steps on Visalia
Courthouse where he harangued strikers, 1933. *Photo:
Courtesy of the Bancroft Library, University of California.*

Caroline Decker, executive secretary of farm laborers'
union at strike headquarters, Tulare, 1933. *Photo: Courtesy
of the Bancroft Library, University of California.*

*several thousand dollars for the coffers of the racketeers, with addi-tional sums to be paid from time to time in dues—should the "strike" succeed.*

*That is the story of the farm labor strike racket in California within the past few months... the various strikes are one in purpose, promoted by a central group presumably principally interested in dues and in advancing the cause of communism... in almost every case the worker—the "comrade—has paid the bill. He is the real victim of the strike racketeer. (Advance-Register, October 17)*

A larger grower said, "Pat Chambers lays tribute on the workers. A picker in conference with growers told me that."

*Growers and their sympathizers also pointed out that more effort was made to bail out and defend Communist leaders than arrested strikers of the rank and file.*

*It has been noticeable, however, and the Mexican cotton strikers are rapidly awakening to the fact that the union has not been so prompt to bail out the ordinary Mexican worker when he gets into jail, and they naturally want to know why. (Journal, October 13)*

A district attorney claimed after the strike that a half dozen trespassing pickets who pleaded guilty, and were given two years' probation,

*have all turned against the strike, at least the women have, and I think the men have, too. They were all Mexicans, and they found the strike leaders didn't care anything about them but left them in jail though their bonds were only $500, while they raised $10,000 to get out Pat Chambers, the white leader. (Interview)*

To the charge of racketeering a Communist leader made answer:

*Not everybody will get his head broken and go around ragged and without decent soles in his shoes. If Pat Chambers had $6,000, why doesn't he bail himself out? The workers didn't believe the charges. They knew Pat Chambers—their Pat. They knew he had no soles in his shoes, that he slept in an arbor back of the house of a friend. They knew he had not made $6,000 on the Tagus strike.*

*American, Negro, and Mexican "stool pigeons" were sent into the Corcoran camp.... Some of our leaders were offered as much as $4,000 to break the strike. Some were offered a contract job to supply labor at $1.50 a head. (Interview)*

It is well known, of course, that a thoroughgoing, idealistic Communist is anything but self-seeking in matters of material personal enrichment, however ambitious he may be in other respects. If these efforts to break the strike with money actually were made, and the report is plausible under the conditions, it must be recorded that neither the emissaries, nor offers of money, nor argument, succeeded in shaking the strike morale. Attempts were made also to invite formation of separate unions or jettison of Communist leadership and direct negotiation with growers. Under the title "Arbitrate with Communists?" a valley editor declared:

*San Joaquin Valley cotton farmers are right when they declare they are willing to submit their wage difficulties with striking cotton pickers to state arbitration, but they will not meet with communistic strike leaders. . . .*

*It is to be hoped the misled workers in the fields will awaken to the fact that their worst enemies are their present communistic leaders and dictators—that under them they can accomplish nothing, for the American people will not long submit to the Mussolini edicts of these un-American vandals who hate not only the American government but as well the very American labor unions which have done so much and are doing so much for the amelioration of labor conditions. (*Bee, October 22*)*

Another valley editor made direct proposal that:

*The cotton pickers have a right to negotiate with the growers and they will find out if they do so directly, cutting out the radical leaders, that the growers are their real friends, not the red agitators who do not hesitate to use them for their own selfish purposes. (*Journal, October 13*)*

Another effort was described by a Communist as follows:

*The growers called in Mr. Elliott. Mr. Elliott is an American and chairman of the Tulare County Board of Supervisors. He talked to the white pickers. He told them they should not associate with the dirty, low-living Mexicans. He said, "Why, if I saw a Mexican dying in the street, I would not help him." You whites must organize your own union—an American union—and act in an American way. But Elliott got no further than Bravo. The workers understood him, too. (*Speech*)*

The ranks of the strikers grew in numbers and kept solid with comparatively few defections to the end. Without becoming Communists, the pickers nevertheless refused to unseat their Communist leaders, or to divide their organization along separate nationality lines.

(8) *The growers endeavored to influence other elements in the community,* including local, state, and federal administrative and law enforcement officials, merchants, and even the general public, to provide protection against picketing and to refrain from rendering relief, aid, or comfort to the strikers. Some of these efforts are discussed elsewhere, but two additional points are set forth here.

It greatly incensed the growers that the merchants should aid the strikers by extensions of credit and gifts. As one grower said, "The merchants gave the farmers more trouble during the strike than any other element in the community." Or, as an official sympathetic to the workers put it, "The small local merchants are among the best friends of the laborers." The growers, regarding themselves as patrons of the merchants, believed they were entitled to full support in resisting a wage advance; they ignored the fact that the pickers are also patrons, the greater portion of whose earnings are spent with local merchants.

So a bitter protest, in the form of a threatened boycott, soon appeared in the *Advance-Register* of Tulare, where union headquarters were located:

*[Paid Advertisement]*
*NOTICE!*
*TO THE CITIZENS OF TULARE*
*We, the farmers of your Community, whom you depend upon for sup-*
*port, feel that you have nursed too long the Viper that is at our door.*
*These Communist Agitators MUST be driven from town by you, and*
*your harboring them further will prove to us your non-cooperation with*
*us, and make it necessary for us to give our support and trade to another*
*town that will support and cooperate with us.*
*FARMER'S PROTECTIVE ASSOCIATION*

Not only did growers seek to bring pressure upon merchants or others who aided strikers or "harbored" them; efforts were made also to influence the tone of strike news which went out of the valley, for the growers resented much of the publicity given by the Bay Area newspapers, especially. To the insinuating suggestion of a growers' leader that "a reporter who would send out news as the growers wanted it sent could make a good deal of money," the indignant reply was made, "Yes, why don't you go and find such a reporter?" (Interview)

The background for the specific tactics employed by the growers against strikers which have been enumerated above, was maintained by incessant proclamation of the well-known and undisputed fact that the principal strike leaders were Communists, sharing the well-advertised aims of Communists.

CORCORAN CAMP

Unplanned circumstances provided the strikers with what was in many ways their most effective weapon in prosecuting the strike—the "concentration camp." Five of these camps of strikers rose like mushrooms in three counties; the largest was that located at Corcoran, Kings County.

The union had never employed a concentration camp in its previous activities, nor did it plan for any in the cotton strike. Union leaders, on the contrary, "advised the pickers to settle on individual ranches and when the strike call was sounded to picket their own jobs." Furthermore,

*The pickers were instructed to remain in the cotton camps after*
*striking, being informed that the growers would find it impossible to*
*evict them for several weeks, if they went to court for redress. (*News,
October 6)

In all previous strikes led by the Cannery and Agricultural Workers' Industrial Union the area involved was small—a single ranch in the Tagus peach strike. Interest centered on this comparatively small area, as on a factory during an industrial strike.

The cotton strike was decidedly different, for it involved several hundred ranches scattered over a hundred miles. If the pickers had

Strikers' camp, Corcoran, 1933. *Photo: Courtesy of the Bancroft Library, University of California.*

Mexican migrant labor camp at Corcoran, 1933. *Photo: Courtesy of the Bancroft Library, University of California.*

been able to follow the advice to remain scattered on the ranches, the completeness of the strike might have been seriously impaired. Union leaders could hardly have reached them. Their morale could scarcely have been as well maintained as when assembled in mass. Growers would have been able more easily to exert pressure on each family. Arrangement of picket caravans and of mass meetings would have been more difficult. But, as described earlier, the growers insisted on evictions. With no other place to go, the strikers gathered in camps erected or enormously expanded by the emergency.

The Mexican, white, and Negro pickers gravitated to the "Mexican towns," which turned into emergency camps at McFarland, Tulare, Porterville, Wasco, and other places, and served as the homes of the strikers, as centers for mass meetings, and as bases for picketing. Each of them resembled, in method of living at least, the most important of them all, the Corcoran encampment.

Corcoran camp began as a refuge for a handful of evicted Mexican workers at the beginning of the strike. Within a week the camp had almost attained its full growth. Union leaders, principally Leroy Gordon, early assumed direction and planned the arrangement and conduct of the camp. They secured permission to use the land from the lessee, Morgan, which led growers to dub the conflict "Morgan's strike."

The camp was located on a vacant field, perhaps four acres in extent, across the tracks on the eastern outskirts of Corcoran. When the camp began to attain substantial proportions, union leaders laid out rows of tents separated by dusty streets, named after towns or heroes of Mexico. Each family provided its own habitation—an old tent or burlap bags stretched between two poles and a car. These makeshift tents, in addition to the family car, cooking utensils, bedding, and the ever-present dog, represented the total possessions of the evicted pickers—with perhaps a goat or several chickens for the more fortunate. Later ten wooden toilets and a waterpipe system, extending through the middle of the "city" with frequent spigots, were added. An irrigation ditch served as the collective washtub and bathtub for the children, too. Garbage was buried in open pits.

The camp was surrounded by barbed-wire fence variously said to be for the purpose of keeping growers out or of retaining pickers within. A single opening faced the Corcoran side of the camp. It was barred by a rope and generally watched by a cluster of Mexicans whose leader's approval must be secured for each entrance and exit. An assembly space with platform was maintained in the center of the camp and a community kitchen was provided for the convenience of single men.

The "Aztec Circus," an itinerant show whose customary audience was in the tent city instead on ranch camps, added a touch of levity with its nightly performances financed by voluntary collections later divided equally between the union and the circus management.

Food, at first, was whatever individual families might be able
to purchase—mainly beans and flour for tortillas—and scattered dona-
tions collected by the Communists and strike sympathizers. Later, the
California State Emergency Relief Administration sent supplies.
Firewood for cooking was procured by scouting parties which hauled
it in truckloads for the entire camp.

A tent school "to take care of about seventy pupils" was opened
on October 11 with two teachers, in an attempt to provide for the
"approximately 800 children of school age. . . ." (*Journal,* October 11)

Camp leaders supplemented the entertainment provided by
guitar players and singers among the Mexicans, by a dance on the hard
ground, and by the circus, with frequent meetings to discuss strike
action, to listen to speakers, or to organize picket caravans.

It is difficult to estimate the number of persons at Corcoran
camp. Generally it has been placed at about 3,000, but more than likely
this figure is too generous, since growers wished to enhance the menace,
law officers the importance of their problem, and strikers the success
of the strike.

There were frequent, and usually unfounded reports of sickness
at Corcoran and the other strikers' camps. Three deaths did occur in
the Corcoran camp. Two were of young children suffering from
malnutrition caused by weeks of starvation prior to the strike. The
third was of a young mother, afflicted with pneumonia. . . . the strike
had nothing to do with her death." (*Advance-Register,* October 19)
These fatalities were more the product of the conditions usually prevailing among Mexican migratory workers than a result of the particular
situation in the Corcoran camp. However, the press generally blamed
the Corcoran camp. *The Los Angeles Times,* for example, drew an
exaggerated picture:

*This camp is the danger spot. I visited it today, and it is a dread-
ful place. I don't wonder that the residents of the town are terrorized.
No one in state employ with jurisdictional authority should consider
that mass of corruption with anything but shame.*

*Thirty-seven hundred men, women, and children are herded in
a ten-acre barren field on the edge of town. There is no shade and the
sun is cruel. At night it is cold. The equipment consists of a few ragged pup tents but mostly a shake down on the ground. There are no
sanitary precautions. No water for bathing; not much more for drink-
ing. Three or four latrines for 4,000 persons. Long lines of misery-marked
humanity await their turn. There is some sickness. There is grave
danger of epidemic. Promiscuity is unlimited.*

\*　　　\*　　　\*　　　\*　　　\*　　　\*　　　\*

*At the main entrance and at various gaps in the barbed-wire fence
Mexicans armed with clubs keep people out and in. Inmates are practically prisoners. They are harangued at frequent intervals by wild-eyed*

Mexican migrant labor camp. *Photo: Courtesy of the Bancroft Library, University of California.*

Cotton strikers' camp headquarters at Corcoran, 1933. *Photo: Courtesy of the Bancroft Library, University of California.*

*orators with a gift for gab, and at night picked crews are loaded onto trucks and started on their raids of sabotage and violence.*

Similarly, citizens, growers, and law officers all sought abatement of the tent city, ostensibly for the health protection of the Mexicans. In Corcoran "committees representing the women's club, PTA, Legion Auxiliary, and American Legion" met on October 18 and "unanimously passed a resolution to declare the camp a health menace." *(News,* October 20)

It seems plain that the impetus for the abatement of the camp on grounds of danger to health came mainly from those who sought dissolution of the camp as a step in breaking the strike. After the strike a district attorney explained:

*The camp wasn't so bad. It was just about as sanitary as other cotton camps and these growers who kept wanting it condemned for being unsanitary lived six miles on the other side of town. What difference did the sanitation make to them? They just had it in the back of their minds that if they could get the camp broken up the pickers would go back to work at 60 cents. (Interview)*

The *Hanford Journal* hinted at the possibility of the forced evacuation of the camp as early as October 10:

*Meantime the tent city at Corcoran with its school and food and sanitation complications will bear close watching by the authorities. It is a menace in more ways than one.*

*State labor camp inspectors would not allow comparable sanitation conditions in the cotton camps on ranches. It is unbelievable they will permit them in the Corcoran tent city for long.*

The hint was followed promptly by a threat of forced evacuation:

*Drawn up by District Attorney Clarence H. Wilson, formal notice to make improvements in the toilet, garbage disposal, and water systems at the big cotton strikers' camp in Corcoran or vacate the property by October 17 was served on the strike leaders and on the lessee of the property yesterday. Sheriff Buckner served the notice upon J.E. Morgan, who leases it from the Santa Fe Railroad, and upon Al Gordon, representative of Pat Chambers, strike leader. Chambers was in Visalia yesterday.*

*The notice to clean up the camp or vacate was based upon recommendations of Edward T. Ross, chief of the Bureau of Sanitary Inspection, State Department of Public Health, who visited the camp Monday.*

*It declared that the camp is a public nuisance as it now exists, owing to the fact that the 1,200 to 1,500 persons estimated to be occupying the premises have no sanitary toilets, no adequate water supply, and no sanitary garbage disposal system.*

*The cotton strikers and owners of the land (directly east of Corcoran) are notified that unless they carry out the following provisions they must vacate the property or be prosecuted to the full extent of the law.*

Mexican migrant labor camp at Corcoran. *Photo: Courtesy of the Bancroft Library, University of California.*

Mexican migrant labor camp at Corcoran. *Photo: Courtesy of the Bancroft Library, University of California.*

*1. They must build at least ten screened, sanitary, fly-tight toilets. 2. Must provide an adequate, sanitary water supply by installing a water storage tank with pipelines and faucets, the exact number of faucets to be fixed by state authorities. 3. Must provide sanitary, covered, fly-tight receptacles for garbage which must be disposed of at regular intervals in accordance with good sanitary practice.* (Journal, October 12)

The eviction threatened for the seventeenth did not occur, but instead District Attorney Wilson issued a second ultimatum on the nineteenth "that unless all of the requirements of the original notice regarding water tanks, faucets, pipelines, etc., were fulfilled by tomorrow night, arrests would be made." (*Journal*, October 20) At about the same time it was rumored that George Creel, NRA chief, had stated following a visit to the camp that:

*... he would get in communication with Governor Rolph and the state board of health... urging upon them the necessity of abolishing the camp of striking cotton pickers at Corcoran.* (News, October 20)

Evacuation threats came from still another source on October 19:

*Dr. Giles Porter, state health director, today ordered abatement of the San Joaquin Valley cotton strikers' encampments unless certain conditions were fulfilled immediately....*

*Porter ordered construction of ten sanitary latrines, installation of a sanitary water supply system with storage tanks, pipelines and faucets, and installation of garbage receptacles.* (Advance-Register, October 19)

Three days later, however, he put his approval upon the camp conditions:

*Dr. Giles Porter, head of the state health board, spent the day at Corcoran in company with Dr. C.G. Newbecker, county health officer, taking personal charge of the health protection work of the state. He informed Dr. Newbecker and S.E. Railsback, chairman of the board of supervisors, that he found sanitary conditions at the Corcoran camp better than the average temporary camp in the state, thus definitely removing the threat of abatement of the camp as a public nuisance.* (Journal, October 22)

Naturally the strikers protested against these continual threats:

*Every civic body and governmental authority has worked in an effort to disband this camp. The strikers have taken every sanitary precautionary measure, and daily the authorities find new excuses to threaten eviction. Today, the occupancy of the camp by the strikers depended upon their ability to meet with an admittedly (by health authorities) unnecessary measure—the establishment of a water tank and pipe and faucet system; while previous to this, health officers have approved the existing water system. From previous experience, even if these demands are met with by the strikers, some new grievance on the part of the authorities will arise.* ("Brief history of the San Joaquin

*Valley cotton strike," presented to fact-finding committee, Visalia, October 20, 1933.)*

As strike tension increased, growers planned to clean out the camp by force, if necessary:

*Only the timely arrival of Kings County sheriff's officers and state highway patrolmen prevented Kings County ranchers from "cleaning out" the Corcoran cotton strikers this morning, where close to 3,000 striking cotton pickers are encamped....*

*Sheriff Van Buckner and E. Raymond Cato, chief of the highway patrol, arrived shortly after the ranchers began to converge on Corcoran and called a meeting in the city hall. The ranchers were "talked out" of their march against the strikers, but thirty-five to forty highway patrolmen joined Kings County officers in patrolling the district.* (Times-Delta, *October 24*)

The final attempt to abolish the camp was successful. However, it was not based on menace to health, nor threats of force by growers. It came only after efforts of state and federal officials to end the strike following the growers' acceptance of the governor's fact-finding committee's proposal on October 25. The next day federal relief to strikers was discontinued. This action, coupled with last-minute appeal by State Labor Commissioner MacDonald, forestalled forcible evacuation of the camp by the Kings County sheriff.

The sheriff originally had set the deadline for evacuation at 3 P.M. October 26:

*Camps of striking cotton pickers in the Corcoran area will be cleaned out today, according to a statement made by Sheriff R.V. Buckner of Kings County last night.*

*All occupants of the camps, which the state health department considered likely places for breeding of epidemics and a menace to public health, will be offered work in the cotton fields.*

*Regardless of whether the inhabitants go back to work or not, state and county officials have declared the camps must be deserted tonight.* (Times, *October 26*)

Sheriff Buckner prepared his forces to tear down the camp at 3 P.M. as announced. He and his men lined the side of the Tulare-Corcoran road north of the camp as the time drew near. A loudspeaker was secured over which the sheriff planned to broadcast the offer of the growers to pay 75 cents a hundred for picking. All those unwilling to accept the offer were to be forcibly dispossessed. The situation was tense. Labor Commissioner MacDonald realized its seriousness and prevailed upon Sheriff Buckner to desist for at least a day. An hour's wait for the arrival of the Hearst Movietone News to photograph the impending combat gave MacDonald sufficient time to win his point. The sheriff conceded and announced over the loudspeaker his desire to speak with several camp leaders. The strikers shouted back, "We are all leaders." Several, however, came forward and received the sheriff's offer of a day's grace. Leroy Gordon, one of the leaders who presented himself, was arrested at this juncture despite the evident truce which had been called. MacDonald then addressed the strikers:

*A number of factors conspired to prevent the wholesale eviction of the Corcoran camp which at one hour yesterday seemed a certain thing. The factors included: waiting for a decision by the strike committee on the 75-cent rate, in connection with negotiations by State Labor Commissioner Frank MacDonald and his deputies; waiting for a reply from ex-President Calles of Mexico to a telegram from the strikers concerning their possible repatriation in Mexico; a statement by Highway Patrol Chief Raymond Cato that highway patrolmen were authorized to take no part in the wholesale eviction; and lack of support to the eviction by health officials and district attorneys' representatives. Labor Commissioner MacDonald made the final dramatic announcement that he had secured from Sheriff Buckner a twenty-four-hour postponement of the eviction.* (Times, October 27)

This action by MacDonald was partly responsible for criticisms of him resting on but the slightest pretext, and ignoring that he had brought peace and evacuation of the camp:

*But there is nothing for the state administration to pride itself on in Deputy Labor Commissioner MacDonald's handling of the situation at Corcoran—his action was an encouragement to disorder and seems difficult either to explain or excuse.*

*The spectacle of a state officer haranguing a group led by reds and calling them "comrades" is not an edifying one.* (Los Angeles Times editorial, reprinted in Visalia Times-Delta, *October 31*)

On the same day the camp was addressed by the labor commissioner, the union decided to call off the strike and posted a sign in the Corcoran camp reading "The strike is over." Immediately the camp began to break up, and in three days was deserted.

*The strike camp at Corcoran was rapidly breaking up this afternoon as processions of rickety cars carrying pickers and their few belongings left the Corcoran district for cotton fields in other sections of the San Joaquin Valley. The camp, which for the past three weeks has housed nearly 4,000 men, women, and children, was expected to be entirely disbanded by 6 o'clock tonight, the deadline set by Sheriff Van Buckner of Kings County.* (Times-Delta, *October 28*)

*The last inhabitants deserted Corcoran's deserted tent city of strikers about four o'clock Saturday afternoon, and the site upon which thrived a tent city of three thousand persons during the past few weeks was returned to an uninteresting tract of barren ground.* (Times, *October 29*)

During the entire life of the camp, reports persisted that many of the Mexicans were being held virtual prisoners. On October 14, Sheriff Buckner said:

*. . . that one of the guards told him that they (the guards), armed*

*with long billy clubs, some of them with iron bars, had been given orders to permit no strikers to move out.* ... *(Journal, October 14)*

A reporter declared, "As nearly as I can estimate the feeling, at least 80 percent of the strikers are willing and anxious to return to work, but they are in deadly fear of the leaders." *(Los Angeles Times, in Times-Delta,* October 26)

These reports gained additional favor at the time of the dissolution of the camp. It was reported on October 29 that several local officers stated they had been,

*told by various Mexican strikers that they had been held prisoners in the camp, that information regarding the settlement of the strike had been withheld from them, that many of those who broke away from the camp and went to work had been beaten by white and Negro leaders and that others had been threatened with beatings or death if they went to work in defiance of strike orders.*

*Many of those coming from the camp believed until yesterday that the 60-cent scale for picking was still in effect, the leaders having held out the information that the growers had agreed to the 75-cent scale. (Journal, October 29; also* Times-Delta, *October 28, 30)*

These reports cannot be accepted as statements of fact. All available evidence points to the conclusion that the inhabitants of Corcoran camp were not held by threats of violence, that the Communists did not rule by force, and that the Mexicans were not kept in ignorance of compromise offers.

One other strikers' camp, located at McFarland in Kern County, was threatened with eviction. The sheriff prepared to dissolve the camp at one time and build two bull pens to hold the prospective arrested Mexicans, but thought better of it and desisted.

*We were ready to clean them out there. We built two bull pens, one for the women and one for the men, and we were going in after them but they disarmed before we had to. (Interview)*

All of the camps disintegrated as pickers drifted back to their work. A new camp, unconnected with the cotton strike but evidently arranged by the union, rose near Portersville in Tulare County, where Mexicans were collecting to await the orange harvest. However, no strike developed and the camp was abandoned. *(Times,* October 20; *Times-Delta,* October 28)

## MEXICAN CONSUL

Since most of the striking pickers were Mexicans, since three Mexican citizens were shot to death, since Mexicans were thrown into jail, and since hundreds of others were evicted from their temporary ranch homes, the government of Mexico, through its consular representative at Monterey, Enrique Bravo, was soon drawn into the conflict.

After the fatal shootings of Mexicans, Bravo visited the strike area and remained until the strike was settled. On October 12 he gave out his first newspaper interview:

*The Mexican government, through Consul Enrique Bravo of Monterey, today demanded that the State of California protect its nationals by disarming cotton growers.*

*The cotton strikers, 95 percent of them Mexicans, are "unarmed and in perfect spirit to abide by the law," while farmers have shown radical tendencies, using force, the consul telegraphed Governor James Rolph, Jr.*

*Consul Bravo declared that Delfino D'Avila, one of the two Mexicans killed by enraged cotton growers at Pixley, was killed while in discharge of his official duties of investigating the cotton pickers' strike. D'Avila was Mexican consular representative at Tulare. . . .*

*Consul Bravo told the United Press at Visalia that his investigation of the strike disclosed ranchers evicted many Mexican families from their homes in the Corcoran district in 24 hours, instead of three days, as required by law; in many cases, shut off their water supplies.*

*He planned to confer with Pat Chambers, strike leader, who was held in jail on criminal syndicalism charges, and Mexicans held on rioting charges, later today.*

*The consul said he had arranged for state and federal aid for Mexican families who were victims of the strike.*

The text of Bravo's telegram to Governor Rolph was:

*"Honorable Governor James Rolph, Jr.: Having visited several strikers' camps and investigated the Pixley case, I found strikers are 95 percent Mexicans, unarmed, in perfect spirit to abide by the law. On the other hand, farmers have shown radical tendencies, using force, being armed. Suggest you request proper authorities to require farmers to disarm and bloodshed will cease. Remaining here, willing to cooperate and accept your suggestions. Please wire me care sheriff's office. Assure you highest consideration."* (Advance-Register, *October 12)*

Bravo conferred both with the strikers whose leaders later charged him with strikebreaking activity and with the growers. He,

*held a conference with the growers, headed by L.D. Ellett, and was informed that the growers would welcome the workers back on the job at the old rate owing to the fact that they had found the Mexican worker particularly fitted for the job. He said they definitely refused to deal with Pat Chambers and other white strikers, but were willing to deal directly with the Mexican workers.*

*Bravo will also confer with Tulare County authorities concerning the seventeen Mexicans who were arrested at Pixley prior to the shooting and who are held for inciting a riot. He expressed hopes of obtaining their liberty soon with the completion of strike settlement negotiations.*

*Bravo said he had been informed that while American strike leaders who have been arrested in the valley in connection with strikes have been provided with bail by the union almost immediately after their arrests, Mexican strikers who have been arrested have been allowed by the union to remain in jail without bail.* (Journal, *October 12)*

The growers looked hopefully to Bravo to help in undermining the strikers' morale. The varied appeal which he made to his nationals was described in valley newspapers:

*After his meeting with the growers and gin men, Bravo went to the strikers' camp in Corcoran where he addressed some 2,000 workers. He told them a straightforward story of the attitude of the growers and suggested that they deal directly with the growers through their own committee of workers rather than through the white strike agitators. His address did not meet with the approval of the strike leaders, he admitted, but was in conformance with his program of informing the growers of the workers' attitude and the workers with the growers' attitude.*

*Fitzgerald (federal conciliator) accompanied Bravo (Mexican consul) into the cotton fields today to select two representative strikers from each of the camps, who will meet with the arbitration board.*

*At Pixley last night a Mexican consular representative was reported to have attempted to break up the strike union by trying to get Mexican strikers to separate and form their own union. (Bee, October 13, 14)*

The Communist answer was stated by a strike leader:

*The capitalist rulers used the age-old method of "divide and conquer." First, they wanted to separate the Mexicans from the whites and the leaders. They called in the Mexican Consul Bravo and asked him to do it. We knew Bravo. He sold out in the cherry strike, in the Salinas Valley. But the workers did not know him—he spoke their language and came from their country. So we had to tell the workers about Bravo. He went around to the camps and spoke to the Mexicans. We had to permit him to enter the camp. The Mexicans wanted to hear him, and we (strike leaders) thought it better to let him speak and expose himself. Some of them, especially the older Mexicans, wanted to rise and bow when the consul came. His line was, "You Mexicans are not Americans. You are Mexicans. You are only here to work, and participation in the strike might cause international complications. You must abide by the laws of this country. The Cannery and Agricultural Workers' Industrial Union leaders are not leaders. They are misleaders. They will lead you astray. Pat Chambers, one of them, stole $6,000 from you in the Tagus Ranch strike. You must organize your own union—a Mexican union—and go back to work pending settlement." But Bravo spoke only once in each camp. He never went back. The Mexicans understood him. They knew he wanted to break the strike—divide the ranks. They saw the whites and Negroes and Mexicans all working together. They saw the union leaders going without food, without sleep, struggling for their rights and their welfare. They wanted to go on that way. (Speech)*

It is extremely unlikely, however, that the Mexican consul wished to injure the chances of increased pay of his compatriots; it is more probable that he desired to cooperate with American officials in effecting a settlement without bloodshed.

Bravo remained in the region during the remainder of the strike. He advised the pickers again to return to work in the "Aviso Oficial" circulated by Federal Conciliator Fitzgerald, and though repudiated by union leaders, he appeared before the fact-finding committee where he plead for the picking rate of $1 a hundred demanded by the strikers. When the consul left the valley, the *Hanford Journal* reported:

*Bravo's straightforward handling of the strike situation brought him into marked disfavor with the strike agitators, particularly the whites, and it was repeatedly reported that his life had been threatened. Bravo from the first urged his countrymen to obey the laws and to deal directly with the cotton growers rather than through their white agitator leaders.*

*His attitude seemed to have found favor with most of his countrymen in the camp by Friday night when they admitted they had followed their Communist leaders because they had no others. When they learned yesterday for the first time that the 75-cent scale had been adopted by the growers, their confidence in Pat Chambers and his white lieutenants seemed further shaken. (October 29. The validity of the last sentence is very doubtful.)*

The Mexican government, as noted earlier, was introduced to the situation once more when Corcoran camp leaders, threatened with eviction, telegraphed former Mexican President Calles, pleading for the repatriation which valley citizens and law enforcement bodies professed to desire. The telegram to Calles read:

*We, 5,000 compatriots in Corcoran, California, district request your quick personal guarantee for we are disposed to migrate en masse to our own country because of force by business and local authorities.*

*These committees have told us to abandon our camp at 3 P.M. because of unsanitary conditions despite the fact it is in better condition than others in the valley. Compatriots in the valley complain of conditions and ask that a representative other than Consul Bravo be sent to investigate the matter here. (Times, October 27)*

The telegram was later repudiated by the Mexican leader of the strike camp:

*It was learned directly also yesterday that Lino Sanchez, well-known Corcoran Mexican and so-called "mayor of the strike camp," and that the telegram sent to Elias Calles, Mexico's immigration minister and former president had been signed with Sanchez's name without his knowledge or consent by some of the other strike leaders.*

*Sanchez told Enrique Bravo, Mexican consular representative, who was ordered by the Mexican ambassador to check the telegram, that he did not know the telegram had been sent until he received Friday morning a telegram of acknowledgement from Mexico City informing him that General Calles was ill in bed. Sanchez said he protested the unauthorized use of his name to the strike leaders remaining in camp yesterday and almost came to blows over it.* (Journal, October 29)

No move at voluntary repatriation was made by the Mexicans and the Mexican government took no action on the telegram.

## LAW ENFORCEMENT

The problem of maintaining the peace and at the same time protecting all parties to a labor conflict in the exercise of their legal rights has generally proved difficult for American officers. Even when authorities wish to preserve an equal balance between the parties to the dispute, they are confronted with vagueness and uncertainty in the law, and with heavy pressure from interested parties. The problem proved particularly difficult during the cotton strike in communities inexperienced in labor conflict.

The sheriffs and their deputies concentrated their efforts on the following program: (1) suppression of violence, but not including the disarming of growers; (2) prevention of anything but "peaceful" picketing, variously interpreted, with primary consideration for pickers working in the fields; (3) arrest of strike leaders as violators of the law. Also, growers were assisted in eviction of strikers from their temporary camps (described in section on Growers' Resistance), and "undercover men" were placed among the strikers. (Proceedings, California State Sheriffs Association, 1934, pp. 20, 23.)

The program was based on the "axiom" stated by the district attorney of Tulare County, "The crops must be harvested." (*Chronicle,* October 29) The attitude to which this led is suggested by the statements and actions of some of the officers. Sheriff Hill, for example, wished to handle the strike in his own way, declaring:

*I know I can handle the situation, but I don't know whether it would meet with the approval of the growers or the public at large.* (Times-Delta, *October 19*)

He warned the strikers:

*We're going to try to force them to obey the law. . . if they won't obey we're going to have a scrap, that's all.* (Times- Delta, *October 24*)

Hill's son, a deputy sheriff, is reported to have told University of California students when they objected to interference with picketing on the grounds that strikers had a legal right to picket:

*We had a meeting last night and changed all that. We make the law in Tulare County. (Testimony before fact-finding committee.)*

The sheriff of only one of the three counties made active preparation for the strike. According to an undersheriff in Kern County the officers

*knew the strike was coming and we were well prepared. We had two machine guns. We bought one thousand dollars of tear gas. We swore in forty-five deputies during the strike and secured fast cars to*

*cover the county. Cars were better than motorcycles on the rough roads
and the men could protect themselves better. We tried to prevent trouble in every way. As a result there was a 50 percent picking all during
the strike because we protected our farmers. The strikers didn't dare
do nothing here. We had them covered and they knew it. They were
afraid. (Interview)*

The sheriff of Tulare County was reluctant to create new deputies,
not wishing to assume responsibility for their actions. He had but two
deputies at the time of the Pixley shooting and created more only as
the strike progressed and the seriousness of the situation appeared
to demand them.

*The board of supervisors. . . vested Sheriff R.L. Hill with full
power to take all steps necessary to hold the strike situation under control, authorizing him to swear in as many deputies as he wants and
purchase all needed equipment. . . .*

*Shortly after receiving authorization of the board of supervisors,
Hill sent in an order for some gas shells to be used in 12-gauge shotguns.*

*Hill has had no special deputies on duty during the strike, and
his only help has been that of his regular deputies assisted by the
California Highway patrol and the constables of the county.*
(Times-Delta, *October 12)*

However, eighteen special deputies were sworn on October 13,
and fifty-one were on duty by the twenty-fourth. (*Times-Delta*) Sheriff
Buckner of Kings County created four special deputies to take care
of the situation.

The special deputies, which numbered more than a hundred in
the three counties, were even more inexperienced in handling strikes
than the sheriffs, and their judgment was continually in danger of being
warped by their prejudices. Many of the deputies were ranchers, ranch
managers, and gin employees. There is no report that any of them were
from the ranks of the strikers.

The focus of clashes between employers and strikers is commonly
the picket line, and so it proved during the cotton strike. This device
is one of the most conspicuous and tangible of the efforts of the strikers
to increase their adherents, and its defeat is a major aim of employers
endeavoring to maintain active operations. Definition of permissible
conduct, during picketing, therefore, is of high importance to the parties to a labor dispute, and to officers who must enforce the law. In
California the law on picketing was in somewhat the same condition
of confusion as elsewhere in the country, the legality or illegality depending upon such vague criteria as the circumstances surrounding each
case, and the conduct of the pickets themselves. Since the guiding decisions of California, as elsewhere, refer principally to conditions obtaining around factories or places of business on crowded city streets, their
discussions of specific situations are not very helpful to officers confronted with rural conditions. Some have thought that California

courts, notably liberal in holding that all strikes are legal, were not equally liberal in holding that "Picketing always amounts to intimidation." (Commons and Andrews, *Principles of Labor Legislation* [1927] 108, 110.) However, less than two months before the cotton pickers' strike a California Appellate Court specifically denied that California law holds "there could be no such thing as peaceful picketing." In a concurring opinion, one judge stated even more broadly:

> *That picketing, peaceable in fact, if not violative of a statute or ordinance, is not unlawful—and that the word intimidate—refers only to fear caused by threats, abuse or violence and not to the natural effect of picketing. . . . (Lisse v. Cooks, Waiters, and Waitresses. 74 Cal. App. 518, 523-525)*

Without discussing in detail the law on picketing, it is sufficient to stress that although peaceful picketing was lawful, it was left largely on the shoulders of local officers to determine in the light of "circumstances" and the "conduct of the pickets," the line between "persuasion" and "intimidation."

At the beginning of the strike, the sheriffs were unwilling to create large staffs of deputies; to do this would have been costly to the county, and responsibility for the acts of numbers of untrained deputies was something to be assumed only with reluctance:

> *A uniform method of handling the cotton situation was worked out by San Joaquin Valley peace officers at Fresno last weekend. . . . It was agreed that no special deputies would be hired, but that officers would keep a close watch on the situation to prevent any violence.* (Journal, *October 4*)

Within ten days, however, first Kern, then Tulare and Kings counties had sworn in fresh deputies. As the strike opened in Kern County the sheriff's office sent out "flying details of men in fast cars ready to rush to any scene of trouble at a moment's notice." (*Californian*, October 3)

Statements and demonstrations of force behind the law were frequently made by the officials and newspapers. Usually they were so phrased or conducted that they appeared to cast a shadow of illegality upon most of the normal activities of the strike. For example, it was reported: "Strike agitators are thwarted" when they "find the county well patrolled today by deputies from the sheriff's office." (*Californian*, October 4) Similarly:

### CITES RIOT LAWS

> *While he does not expect any serious trouble out of the Kings County cotton strike situation, District Attorney Clarence H. Wilson pointed out yesterday that there are definite laws under which county officers can act to handle any possible trouble. Rioting or inciting to riot are amply covered in the state laws as is also refusal to obey an order from a peace officer to disperse a riotous meeting. If agitators force workers to leave their jobs against their will, they are subject to punishment for a high misdemeanor.*

Faced with the difficult problem of interpreting the law on picketing and public assemblages, the peace officers perforce made their own decisions. The sheriff of Kings County, for example, arrested a striker for failure to address his Mexican audience in English. The incident called forth the following editorial:

*Soapbox orators haranguing cotton pickers in Kings County must do it in one language—American. That is the new rule Sheriff W.V. Buckner has laid down. He invoked it yesterday at Corcoran. A Mexican speaker had mounted a truck there and was hitting it off a hundred miles an hour in the Spanish tongue. His hearers, for the most part, were Mexicans. Drawn to the gathering to see and hear what was going on, and also to make sure that peace and quiet were respected by strikers, the sheriff listened for a few moments without understanding what the orator was talking about.*

*Suspecting him of trying to incite the crowd, the sheriff walked through the knot of people and ordered the speaker to say what he had to say in American or stop talking. Corcoran and Kings are American communities, he explained, and whatever was said and done should be carried out above board in the American language. The request was fair. Moreover, it was enforced. The orator obeyed the order reluctantly. Nor did he linger there. He moved on at the insistence of the law. (Editorial in* Hanford Sentinel *reprinted in* Advance-Register, *October 18)*

One sheriff explained:

*It isn't lawful to obstruct the highways whether to hold a church service or to picket. Picketing on the road like they did is obstructing traffic and you can't tell me that three or four hundred pickets standing in the road don't intimidate thirty or forty workers, even if they don't say nothing. Mass picketing is illegal and I am not afraid to go before any court and prove it. (Interview)*

The following instance indicates the manner in which at various times picketing was interfered with by the officers:

*At Pixley in Tulare County two striking cotton pickers who were picketing a ranch when other ranchers continued to harvest were arrested on charges of disturbing the peace. They were accused of cursing workers who refused to strike. (*Californian, *October 10)*

The law against incitement to riot also was employed:

*Five strikers were arrested near Tulare on the eighteenth on charges of inciting riot, when according to information from the sheriff's office the men were calling to pickers on the Singh Ranch and attempting to get the pickers to quit working. (*Advance-Register, *October 18)*

As the strike wore on, the interpretation of lawful picketing became more stringent. A deputy said: "We allowed strikers to stop at a single ranch for a few minutes only and did not allow congestion of the roads. Men have a right to picket, but they can do lawful things in an unlawful manner." (Interview) The practice at one time in Tulare County was to forbid even stopping:

*Picking was resumed in all sections of the county today as deputy sheriffs patrolled the roads and prevented parading strikers from stopping in the vicinity of fields where pickers were at work, Sheriff R.L. Hill announced today. . . . they are allowed to parade through the cotton districts in automobile caravans, but are not allowed to stop and hold meetings in front of the ranches.*

*While banners urging continuation of the strike are permitted, the strikers are not allowed to shout threats at either the pickers in the fields or the ranchers. Hill said that each caravan sent out by the strikers was accompanied by officers, and that every effort was being made to prevent further violence.* (Times-Delta, *October 17)*

A few days later, after trespassing by pickets had become more conspicuous, the sheriff warned:

*An ultimatum to strikers to cease law violations was issued by Sheriff R.L. Hill . . . as he sent into the cotton belt forty armed deputies who were instructed to resort to force if necessary to secure obedience of the sheriff's orders.*

*Strikers will not be allowed to stop on roads, they will not be allowed to double back on roads, shouting into fields will be forbidden, and none of the strikers will be allowed to get out of their automobiles.*

*Persistent violations will result in the arrest of the driver and confiscation of the car.* (Ibid. *October 24)*

On the same day:

*Accompanied by forty deputies, Sheriff Hill caught up with a caravan of strikers headed towards Earlimart from Corcoran. He halted the trucks, ordered all the occupants into the road, then arrested the drivers and confiscated the ten vehicles. The arrested men and the machines were sent to the county jail under an escort of armed deputies. The strikers were left to make their way back to camp on foot.* (Chronicle, *October 25)*

The method by which trespassing pickets were handled upon one occasion in Kings County is described as follows:

*Sheriff Buckner and his deputies and a squad of fifteen state traffic officers met the huge caravan of strike picketers, some thirty trucks and cars bearing almost 100 strikers. Sheriff Buckner, sensing trouble, had deputized some fifteen citizens. The caravan stopped and began yelling at the pickers in the field, some fifty or sixty of the women later swarming into the fields in an effort to pull out the workers, most of whom ran for cover. When the first man was arrested, a near riot ensued. The strikers roared at officers, piled off the trucks and milled around the officers' cars, some of the officers being grabbed by strikers. One tear gas bomb was thrown into the yelling mob, and several deputies and state traffic officers leapt upon cars, held tear gas bombs high and shouted in both English and Spanish that if the riot didn't stop they would throw them. That halted the mob and the officers soon had them under control, ordering the picketers back upon their trucks and into cars and placing eleven arrested leaders, including the three women, into their cars and sending them to jail in Hanford.* (Journal, *October 24*)

Only the day before, the sheriff is said to have forbidden picket caravans to leave the strikers' camp at Corcoran:

*Threat of trouble was seen when Sheriff Buckner of Kings County declared no cavalcade would be permitted to leave the strikers' camp at Corcoran while Caroline Decker, blond strike leader, asserted, "No man will stop us."* (Chronicle, *October 23*)

That strikers or their sympathizers at times did overstep the law with respect to trespass and personal violence has already been pointed out (see section on Union Attack). They also damaged physical property occasionally; for example, an independent farmer near Tipton said:

*The strikers burned cotton on my ranch. They cut fences and let cattle out, and stole sheep on other farms in the neighborhood. (Interview; also see below.)*

The main fear of the growers, however, was clearly not damage to physical property, but loss of their pickers. Efforts were made to jail union leaders in order to limit the effectiveness of the strike, evidently on the principle subsequently expressed by a district attorney, and thoroughly in accord with the views of most growers, that:

*Tulare County can no longer permit the Communists and radical agitators to move about our agricultural belt unmolested.* (Chronicle, *October 29; also see below.)*

In Kern County it was reported following the Arvin riot that the sheriff "staged a house-cleaning in the farming community in an effort to capture the ring-leaders." (*Californian,* October 11) Pat Chambers, the most conspicuous among the strike organizers until his arrest and the hearings before the governor's committee brought Caroline Decker into prominence, was arrested early during the cotton strike, and all efforts to bail him out or obtain release on habeas corpus were unsuccessful. The "leader of the strike was being held under $10,000 bond. . . on a charge of advocating criminal syndicalism. The complaint was signed by F.E. Peterson, Pixley rancher, and was based on alleged statements made by Chambers" preceding the shooting affair at Pixley. Chambers was arrested in front of the strike headquarters in Tulare. (*Times-Delta,* October 12) His "criminal" record stated that he had been "arrested seven times in connection with his strike agitation activities, but never convicted." The *Fresno Bee* announced with evident satisfaction:

*Hanford officers said with Chambers and Gordon under arrest and Louis Bradley convicted on a Fresno County charge in connection with the grape pickers' strike, all three members of the strike agitation in San Joaquin County are in custody.* (Bee, *October 13)*

The *Hanford Journal* stated editorially:

*With Pat Chambers in jail in Visalia on charges of inciting rioting; with Louis Bradley, one of the principal leaders, found guilty of rioting at Madera and facing two years in jail; and with Leroy Gordon, another leader, in jail in Hanford, a considerable crimp has been put in the ranks of the radical cotton strike leaders.*

*Chambers is a known Communist, and Bradley, who "comraded" peach strikers at Tagus Ranch about in an approved Leningrad style, have been clever enough up to this point to evade the law. Arrested before, they have gained freedom shortly on bail, or obtained dismissal of charges against them by promptly using union attorneys to handle their case. (Journal, October 13)*

The policy of arresting the leaders was termed by the *Western Worker* (November 20) a "racket used by district attorneys to break strikes." And Chambers later filed suit against the district attorney, sheriff, and the rancher who signed the complaint:

*On his complaint Chambers stated that he was a leader in the cotton strike, and that the defendants conspired to break the strike by unlawful means, including the abuse of legal process for the purpose of aiding the ranchers. (Times-Delta, November 9)*

The suit was dismissed.

Arrest of strike leaders proved completely unavailing to break the strike. Although it was harassing to those conducting the strike, they used it as a rallying cry of "persecution" to deepen the antipathies of the strikers against officers of the law.

Efforts were also made by the officials to prevent an influx of new leaders which might increase the effectiveness of picketing activities:

*Steps to prevent an influx of transients called to this county to aid in maintaining picketing were taken by county authorities in conjunction with the aid of railroad detectives as a careful survey of railroad yards and jungles was started today. (Advance-Register, October 19)*

Sheriffs coordinated their activities and shared information concerning movements of strike "agitators":

*A report which Sheriff Emig of Santa Clara County said he had been unable to verify, that armed men were on their way from Communist headquarters at San Jose to aid cotton strikers at Pixley, was transmitted to authorities in San Joaquin Valley by Emig. (Journal, October 17)*

Arrests of pickets in Kings and Tulare counties were frequent. Sixteen were arrested near Pixley on the day of the shooting. (*Times,* October 11) Eleven others were arrested in Kings County on October 23. Smaller numbers of pickets were apprehended at frequent intervals in both counties. Only four strikers were jailed for picketing activity in Kern County.

George Creel, NRA Director, who spoke to the strikers at the Corcoran camp on October 18, advised them that they were within their legal rights to picket. At this the growers and sheriffs were greatly incensed. As one prominent grower of Kern County stated:

*Creel told the Mexicans they had a right to picket. They thought the government wanted them to picket. (Interview)*

And a sheriff declared:

*Conditions are worse in the cotton fields this afternoon than they have been any day since the shooting. . . anything might happen any minute, and conditions tend to get worse instead of better. There are several groups of radical agitators in the county now and they apparently want trouble rather than any settlement of the dispute.*

*We have been having lots of trouble since George Creel made a statement telling the strikers they had a right to picket. They took this to mean that they could do anything they pleased, and strikers in caravans have given officials considerable trouble. (*Times-Delta, *October 19)*

Some violence was in fact precipitated by strikers (see section on Union Attack). They are reported to have burned cotton in the fields in Kern County (*Californian,* October 4, 7); to have attempted to burn some cotton at the Long gin near Corcoran; to have resisted officers trying to arrest a Mexican in the Corcoran camp (*Times-Delta,* October 19); to have done some "night riding" (*Times,* October 25); to have overturned cotton wagons in fields of Kings County (*Times-Delta,* October 23); and to have fired shots into the home of one of the growers indicted for the Pixley affair (*Chronicle,* October 20). Two other reports of strikers' violence early in the strike are as follows:

*J.D. Russell, Pond rancher, and Harry Torrey, driving along the highway, were reported stopped by twenty-five alleged strikers. The windows of the car were smashed and efforts made to drag the men from the car. Mr. Russell, however, accelerated the machine and the two escaped.*

*It was reported that while 1,000 pounds of cotton were being loaded on the P.J. Richards Ranch near McFarland a striker tossed a lighted match into the cotton and it was burned. J.D. Croder, brother-in-law of Richards, is reported to have struck the striker on the head with a pitchfork, but not soon enough to prevent a blaze. (*California, *October 7)*

On the whole, however, the strikers made an attempt to keep the peace and obey the law as their leaders advised, knowing their inability to resist attacks by growers and the feeling they might better secure their ends by avoiding violence.

The first violent clash of groups of men occurred at Woodville when growers sought to disperse strikers and forbid picketing (see also section on Growers' Resistance):

*Seventy-five farmers held a meeting and afterward went over to a strikers' gathering at a local service station and broke up the meeting. The farmers told the striker who was speaking to be out of the county by 9 A.M. Sunday, which he agreed to do. The farmers told the strikers they didn't want to see a picket in the fields at 9 A.M. Sunday, and that they would be around to see that such was the case. Farmers planned to hold a meeting at the Poplar gin Saturday night to complete their plans.* (Advance-Register, *October 7)*

The strikers described the Woodville riot as follows:

*Earlier in the day, the president of the Woodville local was attacked by a group of growers. That evening the strikers held a mass meeting at Woodville. Two truckloads of farmers drove up to the meeting; a deputy with a star on his shirt front stood on the farmers' truck. As the strikers' speaker attempted to speak, catcalls came from the growers' trucks, with the occasional urge—"let's go." While a young striker spoke the growers piled off their trucks and made a wedge-shaped attack on the meeting of the strikers. The strikers defended themselves with the parts of a small table and bench which were quickly dismembered, while the growers struck with pistol butts. One striker had seven stitches taken in his head, a farmer suffered a fractured skull, another striker had two front teeth pushed in, and there were several minor injuries. The growers then changed the purpose of their coming to the meeting and asked to address the meeting. They were granted that. Not being able to prove satisfactorily to the strikers that they could not pay the $1 per 100 demanded, they read a document which was later printed in all the newspapers, and informed the strikers that everyone wishing to pick cotton for 60 cents per hundred would be protected by the growers; all others must leave the state by 9 A.M. Monday morning.*

*One grower present at the meeting, Stark, by name, turned to the strikers and said, facing Caroline Decker: "I will shoot to kill the first striker I see in the road, and it won't be the first man I've killed."* *("Brief history of the San Joaquin Valley cotton strike," submitted to fact-finding committee)*

Groups of growers in the strike area vented their anger and sought to demoralize the strikers by arming themselves and threatening violence. Some had migrated earlier from the cotton belt and brought with them traditions of race domination over cotton workers by force. Immediately upon declaration of the strike, growers were publicly assured that they could protect workers in their fields by force and arms under the law against trespass. This they proceeded to do:

*It was reported that picking was proceeding as usual and that cotton growers were prepared to offer protection to their pickers under the state trespass law. Under this law a man has the right to resist unlawful invasion of his property with force if necessary.* (Californian, *October 3)*

*In some sections of the county, farmers are reported to have armed themselves with guns to prevent invasion of their fields and intimidation of their cotton pickers.* (Californian, October 5)

*Armed San Joaquin Valley ranchers today stood guard over their cotton fields, ready to resist with gunfire attempts of strikers to prevent harvest of their crops.* (Advance-Register, October 7)

The *San Francisco Chronicle* declared on October 13 that licenses to carry concealed weapons had been issued to 600 citizens in Kern County alone.

Well-armed as they were without a doubt, threats of forceful action by the growers carried added weight. Threats to "blow to hell every striker who so much as laid a hand on the fences of their properties" (*Times-Delta*, October 13), appear to have been fairly frequent. Also, the growers employed their guns when forcing eviction of strikers from ranch camps and when protecting their pickers from picket caravans. Moreover, when the ranchers organized into vigilante associations, it only emphasized their promises. (See section on Growers' Resistance.)

The strikers, on the other hand, were almost wholly unarmed. There is little indication that the laborers ever carried guns or threatened use of force against the growers, despite rumors that the McFarland and Corcoran camps at one time were bristling with arms. The leaders continually advocated peaceful activity only and warned against the use of arms of any description.

This armament program of the growers led one sheriff to the opinion that "hell may break loose" at any time. (*Tulare Times,* October 24) In fact it had already done so on two occasions when growers and strikers met: at Pixley, where two strikers were killed and eight growers were arrested on charges of murder; and near Arvin where one striker was shot to death and, strangely enough, nine strikers only were arrested for the death. Both clashes occurred on the afternoon of October 10.

Near Pixley, a small town about fifteen miles south of Tulare where a caravan of pickets had visited a ranch, sixteen of them were imprisoned on ranch property by armed growers collected for the purpose and held by them until sheriff's deputies could arrest the pickets and remove them to town. Soon strikers collected in Pixley to protest the arrests and held a mass meeting across the highway from their headquarters on a vacant lot near the Southern Pacific Railroad tracks. While Pat Chambers addressed the group, aroused farmers arrived in town and partially surrounded the strikers, threatening them with guns. The strikers feared violence. They concluded their meeting and crossed the road en masse to enter their headquarters. As the first of them reached the entrance, a grower's gun was discharged, which was seized by a striker and pointed into the ground. This striker was knocked down by a grower and shot to death while lying there. General

Mexican laborers at cotton camp. Photo: Courtesy of the Bancroft Library, University of California.

firing took place as the strikers fled to cover. A second striker was killed, eight more wounded, and holes were shot through windows, woodwork, and flags at the union headquarters.

The growers then began to depart, unhindered by either state or local law officers who were at hand. As they departed, the officers decided to relieve them of their guns but no arrests were made until later when eight growers were arrested and jailed. A grand jury indictment held them on $15,000 bail, "furnished by friends," for trial on December 12.

*It is reported here that ginning companies and other large concerns interested in cotton are making arrangements to furnish the required bond for the accused men, all but one of whom are cotton growers.* (Times-Delta, *November 2)*

A San Francisco newspaper reporter who witnessed the attack has described it as follows:

*The cotton of Tulare is stained with strikers' blood today.*

*Two short-torn American flags droop over the doorways that framed the brutal shooting of unarmed strikers as they peacefully entered their headquarters at Pixley in Tulare County Tuesday.*

*I saw eleven unarmed persons shot down in cold blood. One was a woman. Two were killed.*

*It had been coming a long time. The farmers knew the strikers knew it. They had appealed to the police for protection in vain.*

*W.D. Hammett, striker and former minister, had protested to the peace officers against the danger of allowing the farmers to carry their rifles and shotguns on the taut streets of Pixley.*

*Mrs. Lillian Dunn—she stood with her baby clutched to her breast inside the strikers' headquarters as the farmers' shots ripped through the building all about her—corroborated this.*

*The slaughter had been sudden, almost like an ambush.*

*Pat Chambers, strike leader, had been on a truck haranguing the strikers.*

*"This is no time for a backward step," he had said. "We must fight and show the farmers a solid front. We will match the farmers with their own violence. Let them start something and we will finish it."*

*Idle words—at least so far.*

*The meeting adjourned. The strikers were slowly walking across the street to their union headquarters.*

*Suddenly a farmer fired into the crowd. Several strikers jumped on him.*

*A few fusilades rang out from the other farmers.*

*The strikers broke, ran into their red brick, two-storied headquarters building. All but a few. They lay in their own tracks where the farmers' bullets had dropped them. Some lay very still. Others weakly pulled themselves up on their elbows, tried to crawl to safety out of the line of fire.*

*Tanks and barbed wire were all that were needed to complete the picture.*

*The farmers barricaded themselves behind a row of parked automobiles—as if there was need for it. Not so much as a water pistol appeared in the hands of the besieged strikers.*

*For several minutes the farmers kept up a sniping attack with their guns.*

*The flags over the doorways danced a grotesque jig as shots ripped through their stars and stripes.*

*Bullets whizzed over my head only a short distance outside the boundaries of the narrow no-man's land.*

*It was a strange and feeble flag of peace that finally ended the battle—the white police car of W.W. Snell, in charge of the state highway patrol at Bakersfield. It drove into the highway from a side street and stopped right alongside of me.*

*Surprised, the farmers stopped firing, staring blankly at the emblem of the law.*

*Then they ran for their parked automobiles and drove past us. Inspector Snell remained seated in his car. I was standing outside.*

*Their shotguns and rifles were poked menacingly out of the windows of their cars at us.*

*The inspector, still seated in the machine, tooted his horn weakly. The long procession of bristling automobiles continued its deliberate, dignified retreat, never heeding the horse-like honking.*

*By this time deputy sheriffs had come alongside the inspector's machine. "What shall we do now?" the inspector turned to one of the deputies.*

*There was some stammering, some hemming and hawing, and finally, after the farmers' cars had passed, one of the deputies got an idea.*

*"Let's go after them!" he suggested with very little enthusiasm.*

*. . . the farmers were stopped by Deputy Sheriff Carl Inside, who searched the cars and removed six rifles, four shotguns, and other small arms, but did not detain the farmers.*

*Other arms were found in abandoned cars around the besieged building. (*San Francisco News, *October 11)*

A striker eyewitness has given his version as follows:

*The farmers opened fire on us from behind automobiles without warning last night.*

*Several hundred of us strikers were meeting on the main street here. We thought Justice of the Peace J.E. Swanson shouldn't have issued warrants and caused the arrest of seventeen strikers held under armed guard.*

*Pat Chambers got up and told us not to do anything violent. He said we'd get farther by peaceful means.*

*A bunch of cotton growers drove into town in ten automobiles. They drove through our meeting and scattered the crowd.*

*We decided to go to the hall across the street—the strike head-quarters.*

*We were crossing the street when farmers stopped their auto-mobiles. They got behind the cars and opened fire without warning.*

*Some of the boys fought with them then. But there on the street were the dead and wounded. There was a lot of yelling and screaming. Then nearly everybody cleared out. I don't know whether anybody threw bricks or not. I know I did not.*

*It all started when one of the farmers took a shot at someone in our crowd. I guess they were old enemies.*

*There was a volley of shots. It was soon over. When the growers and the strikers saw the bodies and realized what happened, most of them ran out of there. Two were dead. (Billy Thomas in* Advance-Register, *October 11)*

W.D. Hammett, Pixley strike leader who appeared before the jury during the trial of the indicted growers, gave testimony as follows:

*As Pat Chambers started to talk on the railroad property across from headquarters in Pixley, a group of armed men drove up, Hammett said. When Chambers completed his speech, the strikers and their leader started back to the hall.*

*They had been in the hall only a short time when someone shouted: "Bill, they're coming in on us."*

*Running to the sidewalk in front of the building, Hammett said he saw a group of armed men headed toward the headquarters.*

*Hammett reached the highway just as the first man in the advancing group stepped on the highway in front of headquarters.*

*I told him not to shoot into the hall among women and children there, Hammett said. He shoved a rifle toward me and I grabbed it by the barrel and pushed it toward the ground. Just then a Mexican fellow grabbed the rifle and I grabbed the pistol the next man had. We started scuffling and wrestled around there in the gutter while I tried to take the gun away and the man hung on to it.*

*While we were scuffling, I heard a shot and then heard Delfino D'Avila shout: "Bill, you better run. They've got me." I let go the gun and ran into the building.*

*I went through the back of the building and then through the fence and started north.*

*"Was the shooting going on while you were going away?" District Attorney Walter Haight inquired.*

*"Yes, I heard it while I was getting away," Hammett replied. "I could still hear the shots when I was two blocks away."*

*"You were running pretty fast, weren't you?" Haight asked.*

*"Well, I wasn't walking," was Hammett's answer. (*Times-Delta, *January 12, 1934)*

The Arvin riot took place the same afternoon as the Pixley

Pat Chambers addressing strikers at Pixley shortly before farmers opened fire on them, 1933. *Photo: Courtesy of the Bancroft Library, University of California.*

Striker at Pixley felled by farmers' bullets, 1933. *Photo: Courtesy of the Bancroft Library, University of California.*

shooting. Arvin is a small town in a cotton growing community about twenty miles southeast of Bakersfield, in Kern County. The initial impetus to the riot came on the morning of the eleventh when more than a score of armed growers assembled to protect working pickers in a field 1 ¾ miles west of Arvin from a large caravan of pickets. From 10 o'clock on, the two sides defied each other. The strikers faced the growers across a dirt road and each group hurled epithets at the other. An undersheriff described the scene:

*There was an imaginary line at the edge of the road and neither group dared cross it. There were thirty armed growers on the cotton field side and about 250 strikers in the road. All the time the growers were just hoping one would put his foot across the line and he would have been plugged full of holes. (Interview)*

Sometime after 3 o'clock a skirmish took place. Opinions vary as to the immediate cause. Intermittent fighting continued for nearly half an hour. Growers employed their gun butts and strikers used grape stakes and clubs. Finally shooting broke out for a brief minute or two and Undersheriff Carter threw a tear gas bomb. When the riot was over, one Mexican lay dying in the road and several others were wounded. A few growers had sustained cuts and bruises.

Testimony presented at the coroner's inquest (in the matter of the inquest held on the body of Pedro Subia, deceased, Bakersfield, October 14, 1933), indicated that only the growers were armed and the consensus of opinion was that all the shots, variously estimated at from five to 100, came from the north and northeast, the growers' side of the road. No one appeared to know who fired the death-dealing shot. One theory held it was fired by a striker and intended for Undersheriff Carter but hit Subia instead. A second version described the assailant as a grower:

*Question: Can you repeat his words again? Answer: He [an armed man in overalls, wearing glasses and speaking to a deputy and growers] said, "I would not have shot him but he was contemplating shooting an officer." (Testimony of Eliza N. Margraeves before coroner's jury.)*

A description of the riot by the *Bakersfield Californian* (October 11) depicts another view:

*Varied versions of the Gary Mitchell Ranch battle were forthcoming but the most consistent was that told by guards and onlookers to the effect that strikers attempted to drag a strikebreaker from the field in which he was working.*

*Mitchell laid aside the gun he carried and barehanded charged the strikers who lined the side of the field. Other growers on the scene, including Jewett, Thompson, and Frick, in an instant had joined the fray.*

*They were outnumbered 10 to 1 by the strikers and as grape stakes, gas pipe, and fists swung the growers soon went down. Women and children scattered among the strikers kept the guards from using their guns, they said. The menacing weapons, however, held a large portion of the strikers at bay and are believed to have saved the lives of the growers.*

*A riot call to Sheriff Cos Walser brought a carload of deputies headed by T.J. Carter, ex-marine, and F. Harlow Wright, also an overseas veteran, armed with tear gas guns, and the army of strikers was forced to retreat.*

*A sniper hidden in an evergreen tree beside the road down which the strikers were retreating is said to have been responsible for Subia's death. Witnesses said the bullet evidently was fired at the back of Deputy Carter as he advanced with a gas gun. Subia walked into the line of fire and crumpled to the ground as the bullet tore through his chest, severing an artery and causing death within a few minutes. . . .*

*Stunned by the spectre of death, the strikers soon retired to Arvin, where they milled about their headquarters in the Adobe Cafe and their camp in the residential district for hours.*

*The tear gas produced by the sheriff's office proved the most effective measure in quelling the rioters. The baptismal came as a surprise to the strikers.*

*The main group of strikers had withdrawn down the highway and congregated 125 yards from the deputies. The range of Carter's riot gun is just 125 yards, and as he fired and the projectile barely dropped at their feet, the strikers jeered and hooted, not knowing it was a gas bomb. Suddenly it bursted and the stinging gas poured over them like a blanket. Choking, gasping, and half-blinded, they took to their heels.*

Nine strikers were arrested on murder charges and brought to trial in November, but none were convicted.

In addition to these major clashes there were the usual sporadic rumors of violence. A Negro striker was reported shot in the neck while driving his car south of Pixley on the day of the encounter. Another striker was said to have been injured in McFarland on October 11 by a grower's gun. (*Bee*, October 11, 12)

*Another rancher, whose name could not be obtained, was reported to have driven strike agitators from his property using a gun.* (*Californian, October 7*)

Pat Chambers, strike leader, charged that the violence and shootings were planned by the growers:

*The shooting itself was an organized attempt and was accompanied by disorders at Arvin and other points in the cotton fields.* (*Times-Delta, October 13*)

It seems unlikely that the shootings themselves were more than spontaneous reactions to a common anger. Yet behind them, making them possible on the scale on which they occurred at Pixley lay the prior organization and arming of growers.

The position of local peace officers, caught between growers, strikers, and the metropolitan public of the state, was obviously difficult. Of course the growers were in the best position to bring pressure. They were stable, taxpaying, voting residents and well organized for years. The sheriffs knew them as friends and neighbors. The strikers, on the other hand, were largely migratory, nonvoting, poor, and hastily organized. The metropolitan press was far away.

The formal organization of pressure began early:

*For the first time since the strike commenced, E.K. Walls, president of the Tulare County Farm Bureau, and a committee of nine members met with Chairman Elliott of the board of supervisors at Visalia in a conference relative to the policing of the affected area.*

*It was the consensus of opinion that Sheriff R.L. Hill be provided with special funds to employ extra deputies during such emergencies as the present.* (Bee, October 12)

The power of the growers was well understood by the authorities, who occasionally acknowledged it in interviews. An undersheriff declared:

*We protect our farmers here in Kern County. They are our best people. They are always with us. They keep the country going. They put us in here and they can put us out again, so we serve them. But the Mexicans are trash. They have no standard of living. We herd them like pigs. (Interview)*

A district attorney explained:

*The growers really were more trouble and danger than the strikers were. We could control the strikers because they didn't amount to anything and couldn't even vote, but the growers were well known and had lots of influence and we were much more afraid we couldn't control them. I guess the growers said things just as likely to incite to violence as Pat Chambers did, but they couldn't be guilty of criminal syndicalism, because they weren't trying to overthrow the government.*

*A grower came to me one day and asked me for a warrant, and I refused it and said he had no reason to arrest the striker. He insisted and I refused. Then he said if there was any bloodshed, it would be my fault. I was on the spot then, so I gave him the warrant but told him he had no right to sign it and if he did the striker would have the right to take action against him for illegal arrest. And I told him that if he was brought into court, I'd tell the jury the same thing as I told him. He went out with the warrant, but I never heard of it again. Why, some of the growers wanted us to arrest the strikers just because they were strikers and for no other reason. (Interview)*

This pressure from growers largely explains why tactics of the authorities so frequently operated to undermine the strike. One of the district attorneys pointed out the use of arrests for this purpose:

*Four other arrests were made in this county. That was when the strike leaders were arrested for vagrancy at Corcoran. The sheriff thought that would break the strike but they were better organized than we thought and it didn't do any good. I was against arresting them all the time because we didn't have any case against them. Their cases were later dismissed. (Interview)*

A similar occurrence in another county later was made the basis for an unsuccessful suit:

*Pat Chambers, strike leader and asserted Communist, today filed suit against District Attorney Walter C. Haight, Sheriff R.L. Hill, and F.M. Peterson, Pixley rancher, demanding $15,000 damages for what he termed malicious prosecution and his confinement in the Tulare County jail.*

*On his complaint Chambers stated that he was a leader in the cotton strike and that the defendants conspired to break the strike by unlawful means, including the abuse of legal process for the purpose of aiding the ranchers.* (Times-Delta, *November 9)*

The *Western Worker* termed the policy of arresting leaders "a racket used by district attorneys to break strikes." (November 20)

The *Hanford Journal* reported that "113 persons have been arrested in connection with the strike." (October 28) Of these only eight were growers who were arrested after the Pixley shooting; the remainder were strikers.

No part of the report of the governor's fact-finding committee was more bitterly resented by growers than that section (see below) which found that the civil liberties of strikers had been violated.

The state highway patrol was used in the valley shortly after the Pixley and Arvin shootings:

*Cato, who has been in the district since the violent outbreak Tuesday night, offered to send eighty highway patrolmen into the community if the sheriff thinks it necessary.* (Times-Delta, *October 12)*

The patrol quickly "took command of the tense situation in Kings County" at Corcoran camp and "relieved Sheriff Van Buckner." *(Times-Delta,* October 24) The presence of the patrol of course relieved pressure for local deputies and shifted part of the cost of policing the strike from the counties to the state. When temporary withdrawal of the patrol was announced the sheriff of Tulare County was immediately affected:

*Hill announced this morning that he had received reports that the California Highway Patrol has withdrawn from strike duty. This will make it necessary to swear in more special deputies to cope with the situation, Hill said. The highway patrol has aided greatly in preserving order in the cotton belt, and patrolmen have been accompanying caravans of picketers every day since the Pixley shooting.* (Times-Delta, *October 21)*

Cato's program included an effort to persuade the farmers to halt picking until peace was restored:

*Chief Cato warned ranch owners not to attempt any picking today, fearing the strikers, grown suddenly ugly-tempered despite the efforts of Governor Rolph's fact-finding mediation board, might resort to further violence.* (San Francisco Call-Bulletin, *October 24)*

Also Cato used his influence, together with that of others, to dissuade the sheriff from entering Corcoran camp with thirty John Doe warrants to arrest leaders, although "some growers were white in the face because the sheriff wouldn't go in." The intensity of the situation, the influence of hereditary backgrounds, and the pressure of growers was described by a leading citizen:

> *Southerners didn't think a Mexican or Nigger as anything but a slave. They said, "We will arm and go in there and clean them out." A grower who had come originally from Georgia said, "You ought to have guts enough in this community to go in and clean them out. The cotton industry in the San Joaquin Valley will never be worth anything unless you do." (Interview)*

The patrol was subjected to some criticism for its work with strike caravans and at Pixley. At Corcoran camp, however, it clearly was a stabilizing influence, and restrained the more hot-headed growers from precipitating what could only have been a bloody and futile battle. But the terms in which the patrol won praise from local newspapers for its work in the valley foreshadowed the growth of hostility from organized labor toward the use of the highway patrol in labor disputes:

> *Whatever the final outcome of the cotton strike, it has already been shown that the state highway patrol constitutes one of the most effective police organizations in California.*
>
> *... an organization comparable to the famous Royal Northwest Mounted Police and the celebrated Pennsylvania State Troopers.* (Times, *October 27)*

In the closing days of the strike there were rumors that the National Guard would be called out. Sheriff Buckner is reported to have sent a "plea for troops to Governor Rolph from Corcoran declaring that the strike had gotten out of control and that unless troops were sent to Corcoran area bloodshed would result." (*Journal*, October 24)Governor Rolph answered he would not call out any troops until absolutely necessary. (*Times-Delta*, October 24) They were never considered indispensable.

### RELIEF

The California Emergency Relief Administration, operating under federal advice, rendered material assistance to the strikers in their dual role as needy unemployed. This was the first large labor conflict in the United States, perhaps the first of any size, in which a federal agency gave food to hungry strikers, and it established a precedent of importance.

Many migratory families, living an always precarious existence, had come to the cotton area two or three weeks before picking season. This period served for many to exhaust their scanty reserves. Thus the advent of the strike found many of them penniless, and as it continued, the situation became grave. Even by the second week, many of the striking laborers had difficulty obtaining food and the threat of starvation of children in the dramatic Corcoran concentration camp attracted the attention of governmental officials and of the public.

The union attempted through its Communist connections to collect both money and provisions at mass meetings staged in metropolitan communities. The *Western Worker* (October 16) declared that the strikers:

> *must have* immediate relief! *Send funds and food! That's the ammunition they need! As soon as San Francisco heard of the strike, a lightning arrangement brought a big meeting to hear the strike leaders. $54.00 and lots of food was collected. YOUR CITY MUST DO LIKEWISE.*

AFofL locals and sympathetic persons also contributed. But the support secured in these ways was insufficient.

Local government relief agencies refused aid. The Tulare County Board of Supervisors on October 12 determined not to assist the strikers:

> *The Board of Supervisors, meeting in special session at the courthouse this morning, approved the action of Chairman Alfred J. Elliott of Tulare in refusing to promise to turn over to striking cotton pickers $5,000 to be used to feed and clothe the workers for the duration of the strike.*
>
> *"We are going to carry on relief work just as we have in the past, but in the past we have never cared for indigents," Elliott said. "If the person applying for aid has resided in the county for the required length of time and is not an indigent, he will be given relief, without regard as to whether he has been involved in the strike."*
>
> *"If we were getting federal money we would have to give aid to these indigents.[9] However, we are not getting federal money and we are not going to apply for it."* (Times-Delta, *October 12*)

The Kern County Board of Supervisors took similar action. Chairman Brite, when interviewed by a union delegation seeking food relief, replied: "We haven't the money." (*Californian*, October 16) Union leaders severely criticized this attitude, which they called "starving us out."

Contrary to precedent the California Emergency Relief Administration stepped into the situation and treated the hungry strikers and their families like other destitute people "willing to work." Thus for the first time on a large scale a public relief agency waived the existence of a labor dispute and aided "strikers" just as it aided other "unemployed."

On October 12 Governor Rolph directed R.C. Branion, director of the relief administration, to give aid:

> *Stark hunger gripped the cotton belt tonight as Governor Rolph overrode NRA regulations to rush relief to the sufferers.*
>
> *Threatened with an epidemic of typhoid fever as a result of the unsanitary conditions, thousands of destitute cotton strikers and their*

*families, camped in squalid tent cities in Kings and Tulare counties, are showing marked effects of malnutrition. More than 4,300 women and children, many of whom have not tasted food all day, are included in the population of the makeshift canvas villages, sprawled like gypsy encampments over the countryside.*

*And in these wretched surroundings some of the women are expected to give birth to babies within forty-eight hours!*

*Alarmed over conditions in the area, Governor Rolph last night ordered R.C. Branion, state administrator of federal relief funds, into the cotton belt to distribute food....*

*"Under national recovery regulations our hands are tied until the strikers agree to submit their difficulties to arbitration," Branion told him.*

*"Arbitration hell!" declared the Governor. "We're not going to force these strikers into arbitration by starving them out. Not in my state! These people are hungry. Get down there—fly down there by plane and feed them as soon as you can."*

*Branion left a short time later to organize relief here in cooperation with agents of the state department of industrial relations.* (Chronicle, *October 13)*

On October 15 assistance was ready. At first it was refused by the strikers:

*While demanding federal relief in the Kings County strike feud in a circular broadcast yesterday, strike leaders refused to accept the proffered relief of R.C. Branion, state emergency relief chief, and a corps of assistants who took milk to the Corcoran camp Sunday for children of strikers. Branion and a corp of women relief workers were reported to have taken 260 quarts of milk for the children but only eighteen quarts were accepted before strike leaders halted the procedure. Wood was also reported to have been offered by Branion and as definitely refused.*

*Kings County officers who visited the camp could explain the refusal only on the grounds that the "history card" the state agency required strikers who accepted milk to sign were interpreted by the strike leaders as binding them to go to work at the 60-cent scale. Another version was that the strikers feared that if their record were thus obtained, many of them would be deported to Mexico.* (Times-Delta, *October 14)*

The questions objected to by the union were dropped and the mere signature of a family head and declaration of need sufficed for receipt of help. The strikers then gladly accepted the food distributed at emergency depots established at all important towns. The *Fresno Bee* stated on October 21:

*Unemployed cotton pickers and their families in most of the strike areas were reported to be receiving food from the federal unemployment relief administration....*

The food was principally milk and groceries.

In the Corcoran camp alone, 2,595 persons in 525 families received food allotments "based on $8.00 a week for families of fourteen and $5.00 a week for smaller families." *(News, October 27)*

The total expenditures by the California Emergency Relief Administration for relief in the strike area were $10,709.26, divided as follows: Kern County, $5,233.48; Tulare County, $1,848.19; Kings County, $3,637.59.

As soon as the governor's fact-finding committee submitted its suggestion of a 75-cent rate for picking, R.C. Branion telegraphed leading growers' representatives on October 25 urging acceptance of the rate determined by that public body, and promised to discontinue assistance to the strikers in the event the farmers yielded:

*Referring to your telegram of October 23 to George Creel, federal relief will be withheld from any able-bodied individual striker who is given a bona fide offer of work at 75 cents per 100 pounds of cotton picked, as approved by the fact-finding committee, and who refuses such employment.* *(Times-Delta, October 25)*

Despite the fact that a "fair" rate had now been approved by a governor's committee, a left-wing group protested the termination of relief to force acceptance of the terms. A telegram to George Creel stated:

*We also demand that relief which has been cut off from unemployed workers in strike areas in disgraceful attempt to force them to scab be immediately restored. We pledge full solidarity with strikers in heroic effort to win a living wage. Rudie Lambert, Chairman.*

The difference between a strike *prior* to adjudication of fair wages by a public agency, and one *after*, and in opposition to its adjudication, was not recognized by these strike sympathizers.

The growers decided to accept the 75-cent rate, and on October 26:

*Sheriff Buckner was informed by Mr. Hughes that he had orders from his chief, Mr. Branion, that those who refused to go to work today would not be fed and authorized officers at Corcoran to notify the strikers to that effect. (Journal, October 26)*

Feeding strikers under rules of the federal relief administration was severely criticized by the growers, who felt that federal support greatly assisted the union to maintain the strike and to force a higher picking rate. In a telegram addressed to federal and state officials, the Citizens and Growers Committee of Kern County called their attention:

*... to bountiful use of federal funds for welfare relief through federal-state agencies, which has made and is making it more pleasant and desirable for labor to accept charity than to work. Little if any investigations are made by welfare workers and we have evidence that practically anyone can obtain help whether needed or not and in amounts greater than necessary. This is keeping many workers from working. (Californian, October 21)*

The chamber of commerce of the same county took the same position:

*The directors of the Kern County Chamber of Commerce unanimously adopted a resolution opposing the promiscuous feeding, such as has been done during the past few weeks in the San Joaquin Valley through state agencies, of any able-bodied person who was offered or able to secure work where there was plenty of it, and refused to accept it. (Letter of L.B. Nourse, secretary)*

A prominent grower objected to relief for strikers on the basis that it led the Mexican strikers to believe that the federal government wanted them to strike and was supporting them in their conflict with the growers. None of the growers saw anything in common between extension by government of agricultural "relief" to growers seeking a better income and "relief" to laborers striking for better wages.

Sheriff Buckner of Kings County made a charge of misuse of federal funds to augment the strikers' ranks:

*... returning from the Corcoran strike area... said he had obtained positive proof that a woman representing herself as a welfare worker from Sacramento, with authority to distribute federal and state funds to unemployed workers, had approached workers in the district and promised to allow each man $5 worth of groceries per week for himself and family if they would leave the job and join the strikers' camp near Corcoran. (Journal, October 21)*

The charge was refuted by C.W. Burr, representative of the emergency relief administration:

*The position of the state emergency relief administration and the federal emergency relief administration in the distribution of food is purely one of relieving distress. No discrimination between strikers and people who may be working in the fields of growers is made. The only condition necessary to secure relief is a reasonable evidence of need.*

*Any statement made by anyone to the effect that any penalty of any kind would result from people who are anxious to work or return to work securing food is purely propaganda. We deal with individuals and family heads and in no sense are we interested in organizations or groups.*

*Any statement to the effect that people who may have returned to work would be barred from securing needed food or that they would be required to cease work by any representative of the administration is entirely false. Our position is to relieve distress. The issues of the strike are in no sense any responsibility of the emergency relief administration. (Californian, October 21)*

There is no doubt that the extension of relief to the strikers helped them to continue the strike. Public relief policy, moreover, was now starting to remove fear of starvation from the list of legitimate pressures in labor relations.

## SETTLEMENT

The growers, angered at the disaffection of their formerly uncomplaining workers, conspired to "stand pat" as a unit. The pickers, enraged by the summary methods of eviction and threats meted out to them, determined to pick "not a pound for less than a dollar a hundred." The farmers believed they could break the strike. The strikers thought they could batter down the ranchers' resistance, supported by the growing threat of unfavorable weather as the season advanced. Each side was urged by its small group of leaders to hold fast to its original demands. The small growers were kept in line by the large ranchers and gin operators. On the other hand, the Communists bolstered any sags in the spirit of their followers. The ill-feeling engendered by the Pixley and Arvin fatalities, the riots, the threats, and the gun-carrying all galvanized the stubbornness of the contending groups and set the mold of opinion more firmly.

Four principal attempts to settle the strike were made: first, by Frank MacDonald, state labor commissioner; second, by Edward H. Fitzgerald, federal conciliator; third, by Timothy Reardon of the state department of industrial relations; and finally by the fact-finding committee appointed by the governor and supported by the NRA in California. The labor commissioner's staff offered its services as mediator in the strike as early as October 6 through E.B. Daniels, deputy commissioner for Kern, Kings, Tulare, and Inyo counties. Daniels addressed a communication to both farmers and strikers as follows:

*I have been requested by Frank C. MacDonald, state labor commissioner, to offer the services of the state department of industrial relations and the labor commissioner's office in the matter of mediating the dispute which has arisen between the San Joaquin Valley cotton growers and their picking labor. (Bee, October 6)*

The flat rejection of this offer by representatives of the growers was condemned by the labor commissioner:

*I think their refusal to allow any officials, state or federal, to act as mediators is unjustifiable and tends to encourage communism and to precipitate such dangerous conditions as have developed in the Lodi district. (Bee, October 8)*

The strikers accepted with some reservations. Daniels is reported to have received:

*requests from the McFarland, Shafter, and Wasco strikers to use his efforts to mediate the strike, and that he had been informed a similar request had been sent by mail from the Arvin workers' group. (Bee, October 10)*

Deputy labor commissioners made new proposals for mediation to the growers on October 9 at Corcoran, which again were declined as Chairman Ellett of the Corcoran growers' committee declared:

*The growers of this district talked over the situation this morning and decided to sit tight. (Bee, October 10)*

MacDonald himself entered the strike area at Governor Rolph's request to seek a settlement on October 11, and stated shortly:

*Developments since my arrival here cause me to feel confident of mediation. The serious complications and possibilities of tremendous financial loss, coupled with the sobering effects of the tragic*

*occurrences during the past two days, have brought home a realiza-*
*tion that violence will not settle the controversy and that mediation*
*must be resorted to immediately.* (Bee, *October 12)*

Even this endeavor was rebuffed by the growers when Frank J.
Palomares, manager of the San Joaquin Valley Agricultural Labor
Bureau, representing the growers, telegraphed the governor on October
13:

*Leaders among the cotton farmer group are not favorable to the*
*state department of labor conducting such a hearing as they do not*
*have confidence in the impartiality of this department and think they*
*would be unsuitable for working out a solution of the problem.* (Journal,
*October 14)*

A more colorful statement appeared in the valley press:

*"Why should we mediate with any of Governor Rolph's agents?"*
*one grower demanded. "Every one of them is on the side of the strikers.*
*They can't see our side of it at all. All they want is to get something*
*for the strikers. We can't and won't buck that combination."* (Advance-
Register, *October 11)*

Thus ended efforts by the labor commissioner to mediate, but
deputies remained in close touch with the strike throughout the conflict. MacDonald himself played an important role in the closing days
of the strike when he helped to prevent armed eviction of the Corcoran
campers and to persuade strikers to accept the report of the governor's committee.

The commissioner drew criticism from both sides. By the *Western*
*Worker* he was charged with "strikebreaking." (November 20) The *Los*
*Angeles Times* characterized his manner of persuading the strikers to
settle as:

*an encouragement to disorder (which) seems difficult either to*
*explain or excuse.... The spectacle of a state officer haranguing a group*
*led by reds and calling them "comrades" is not an edifying one.*
*(Reprinted in* Times-Delta, *October 31)*

Timothy Reardon, director of the California Department of
Industrial Relations, also tried to settle the strike, declaring after the
Pixley and Arvin shootings that "Order must be restored and the strike
must be settled immediately." (*Bee,* October 12) Ten days later, after
a brief visit to the strike area, he offered an ill-advised plan that he
said would "settle the strike in twenty-four hours":

*Pay cotton pickers 80 cents per 100 pounds and induce the federal*
*government to make up the difference of 20 cents between that and*
*the present rate, possibly out of funds now spent for relief among*
*strikers' families. (*Bee, *October 22)*

This plan would have been satisfactory to the growers but less
certainly so to the strikers. Clearly the federal government could not
accept a proposal to supplement wages directly. The precedent would
have been impossible to follow. Generally it was accorded no more than
brief attention by growers, strikers, or the public. But Reardon, like

MacDonald, was attacked by those who took the agricultural employers' side.

*. . . it is understandable why farmers do not care to leave it to Rolph's men.*

*For instance, men like Tim Reardon. Tim is a San Francisco political leader. Need more be said.*

*As an advocate and battler for labor he is doubtless a whiz, but as a calm, judicial arbiter looking at both sides dispassionately and making decisions broadly he is probably overpriced at a dime a dozen.* (Pacific Rural Press, *October 21)*

Another settlement was advanced by the manager of the state free employment service in Bakersfield. As early as October 10 he proposed a compromise at *"75 cents for first picking." (Bee,* October 10)

*I settled the strike in Kern by getting the growers to pay 75 cents. That is why they were picking here before the committee reported. All but three or four growers were willing to pay it. I did not send any pickers out at 60 cents. They did not want to go. (Interview)*

The efforts of Edward H. Fitzgerald, of the United States Conciliation Service, opened the last phase of the strike settlement. Fitzgerald arrived in the San Joaquin Valley fresh from conciliation in the cotton pickers' strike of the Salt River Valley, Arizona. In the Arizona dispute, his work culminated in the return of the pickers to work at the rate against which they struck (60 cents for each 100 pounds of short staple and $1.00 for long staple), with provision for them to share in any further increase in the market price of cotton. *(Advance-Register,* October 13)

The federal conciliator reached Visalia on Friday, October 13, and immediately urged a group of growers to accept a fact-finding commission. The growers finally yielded but protested the personnel of the board suggested. Whereupon Fitzgerald intimated that another more suitable to them would be appointed. He then prepared to secure individual pickers, but not union leaders, to represent the strikers during negotiations. Immediately there was premature publicity that the strike had ended:

*"The San Joaquin Valley cotton strike is over. Pickers will be in the fields Monday."*

*These were the words of the Federal Conciliator Edward Fitzgerald today following an all-night conference with sixty ranchers that ended in the early hours this morning.*

*Fitzgerald announced the growers had agreed to the appointment of a committee to make a survey of the cost of production of cotton and the wages ranchers are able to pay for picking.*

*He declared a fact-finding commission suggested by State NRA Administrator George Creel and James Rolph, Jr., and designed to include Archbishop Edward J. Hanna of San Francisco, O.K. McMurray, head of the law school of the University of California, and Tully C. Knoles of the College of the Pacific, had been suggested but had not met with the full support of the growers.*

*Fitzgerald said a new commission probably would be suggested by Creel or Rolph today. The principal objection raised to Hanna, McMurray, and Knoles was by Edson Abel, attorney for the California Farm Bureau Federation, who pointed out none of those named had had previous experience in agriculture labor disputes.*

*The agreement for a fact-finding committee followed a meeting in which the federal conciliator warned that grave consequences might result from delay in reaching a settlement.*

*"This controversy must be settled peacefully or else somebody is going to get hurt," Fitzgerald declared. "The government has made up its mind to settle this dispute and there is to be no more quibbling. I know what the government will do if this situation is not immediately taken care of, but I will not state that course now. . ."*

*The [Mexican] consul agreed to cooperate with the movement for arbitration and said he would urge his countrymen to return to the cotton fields pending negotiations.*

*Fitzgerald accompanied [Consul] Bravo into the cotton fields today to select two representative strikers from each of the camps, who will meet with the arbitration board. (Bee, October 14)*

Fitzgerald concluded his trip into the area with publication and distribution to growers and strikers of an official notice in English and Spanish. The notice announced to all parties concerned that a fact-finding board had been appointed and accepted by growers and strikers with the following commissioners:

*Archbishop Edward J. Hanna, San Francisco; Professor O.K. McMurray, Dean of the School of Jurisprudence, University of California; and Dr. Tully Knoles, President of the College of the Pacific. . . .*

*It therefore becomes the duty of the striking cotton pickers to proceed with the picking of California's cotton crop subject to the decision of the federal-state arbitration commission's findings and decisions.*

*It is also the duty of the cotton growers to forthwith reemploy the cotton pickers who have been on strike.*

*The governments of the United States of America and the State of California have authorized their representatives to furnish food, clothing, and, if necessary, medical attention to cotton pickers and their families who are unable to earn sufficient money for these necessities for themselves and families.*

*The consul of the United States of Mexico has agreed to help to prepare and to present evidence and data to prove justification of the wage rate which the striking cotton pickers claim should be paid them.*

*Because of the above stated arbitration arrangements and the acceptances of arbitration by the interested and affected parties, the cotton growers and the cotton pickers are requested to proceed with the picking of California's cotton crop beginning on Monday, October 16, 1933.*

The notice carried statements approving the proposal from George Creel, chairman, California Division of NRA; Governor James Rolph, Jr.; Enrique Bravo, Mexican consul; Federal Conciliator Fitzgerald; F.C. MacDonald, state labor commissioner; San Joaquin Cotton Committee of the California Farm Bureau Federation; and R.C. Branion, Federal-State Emergency Relief Administration of California. Following the issuance of the communication, Fitzgerald returned to his office in Los Angeles for the remainder of the conflict. The growers approved of his plan. The settlement of the Arizona strike had favored the farmers, he had conferred with the growers and attempted to secure a commission satisfactory to them, and he had refused to treat with the Communist leaders, dealing instead with the Mexican consul and individual strikers. Finally, he advised the return to work under the status quo until a report could be rendered by the commission. Consequently, the growers desired to secure his return to the valley later when the attitude of the fact-finding committee appeared unsatisfactory to them. The Citizens' and Growers' Committee of Kern County, in fact, telegraphed Washington:

*State efforts have been unavailing and growers have lost confidence in these officials and their work. Growers have expressed confidence in Edward Fitzgerald, federal conciliator in Los Angeles, and urge you to instruct him to enter this controversy with authority necessary to get results. (Californian, October 21)*

Governor Rolph and NRA Administrator Creel cooperated in selecting the fact-finding commission and continually sought to settle the dispute as quickly as possible:

*After conferring for two hours with representatives of the strikers, Governor Rolph urged them to agree to arbitration or mediation if the growers likewise would agree. The strikers were told that only through such steps could the state assure relief in the way of food to destitute workers.*

*After his conference with the strikers, the governor sent the following message to Frank J. Palomares of Fresno, representing the growers:*

*"In the interests of California, I earnestly request that mediation or arbitration be immediately agreed upon between the cotton growers and the cotton pickers in the existing affected area.*

*"I have the assurance of Mr. George Creel as representative of the federal government that he will cooperate with me to the fullest extent possible in attempting to bring an amicable adjustment of the pending controversy between the cotton growers and cotton pickers."* (Journal, October 13)

George Creel became active in the strike upon—

*receipt at San Francisco of a telegram from the national labor board asking him to represent it in the San Joaquin Valley cotton strike and to mediate.... [Immediately he] notified Governor Rolph the full*

*power of President Roosevelt's labor mediation board is ready to be thrown into efforts to bring industrial peace.*
*"Immediate suspension of hostilities is imperative," Creel said. He added that if Governor Rolph and state officials fail to take drastic peace measures, the government will.* (Bee, October 12)

Following acceptance by growers of the fact-finding commission proposal, Creel announced, "The strike is over." (*Advance-Register*, October 14) When this did not prove to be the case, he went to the valley to arrange for a settlement:

*"I am not here to settle the strike, but to set up a procedure by which it can be settled by the government commission on arbitration which is due here tomorrow. I want to be able to give the commission an outline of facts on which it can work to restore industrial peace in the cotton fields. We will want to know what the growers are able to pay, what is the limit of their capacity to pay, and whether that is sufficient for the workers. This strike is going to be settled in a way fair to all; but the federal government is going to insist on a settlement."*

*Mr. Creel's plans are being formed as he moves along. First he was to interview Pat Chambers, strike leader in jail at Visalia. Then he proposed to proceed to Corcoran and look into conditions at the strikers' concentration camp there housing 3,700 Mexican nationals. Afterwards he would return to Visalia for a conference with growers which is being arranged by President Ed Walls of the Tulare County Farm Bureau. This itinerary completed, he intended to fly back to San Francisco.* (Times-Delta, October 18)

By now neither the growers nor the strikers were as adamant against talking of an agreement as they had been and arrangements for a fact-finding committee were advanced.

Some difficulty was experienced in securing the personnel of the commission. The committee originally proposed on October 14 to include Archbishop Hanna, President Knoles, and Dean McMurray did not meet with the approval of the growers but was nevertheless in the official notice of Conciliator Fitzgerald. Soon it was announced that:

*. . . R.L. Adams, cotton expert, and professor of farm management at the University of California, has been substituted for Prof. O.K. McMurray, who was called East.* (Times-Delta, October 18)

Professor Adams, in turn, was unable to serve, and at the last moment Professor Ira B. Cross of the Department of Economics at the university was requested to take his place.

Neither growers nor union would bind themselves in advance to accept the recommendations of the commission. Both groups reserved the right to reject all or part of any forthcoming proposal as each saw fit. Neither of them realized the power behind the fact-finding committee, which was not evident until later when pressure was brought to bear on both sides to accept its recommendations.

The growers' case, presented by Edson Abel, attorney for the Farm Bureau, began with an attack on the governor's committee:

*. . . on behalf of the growers it is my duty to state that they do*

*not regard that their case will be considered with impartiality by the personnel on the committee. Many growers are not satisfied the problems of the farmer will be given fair consideration.*

*The position of the growers may be stated in a very few words. In spite of the demands for higher wages being put up to the growers by the pickers, the price fixed by the Agricultural Labor Bureau of 60 cents per 100 pounds is all the price of cotton will stand. The price of cotton is a world price. It is fixed by competition between the various growing areas of the world and California must compete in that market. The growers must do their best to come within this world price. (Hearings)*

The growers' case rested principally upon a series of individual financial statements purporting to show that increase in the picking rate would cause losses. The committee made some inquiries on its own account which raised doubts of the representative character of these estimates and of the propriety of their base from an accounting viewpoint.

In general, the growers accepted the conditions of the hearings with good grace. Several times growers protested against the presentation of the pickers' case by the Communists, nonpickers, and agitators instead of workers. For example, H.C. Merritt, of the Tagus Ranch, at first refused to be questioned by Pat Chambers, stating: "I didn't come here to be insulted by being asked questions by a dirty scum of a Communist." (Hearings) He retracted his declaration, however, when the chairman pointed out that the union leaders had been chosen by the strikers as their representatives and accepted as such, and that it is customary for laborers to be represented by nonworkers who can devote their time and ability without fear of losing their jobs, and for witnesses to submit to crossquestioning by representatives of the other side. Also the Communists were accused of coaching their witnesses. Miss Decker retaliated by offering to place any picker in the room, chosen at random, on the stand.

The witnesses presenting the growers' case were either large growers or were connected with gins or finance companies. No "small growers" were represented. Seven of the twelve witnesses grew cotton and stated their cotton acreages which ranged from 300 to 1,200, with an average of 575. The average cotton grower in the three cotton counties in 1929 had only about seventy acres. Four of these seven men also were connected in an official capacity with banks, gins, finance companies, or growers' labor agencies. Four of the other five witnesses were: a gin employee, a gin owner, a farm manager with no cotton plantings, a landowner renting out "twenty-five to thirty" farms, and a cotton farmer who did not state his acreage.

The growers centered their case on two points: first, the Mexican pickers can live on the 60-cent scale; and, second, the farmers cannot increase the rate of payment.

The growers sought to establish the sufficiency of the 60-cent rate by a statement of the estimated earnings of a Mexican family at that scale, and by comparing the 1933 scale in California with that paid in other sections of the United States, with the rate paid in 1932 for the same picking in California, and with that paid to labor engaged in other agricultural work. The California rate was said to be the highest in the United States with the exception of that prevalent in Arizona. The 1933 rate was stated to be a higher one, compared to the price of cotton, than in the two previous years. The 1932 scale was 40 cents based on 6-cent cotton, and in 1931 it was 50 cents. The 1933 rate, then, was a 50 percent and a 20 percent increase, respectively, over the two previous years.

*L.W. Frick: The [San Joaquin Valley Agricultural Labor] Bureau has never established any wage scales. We supply labor when the farmers need it; make recommendations to farmers as to prices to be paid for getting employers help. Of the cotton acreage in the valley there was about 90 percent present. A price of 60 cents was settled upon for the 1933 crop. Last year's price was 40 cents on the basis of 6-cent cotton and this year it is 50 percent higher with only a 35 percent increase in the price of cotton. (Hearings)*

*A.L. Wirin: Do you consider that a fair American rate?*

*J.W. Guiberson: I can answer that by asking you whether it is fair for the American farmer to have been working for nothing for the past few years.*

In general the information offered by the growers concerning the pickings and earnings of the laborers was of scant value, which was explained by Attorney Abel:

*Well, it is due to difference of viewpoint. The growers are only incidentally interested in the days of work of pickers. (Hearings)*

Caroline Decker opened the strikers' case by reading several typewritten statements on a history of the strike, on the organization of the Cannery and Agricultural Workers' Industrial Union, on a comparison of the Mexican pickers' standard of living with certain minimum cost of living studies, and on the demands of the union. These demands of the union were:

*1. That the federal government, through its authorized agencies, immediately cancel all cotton contracts between growers and finance companies, cotton gins, or other agencies which are now financing cotton growers in the San Joaquin Valley.*

*2. That in conjunction with the cancellation of above-mentioned contracts the federal government, through the proper agencies, establish a minimum price for cotton to the growers of not less than 12½ cents a pound.*

*3. That a minimum scale of wages for all cotton pickers be established and set at not less than $1 a hundred pounds of cotton picked.*

*4. That the cotton growers recognize the Cannery and Agricultural*

*Workers' Industrial Union, as representative of the agricultural workers in the state of California.*

*5. That there shall be no discrimination in rehiring because of race, color, creed, union, or strike activity.*

*6. That the inalienable right of the workers to organize, strike, and picket be upheld by federal, state, county, and local officials.*

*7. The immediate unconditional release of Pat Chambers, chairman of the strike committee, and all arrested cotton strikers.*

*8. Conviction for first degree murder of growers identified in the shootings at Pixley and Arvin.*

The strikers' case rested almost entirely on the ground that cotton pickers and their families cannot support themselves at the 60 cents a hundred rate. It was contended also that the farmer could pay more than this scale only if the "stranglehold of the gins and finance corporations" were released by action of the federal government.

The union desired the cooperation of the small farmer:

*In all its activities, the union has called upon the poor and small farmer to support the strikers in their demands, pointing out to the farmers that they must not attempt to take their own miseries out on the hides of the workers, since the workers have nothing, but that they, the small farmers, must organize to combat the stranglehold of the gins and finance corporations. The majority of growers testifying today and yesterday are large growers, bankers, and holders of large interests in finance corporations and gins. ("The Union's Position on the Farmer," typewritten document read before the fact-finding commission. In 1933, efforts were made to organize small farmers in the San Joaquin Valley into the United Farmers' League, to protest farm mortgage sales, power rates, etc.)*

The union therefore attacked the gin and finance companies as responsible for the desperate situation:

*We also contend that the cotton gin operators and finance companies have been exacting their pound of flesh from the cotton grower, and he, instead of fighting the injustice that has been inflicted upon him by these merciless financial interests, has proceeded to exact two pounds of flesh from the unfortunate cotton picker—the man and woman lowest down, the man and woman without defense, the man and woman whose condition has been ignored until this time, and is now only called to public attention because their lives have been threatened when they refuse to pick cotton at 60 cents a hundred pounds. ("Arguments Submitted in Justification of the Demands by Striking California Cotton Pickers for Wage Increases"; document read before fact-finding commission.)*

The strikers' case was summarized as follows:

*We appear today to ask for justice for one of the most unfortunate and lowest paid groups of workers in America. . . .*

*Striking cotton pickers have interviewed many of the growers who have frankly told them that 60 cents was too low; that they can afford to pay 75 cents per hundred pounds for picking cotton, but that they do not dare do so because if they do they will be punished and possibly ruined by the cotton gin operators and the financial companies. . . .*

*It should be borne in mind that with the tremendous increased cost of living, that such a miserable, un-American, and, in our opinion, unlawful wage standard condemns the cotton picker, almost the moment he leaves the cotton fields, to apply to the state relief agencies for food to keep himself and family from starving, and thereby forces the citizens of the state to pay for the low wages that the cotton grower says is the most he can afford to pay. This they ask you to approve. . . .*

*We call your further attention to the fact that the vast majority of the cotton pickers are Mexican citizens who were induced to come to pick California's cotton crop by the alluring untrue promises made by the financial interests that have grown rich through control of the cotton industry. . . .*

*You are asked to put your approval on a condition of peonage in America, and a condition, we believe, of illegal domination of the cotton industry by its financial exploiters.*

*We are sure that at this time when America's hope lies in the National Recovery Act that the American people will expect your honorable commission to tear the lid off and expose the viciousness that lies back of this condition, and to do justice to these poor, unfortunate cotton pickers that ask for a wage that will barely enable them to live. (Hearings)*

The union representatives pointed out also the seasonality of the pickers' employment, the low value of perquisites furnished by growers, the rising cost of living, and the disparity between cotton pickers' earnings, and the state minimum wage for women (in industry) and to various standard family budgets.

Consul Enrique Bravo, though repudiated by the union leaders, supported the strikers' case with testimony of his own. He said in part:

*It is my desire to interpret the desires of the Mexican pickers. In 1917, during the war, Mexicans were brought here to work while others were at war. The Mexican laborer has been here for many years, long before cotton was planted in this valley. . . .*

*The Mexican people with whom I have been in contact state that they are willing to work for 60 cents, but 60 cents for 60 pounds. . . . The children usually have to work to help in the support of their families. . . .*

*My information from Mexican women pickers is that they cannot pick over 150 pounds a day and then they must have time out to fix dinner. This would be 90 cents per day; 5½ days would make $4.95 per week; 52 weeks, $237.40. This would be about $580 per year for both man and wife. . . .*

*The Mexican has been an honest, just, and loyal worker. He is liked by the grower. He is easy to handle. In case of war, they would then be willing to cooperate. They are obedient to the laws of this country. Due to the increased costs under the NRA, this year he needs higher wages. I wish to reach a just and fair amount of wages for these laborers which they need for the support of their families.* (Hearings)

As the hearings drew to a close, Chairman Cross, the only member of the governor's committee able to be present throughout the hearing, attempted to get the two sides to discuss with each other plans for a settlement. The strike leaders agreed but the growers refused:

*Miss Decker: The feeling is only that the people cannot live on the 60 cents per hundred rate. The strikers are entitled to hold out for more than 60 cents. They have organized their picket lines and are trying to get the scabs out of the fields. If you wish and the growers wish, we can meet in a small group with you or them and then submit any proposals to our strike locals.*

*Attorney Abel: But Miss Decker has no proposal.*

*Decker: We have our proposal.*

*Cross: Mr. Abel, will you meet with a small group?*

*Abel: I will say right now that until the grower is provided with more money for his cotton, he cannot afford to pay more than 60 cents. When prices are higher, then they will pay more for picking, but only when conditions will permit.*

*Cross: Then there is no possibility of a compromise being effected?*

*Abel: You have seen the cost records. If you can show how the farmers are going to pay $1.00, the farmers will be glad to have your method explained to them. The farmers are faced with a set of facts in this matter, not with theory. . . .*

*Decker: May we take a definite answer to our proposal to our strike locals as to the position of the growers assuring us that they will meet with us in a smaller group or that they will do something about it, or some definite answer?. . .*

*Guiberson: The growers wish a proposal which comes honestly from the pickers.*

*Cross: What do you mean "honestly?"*

*Guiberson: I mean coming from the pickers.*

*Cross: But we would have to work through representatives. The strikers are organized as are the growers and use committees to carry out their ideas.*

*Guiberson: We would like to have a committee picked from real representative pickers and not from those who are out for what they can get.*

*Cross: All labor is now represented by business agents who never do any of the work of the industry and in this case are not pickers.*

*Decker: Of the officials of the union in the valley all but two are elected by the workers. The union has been unanimously backed by the pickers....*

*Cross: I was hoping that we might be able to arrive at some sort of an agreement between the parties that would lead to a settlement of this matter.... We have been notified that the strikers will strengthen their picket lines. We are wondering what the growers are going to do. Is this cotton belt of ours going to be an armed camp? The strikers are willing to listen to a proposal. Have you [growers] any suggestions to make to us? If the suggestion is made, we will probably deal through mediation.*

*Guiberson: In order to give Dr. Cross a chance to investigate conditions for a few days, I would suggest that in the meantime we declare an armistice. We have nothing against the pickers. They have a right to do all the things they have done but we do not wish to listen to tales we know nothing about. If we can get together, we shall be glad.... We only want a fair proposition....*

*Decker: I would like to ask Mr. Guiberson what he means by an armistice.*

*Guiberson: I mean for the pickers to withdraw from the picket lines and go back to their camps for a few days until this committee has a chance to study the facts.*

*Decker: Will the growers suspend picking for that length of time?*

*Guiberson: We could not do that.*

Dr. Cross then thanked the meeting for its conduct during the hearings, stated that the invitation to mediation would remain open, and adjourned the hearings.

Even before Chairman Cross left the strike area, the San Joaquin Cotton Committee of the California Farm Bureau Federation issued a statement attacking the personnel and conduct of the board, and attempting to prescribe the nature of its decision:

*The fact-finding committee resulted from the efforts of NRA Administrator George Creel to settle the strike. The basis for the injection of the committee was that there should be ascertained what price farmers could afford to pay for cotton picking and what wage was necessary to enable cotton pickers to decently support themselves. If it became evident that there was a spread between the two, the national and state governments would find some way to take up the slack.*

*On that basis the cotton growers were willing to present the facts of the case to the committee as it was originally constituted. The personnel of the committee was subsequently changed without the consent of the growers and at the subsequent hearing just concluded, the committee went outside of its functions as agreed upon and attempted to bring about a settlement before it found facts.*

*At the hearing before the committee, it was established without dispute that the general run of cotton growers in the valley cannot pay more than 60 cents....*

*Despite this very obvious fact, some of the committee are put-*
*ting as much pressure as can be developed on the growers to force an*
*acceptance of a higher wage scale. In other words, the slack which it*
*was understood the state and national governments were to absorb is*
*now to be taken out of the cotton growers. The individuals responsi-*
*ble for this violation of the understanding have not even suggested*
*the sources from which cotton growers are to obtain the money to pay*
*this added cost.* (Times-Delta, *October 21)*

Dr. Cross replied to this published objection in part as follows:

*No attempt was made to arbitrate, i.e., to force the acceptance*
*of an award, in the present controversy, but a sincere effort was made*
*to assist the parties concerned to compose their differences. Manifest-*
*ly such efforts could carry no compulsion, nor has any been attempted.*

*The committee leaves the community regretting exceedingly that*
*certain attacks have been made upon its personnel, integrity, and ability*
*to render an impartial service.*

*The findings of the committee have not been determined. Any*
*statements by parties outside of the committee must necessarily rest*
*upon conjecture and are untimely and unfair. The public may await*
*with confidence the further deliberations of the committee and the*
*publication of its report.* (Times-Delta, *October 23)*

While the committee conferred in San Francisco, renewed
activities of both farmers and strikers resulted in a series of riots and
near-riots in Kings County and elsewhere. A Tulare County paper
reported:

*"The patience of the farmer is about exhausted, and if the pres-*
*ent conditions continue we may see slaughter within the next three*
*days,"Sheriff R.L. Hill said this morning in commenting on the strike*
*situation.*

*Reports received from the cotton belt today tend to bear out Hill's*
*statement. Picking was almost at a standstill as picketing strikers*
*called the workers from the fields.*

*At the B.A. Overland Ranch in the southern part of the county*
*eighty pickers deserted the field at the blasts from a bugle in the hands*
*of picketers, estimated at 300, who stood opposite a field where pick-*
*ing was in progress.*

*Picking has been suspended on the Tagus Ranch, reports indicate,*
*while at the California nursery property a few white men are picking.*

*That some of the ranchers plan to resort to force if picking is*
*delayed much longer was revealed by the statement of a wife of a ranch-*
*er in the Pixley area. She said her husband planned to start picking*
*and if picketers appeared, intended to seize the leader and hold him*
*as hostage until the picking was completed.* (Times-Delta, *October 23)*

The committee deliberated promptly and made its report to
Director Creel and Governor Rolph as follows:

*Your fact-finding committee appointed to investigate strike conditions in cotton areas of the San Joaquin Valley, after a two-day session at which both sides had full and ample opportunity under leadership of attorneys and other representatives to present their cases, begs leave to report as follows: It is judgment of committee that upon evidence growers presented, growers can pay for picking at rate of 75 cents per 100 pounds, and your committee begs leave therefore to advise this rate of payment be established. Without question, civil rights of strikers have been violated. We appeal to constituted authorities to see strikers are protected in rights conferred upon them by laws of state and by federal and state constitutions.*

*(Signed) E.J. Hanna, Chairman, Ira B. Cross, Tully C. Knoles*

Creel immediately acquainted the growers and strikers with the action of the committee and added his own approval to that of Governor Rolph:

*As representative of National Labor Board and National Recovery Administration, I approve recommendation of committee and urge its acceptance by growers and workers as an equitable adjustment. Governor Rolph also states: "I feel recommendation of committee represents fair compromise and endorse it fully. I hereupon call on both sides to accept settlement sincerely and patriotically." (Telegram to chairman, Kings County NRA)*

State and federal officials added weight to their advised acceptance of the 75-cent scale by sending members of the state highway patrol to police the region, by using the influence of the Federal Intermediate Credit Bank to urge on the growers to accept, (*Chronicle*, October 25) and by withdrawing food relief to encourage acceptance by the strikers.

The committee's report was made public on Monday, October 23, but was not finally agreed to and the strike called off until Thursday. During this interval, as described earlier, picketing continued and in several instances resulted in rioting, growers became increasingly incensed and threatened to clean out the Corcoran camp by force, and state highway patrolmen were again used to augment local forces in preserving peace.

Representatives of the farmers immediately objected to the committee's report. E.K. Walls, chairman of the Tulare County Farm Bureau, and Edson Abel, attorney, California Farm Bureau Federation, telegraphed President Roosevelt, "All state efforts have shown marked bias for strikers," and requested return of Federal Conciliator Fitzgerald. (*Times-Delta*, October 23)

Representatives of growers in five San Joaquin counties met at the farm bureau office in Visalia and sent the following telegram to Creel:

*Findings of the governor's fact-finding committee with comments by Governor Rolph and yourself have been received by us. Cotton*

*growers in this valley reiterate dissatisfaction in governor's commit-
tee and their findings, which are not supported by the facts submitted
by either side. At the start of this season growers voluntarily increased
picking rates from 40 to 60 cents per hundred. Now you are asking a
further increase in rates without any assurance that the crop can be
picked at this or any other figure.*

*What assurance can you give growers that federal-state welfare
aid will not be continued for those who refuse to go to work and that
intimidation of labor and threats of violence to workers and growers
will not be continued? These points must be cleared up before the findings of the governor's committee can be recommended for the consideration of growers. E.K. Walls, president Tulare County Farm Bureau;
H.V. Eastman, chairman Regional Cotton Committee; H.E.
Woodworth, chairman Valley Citizens and Growers' Committee.* (Times-
Delta, *October 24)*

The Farm Bureau appears to have led the growers' criticism of
the commission:

*Groups of growers threatened retaliation because of the fact-find-
ing report by a "tax strike." H.V. Eastman, chairman of the regional
farm bureau, issued a statement asserting the findings of the committee had "no binding force, either legal or moral," and declaring that
the committee had "made a joke of its duties" and was biased against
employers of all kinds.* (Chronicle, *October 23)*

Nevertheless, growers' representatives held a valley-wide meeting
at the office of the Agricultural Labor Bureau of the San Joaquin
Valley in Fresno on Wednesday morning where, after discussion, they
accepted the 75-cent scale, "in the interests of good American citizenship, law and order, and in order to forestall the spread of communism
and radicalism and to protect the harvesting of other crops." (*Times-
Delta,* October 25) Acceptance of the 75-cent rate was encouraged by
such reports as the following in the *Tulare Times* for October 25:

*Governor James Rolph, Jr., last night strove to bring striking
cotton pickers and growers to a settlement on a wage of 75 cents per
hundredweight by announcing that strikers who refused to accept the
wage would not receive federal aid, and growers failing to pay the wage
will not be allowed loans from the Farm Loan Bank of Berkeley. . . (and)
the assurance (by George Creel) that strikers who go back to work will
be protected against intimidation and violence.*

Following their acceptance, E.K. Walls of the Farm Bureau, and
himself a former strike leader for the Iron Molders' Union in
Massachusetts, explained the growers' position:

*My judgment is that growers immediately should resume pick-
ing operations on the stipulated 75-cent price—that every possible effort
should be made to move the balance of the crop before rains set in.
Growers should cooperate in getting every picker possible into the
fields, with the assurance to us by Governor James Rolph, Jr., George*

*Creel, and R.C. Branion that law and order will be maintained in the cotton area. . . .*

*We are going to resume picking operations and we are going to expect federal and state agencies, as well as our county officers, to maintain order among farm employees.*

*The 15-cent price raise for picking will cost the growers of the San Joaquin Valley an additional $450,000—nearly half a million dollars—and certainly many of our growers can ill afford to pay it. The least we can ask is that there shall be no further retardation of the cotton harvest. At 75 cents per hundred the pickers will realize $2,250,000. Many families of pickers are going to make more net money than will the growers, whose investment as well as months of labor are tied up in the crop.*

*The Farm Bureau has consistently stood for maintenance of law and order and now, in view of the part it has played in the conciliatory moves, will unequivocally demand full and complete protection for harvest operations.* (Times, October 26)

The strikers, who had been less opposed than the growers to conciliation, now offered greater resistance to final settlement, and delayed conclusion of the strike another day and a half. The final acceptance by the union appears to have been influenced by the discontinuance of food relief by the California Emergency Relief Administration, cooling of the ardor of the strikers after three weeks of hostilities, and general assent by the rank and file of workers to the 75-cent rate. Threats of importation of new workers and more arrests of leaders likewise seem to have had their effect.

The delay of the union leaders in advising termination of the strike has been ascribed to Communist strike policy at the time of obtaining enough in a settlement to confirm the strikers' faith in Communist leaders but to engender continued dissatisfaction toward employers by holding out unfulfilled demands. The manner of reaching this settlement supports this opinion. The central strike committee of thirty members, under leadership of Caroline Decker, decided, before acceptance by the growers, to counter the proposal of the fact-finding committee with one of their own:

*1. That 80 cents per 100 pounds of picked cotton be adopted as the wage for picking cotton in the entire strike area. 2. Recognition of the Cannery and Agricultural Workers' Industrial Union. 3. No discrimination in rehiring because of race, color, creed, or union, or strike activities. 4. Immediate unconditional release of Pat Chambers and all the rest of the strikers.*

The strike committee promised continued picketing activity in the event that this proposal met with refusal. These recommendations were presented to the membership of the strike locals on Tuesday evening and approved.

The following day State Labor Commissioner MacDonald notified the union that the growers had accepted the recommendation to pay 75 cents:

*I am authorized by the governor to advise you of the cotton growers' action. Inasmuch as your union was a party to the findings of the commission, it therefore becomes equally obligated and subject to the decision.*

*You are therefore hereby officially requested to declare off and terminate the cotton pickers' strike and authorize your members to complete picking of the cotton at the rate of 75 cents per 100 pounds. (*Times-Delta, *October 26)*

The central strike committee remained steadfast, arguing in substance that:

*1. The fact-finding body was not considered by it as an arbitration board and the union had never agreed to accept its proposal. Thus it was unjust to demand acceptance of the decision or try to force acceptance by terminating food relief.*

*2. The state and federal representatives had entirely ignored the union demands for recognition and absence of prejudice in rehiring workers. These proposals deserved consideration.*

*3. The Fresno meeting of growers represented only 20 percent of the cotton acreage in the valley and was controlled by gin and finance company operators.*

MacDonald renewed his efforts to obtain union assent on Thursday when he addressed the strikers gathered in the Corcoran camp at the time of the threatened invasion of the tent city by Sheriff Buckner. He pointed out that the difference between the proposed 75-cent scale and the demand for 80 cents amounted to only 10 cents a day in individual picking wages and that much of the crop was being picked by nonstrikers. The central strike committee finally capitulated on Thursday night and on Friday morning a notice reading "The strike is over" was posted in each of the concentration camps.

Upon concluding the strike, Miss Decker stated:

*Today brings to a close the third week of the strike of 12,000 cotton pickers in the San Joaquin Valley. During this period every form of intimidation and terror has been employed by the growers and government officials to break our strike. The government, acting for the finance corporations and large gin interests, has used its armed forces in an attempt to force the strikers back to work, and today they are threatening to take by armed force the miserable shacks and tents the cotton pickers call home. Throughout this terror, the workers have remained a solidified unit through their own union, the Cannery and Agricultural Workers' Industrial Union. The representatives of the government have made clear to us that the government does not wish to recognize the union. It is clear to the workers that the government will not recognize any union which has a militant policy of struggle for the working class. We also understand that only the mass organiza-*

*tion of the workers into the union will force the government and employers to recognize us even against their desire.*

*We are, therefore, issuing this statement as a result of a majority vote in every strike local; and the statement becomes the basis upon which we officially call off the strike of the cotton pickers:*

*1. That 75 cents become the minimum wage for picking 100 pounds of cotton in the San Joaquin Valley.*

*2. That we demand immediate withdrawal of armed forces from the strike area so that the strikers shall return to work in an organized manner. We call the government to task on this, in face of their assertions that they wish the strike ended in a "peaceful and orderly manner."*

*3. That cotton pickers shall be hired by the growers free of charge from the locals of the Cannery and Agricultural Workers' Industrial Union in their respective territories.*

*4. No strikers shall return to work until they are placed on union-contracted ranches by their local union.*

*5. An intensified continuation of the mass defense and fight to free our comrades who are rotting in jail because of their militancy in the interests of the strike.* (Times-Delta, *October 27)*

The strike was over but the reverberations continued.

With scarcely an exception, the newspapers of the valley supported the position of the most unyielding growers. When growers at first rejected the report of the governor's committee, the *Tulare Times* published an editorial entitled "No Compromise Wanted":

*Any compromise whatever with the strike agitators means bankruptcy for the farmer and the end of cotton raising as a major industry in this section—the abandonment of approximately one-third of the farms before next year—when there would be a much larger crop of radical troublemakers with a brand new set of impossible "demands."*

*If the "comrades" pay tribute to the communistic influences guiding the strike, and the farmer pays the "comrade," that means the farmer would be paying tribute to the communists. This is enough to make the blood of any loyal American boil. We want none of it. Neither do the farmers. Our slogan should be: "Millions for defense, but not one cent for tribute." (October 21)*

The *Hanford Journal* also supported the growers' case editorially as the hearings closed with the declaration: "The 60-cent picking scale is fair. . . ." (October 21) The *Journal* announced the failure of the efforts of the fact-finding board to bring a settlement in an editorial the following day:

*Growers and strikers who had hoped that the hearing of the federal-state fact-finding board at Visalia would point the way to peaceful settlement of the cotton strike which has seethed in the San Joaquin Valley recently, bringing death and violence, will have to take another notch in the belt and get set for the real crisis.*

The *Visalia Times-Delta* also joined in the growers' attack on the committee:

*Meanwhile, the report of the erudite committee sent down here by Governor Rolph, which gives the strikers a 25 percent picking rate increase, ends with the statement: "Without question the civil rights of the strikers have been violated. . . .*

*By all that is fair and just, have the American farmers no rights over Communists and aliens? Are their ranches to be trampled on, their employees beaten and carried bodily from their fields, their cotton scattered and destroyed and their harvest left to the elements? And all they get for their year's work is to hear a commission of highbrows prate of "strikers' violated civil rights, " while a complacent government feeds the farmers' enemies as they are effecting his undoing. (October 24)*

In the southern end of the cotton area, the *Bakersfield Californian* also attacked the findings with an editorial entitled "A Discredited Report":

*Before the ink was dry upon the report filed yesterday by the governor's mediation committee in the cotton strike and at the very hour that the governor and regional director of the federal government were signing their approval of the finding that "without question the civil rights of the strikers have been violated and we appeal to the constituted authorities to see that the strikers are protected in rights conferred upon them by the laws of the state and federal constitution, " tragic events were moving swiftly in the northern cotton fields; families of wage earners were kidnapped; night riders representing the so-called strikers are adding to the terrors in the disturbed region, and the sheriff and other officials of one county, Kings, have already been compelled to appeal to the state for relief in a situation which they declare has gone beyond the control of local authorities.*

*The masses of unprejudiced people will not be disposed to quarrel with the finding that the grower can pay 75 cents per hundred for picking. From the viewpoint of the latter, that question is debatable, but any conclusion reached in that connection is of far less consequence than is the gratuitous statement that lawless interference with peaceable workers and concerted activity that threatens a great industry and menaces life represent "civil rights that call for protection under the law and the constitution. " The finding of the committee and its official endorsement are simply an invitation to rioting and lawlessness, and that is exactly what followed, and followed swiftly, when word of the verdict reached the areas where the situation was already acute and which, since then, is at a stage that impels local authorities to declare that overt acts menace the social order of entire communities. (October 24)*

Two days later the *Californian* added to its attack on the "civil rights" section of the committee's report a note of praise for the unselfish acceptance by the growers of the rate set by the board:

*The farmers of the valley are to be congratulated for their prompt
acceptance of the demand that the price of picking be increased 15 cents
a hundred. Recognizing their obligation as citizens, and realizing that
that demand, even though advanced without intelligent investigation
and without regard to the capacity of the growers to meet it, created
a situation that made acceptance a prerequisite to the resumption of
peaceful conditions in the disputed area, they preferred to sacrifice their
anticipated profits to such an end.*

*And now the governor and the state administration, by firmly
pursuing their promised policy of maintaining law and order, give
assurance of resumption of work in the fields. Upon that depends the
harvesting of a ten million dollar crop which was so vexatiously
interfered with by those who were without understanding of the situation and who seemingly held the belief that the premier issue involved
was the "violation of civil rights" by reckless leaders. . . . (October 27)*

Professor Cross in particular, who was the only member of the
committee not a clergyman, was subjected to much abuse by growers
and their sympathizers. Their highly emotional state and lack of critical
judgment are exemplified by the absurdities uttered by a gin foreman
during an interview after the strike:

*Cross is the cause of all this trouble. He ran the thing wrong from
the start. We knew we wouldn't get a square deal. Cross had no business
listening to the Communists in the first place. He had no business letting Chambers question the growers—the dirty scum. He was an IWW
of the worst sort when he was a student. He's a Communist now. He
ought to go back to the country where he belongs. The growers and
finance companies gave him figures, and figures don't lie, but he
believed Chambers instead. You tell him it won't be healthy for him
if he comes down into the valley—the respectable citizens will take care
of him. (Interview)*

The local growers expressed no gratitude that the committee's
work had ended the strike and permitted the harvest. A single large
grower did say after the strike that Knoles and Cross were "absolutely fair." (Interview) Some small growers and less vocal large growers,
however, appreciated the settlement. One small grower, for example,
thought the committee "did the best that it could." Another said it
was a "fair decision," and another said:

*All the members of the committee were fine. The doctor [Cross]
was as fine as you could want and he knew all the time he was going
to get in wrong for it. (Interview)*

Many of the farmers with small acreages also attacked the committee, as did one who said of Dr. Knoles:

*Dr. Knoles made a bad mistake when he lectured over the radio
at the Commonwealth Club. They say he's a minister but I call him
a liar. Anybody would know that what he said about raising cotton
was a lie. (Interview)*

In general, the growers and their allies operating gins and finance companies have censured the board violently, though the small farmers have tended to be more favorable to the commission. The deep feeling with which the agricultural interests have expressed themselves would indicate that they will not forget their grievance in the near future.

Local law enforcement officials naturally attacked the report of the fact-finding committee on "civil rights," which was a reflection on them. Their criticisms (in interviews) were directed especially at Professor Cross:

*A sheriff: I know too much about that _____ _____*

*Cross. He's a Communist pure and simple. He's on their payroll. He's a Pat Chambers man. I can't see paying taxes to give salaries to men like him. Something ought to be done to put a stop to it. He wouldn't stay long at the university, if I had my way about it. Anyway, he, nor none of the others knew anything about cotton. They shouldn't have taken the job.*

*A district attorney: The recommendation of 75 cents was all right. Most people believed all the time they ought to pay that. Then at the end some of the growers wanted to pay 75 cents but the gins wouldn't let them.*

*But so far as Kings County is concerned at least this charge of the strikers not getting their constitutional rights is just not true. However, there isn't any feeling against the committee as individuals.*

*A sheriff: The committee made an ass of itself. Anybody could have found the facts. All the farmers keep records. They know what every pound of cotton costs and what they can pay. Instead the committee let Sacramento politics run it.*

*A district attorney: It seems to me they were entirely out of their jurisdiction to state that the civil rights of the strikers had been violated. The principal criticism of the committee has been on that score. They did not call in Hill, Snell, Cato, or myself, who were most concerned. They condemned us without a hearing.*

*I realize they had a difficult time. It is almost impossible to set a rate which is fair to all. Some can always afford to pay more and some cannot afford to pay anything at all.*

Labor and liberal groups in the valley supported the committee but probably local public opinion preponderantly "resented the fact-finding board, particularly its findings about the violations of civil rights. The people haven't forgotten about it yet, though it is a lot more quiet than it was." (Interview, December 21)

This strike and the method and results of the settlement stirred emotions in the southern San Joaquin Valley probably more than any other series of local events since the Muscleslew "massacre" of farmers by railroad agents fifty years before. (Cf. Frank Norris, *The Octopus*) The entire population of the region, as is seldom true in urban industrial strikes, felt itself involved.

## AFTERMATH

Upon termination of the strike the pickers soon resumed harvest. The delay had allowed most of the bolls to open, picking conditions were excellent, and many fields were picked but once. The delay also allowed many workers freed upon conclusion of the grape and other harvests to join the cotton pickers. Consequently the crop was gathered rapidly and daily earnings were high. However, the season of employment was brief and more pickers than usual shared in the work. The strikers, therefore, did not themselves receive the full benefit of the increase from 60 to 75 cents. But undoubtedly the example of the cotton strike held up wage rates in a succession of harvests which followed. Growers obtained a rapid and brief harvest because of the strike, but at an added cost of approximately $450,000. Losses because of deterioration in grade of cotton were negligible.

Friction engendered by the strike did not end with its termination. For a brief time growers near Corcoran and Pixley had some difficulty obtaining pickers because of resentment against their treatment during the strike. (*Tulare Times,* October 29) On their side "... a number of growers indicated the sentiment they would get along without hiring known strikers if possible." (*Times,* October 28) White and Negro strikers interviewed in November and as late as January testified to the difficulties of obtaining jobs:

*Negro union leader at Pixley: Some of our leaders have had a hard time to get jobs. Bill Hammett tried at Pixley and Tulare and then had to go 100 miles to Buttonwillow. The growers will never hire some of us again so we will have nothing to lose if we strike.*

*White union leader at Pixley: Some of us had a hard time getting jobs, but if one farmer wouldn't hire us another one would.*

*White strike leader, long resident at McFarland, interviewed while preparing to leave: No one here will ever give me a job again. Many other strike leaders have found out the same thing. We have had to leave the districts where we struck. The growers and gin operators are very bitter.*

Ten days after settlement, the strike threatened to break out again around Pixley and Woodville:

*Resumption of the cotton strike in the Woodville and Pixley areas was expected today as cotton pickers demanded full recognition of their union and increase of their pay to 80 cents a hundred pounds. ...*

*Strike leaders have caused trouble on several ranches in the cotton belt by insisting that the ranchers hire union members only. It is reported that strike leaders brought a crew of union pickers upon a ranch where picking was in progress and ordered the owner to discharge his non-union crew.* (Times-Delta, *November 2*)

Four days later the threat of importation of Mexicans from Los Angeles into the Pixley neighborhood caused the threat of another minor disturbance:

*A new tenseness was injected into the cotton field situation south
of here today when it was learned that 4,000 Los Angeles Mexicans
were on their way into the valley to break a threatened strike in the
Pixley district scheduled for tomorrow....*

*Spokesmen for the far-from-pacified pickers declared the growers
were systematically letting out workers they have already taken back,
and are fostering an infiltration of fresh Mexican labor from the south.*
(Chronicle, November 6)

The new strike did not materialize and few, if any, of the Los
Angeles laborers arrived in the cotton belt:

*Some hostility between strikers and nonstrikers survived the set-
tlement.*

*Ill feeling between strikers and strikebreakers in the cotton fields
almost developed into a gang fight at a Mexican dance at Armory Hall
last night. City police intervened after two were injured and closed the
dance to prevent further bloodshed.* (Journal, October 29)

*The scabs are still scared and won't go near the union members.*
*(Interview with local union leader, January 1934.)*

A committee of growers from five counties went to San Francisco
on October 27 to confer on the cotton strike and lay plans against future
strikes with Governor Rolph, Timothy Reardon of the State Department of Industrial Relations, U.S. Senator Hiram Johnson, and NRA
Director George Creel. One of the committee, Mr. Tom McManus, chairman of the Americanism Committee of the National American Legion
(in 1939 executive of the Citizen's Association of Bakersfield):

*... reported a cordial reception of the committee, particularly by
Governor Rolph, Senator Johnson, and Director Reardon.*

*"We reviewed the entire agricultural labor situation," he stated,
"and succeeded in bringing forcibly to the governor's attention the question of whether the sinister and vicious influence of communism is to
be controlling factor in agricultural labor conditions in California. ..."*

*It was the unanimous report of the committee that the conference
with George Creel had not been on as cordial terms as with the others.*
(Californian, October 28)

Growers became highly sensitive to the cricitism of their actions
from metropolitan centers. After President Knoles of the governor's
committee addressed the Commonwealth Club in San Francisco:

*Kern County Farm Bureau called upon the Commonwealth Club
to fix a date when a representative of the agricultural interests of the
valley may appear and give the organization the true facts relative to
the strike situation which existed in connection with the cotton harvest.*
(Californian, November 4)

For some months the conflict was debated back and forth before
the Commonwealth Club and other forums.

The court trials of persons arrested during the strike served to
keep the conflict before the local communities. The strikers were

defended in the courts by Attorney A.L. Wirin of the American Civil Liberties Union. Communists sought to build up a "defense fund" to assist in supporting the strikers' case.

*The workers, back on the fields, with a 25 percent increase, have not forgotten those who sacrificed most to get the gains, and are now behind the bars. They are each donating five cents out of each day's wages towards the defense fund.* (Western Worker, *November 13)*

The International Labor Defense established local defense committees to gain support for the jailed strikers:

*Defense committees to cooperate with the ILD are responsible for the defense work in every local of the C&AWIU. Is your committee set up, and is it active?* There are Defense Stamps *to sell. They are to be pasted in the union membership books. They are 25 cents each. The Porterville, Tulare, Visalia, and Farmerville locals have done their best so far. All money from the stamps goes for the defense of the cotton strike prisoners. Defense committees should see that leaflets and defense folders are widely distributed, and that prisoners are written to, and visited. (Bulletin No. 2, issued by International Labor Defense, December 8, 1933.)*

In Kern County, fourteen strikers and no farmers were arrested. Five of the strikers were released at the conclusion of the conflict and nine stood trial accused of the fatal shooting at Arvin. None were convicted for murder.

"Twenty-two or twenty-four strikers were arrested in Tulare County according to the sheriff. Several were released without trial. Of the seventeen Mexicans arrested on the Taylor Ranch previous to the Pixley shooting, nine pleaded guilty and got ninety days." (Interview with a district attorney) The union attorney charged the judge with "vindictive attitude," and declared:

*Tulare County has had its Scottsboro case, A.L. Wirin of the International Labor Defense and attorney for the convicted men said in a statement issued following the announcement of the verdict.*

*What the South does to its Negroes, California has done to its exploited cotton pickers. (*Times-Delta, *November 21)*

The last trial of the strikers was that of Pat Chambers, accused of violating the Criminal Syndicalism Act and that section of the act, in particular, "referring to a change in industrial control." (Defendant's Instruction November 11, in re John Ernest Williams, alias Pat Chambers.) The ranchers advancing the charge quoted Chambers as saying:

*Fellow workers, we'll need every man to win this strike. This is no time for a backward move. We'll give Pixley more publicity than it has ever known. We'll make Pixley as bloody as Harlan, Kentucky. We'll take the law into our own hands. We don't want any more arrests. If anyone gets in our way, put him in the hospital to stay. (*Times-Delta, *November 29)*

The *Western Worker* charged that the trial was held "before a court full of armed patrolmen and deputies, with machine guns mounted to prevent the workers from attending." (November 27) The union sought to dramatize the trial by the strategy employed at the IWW trial in Centralia:

*A workers' jury selected by the strikers at a meeting in Hyde Park yesterday afternoon filed into the courtroom as the selection of the jury started yesterday afternoon. The twelve persons selected by the strikers will listen to the entire case and will return their own verdict on the charges against Chambers after the testimony is completed.* (Times-Delta, *November 22)*

The right of workers to organize as declared by section 7a of the National Industrial Recovery Act was advanced as one of the principal justifications of Chambers' conduct.

The jury disagreed six to six and a retrial was called for February 6, 1934. Judge Lamberson was generally held to have been fair to Chambers and a "judge above all things else." One defense instruction to the jury allowed by the judge questioned the application of the Criminal Syndicalism Act to conditions in 1933:

*"You are instructed that the Criminal Syndicalism Act was an emergency measure passed by the legislature of California in 1919 on the grounds that it was necessary for the immediate preservation of the public peace and safety." (Defendant's Instruction, November 16)*

The trial of the eight growers held on murder charges growing out of the Pixley fatalities was held in January. Attempts were made to have laborers picket the trial, and the *Western Worker* charged that "Every attempt is being made to turn the trial into a whitewash." (January 8, 1934) By this time, however, feelings were cooling on both sides. (*Times-Delta,* January 12) The growers were acquitted, and soon thereafter Pat Chambers was released.

In Kings County the sheriff arrested eleven persons during the strike:

*One arrest was more or less accidental and was released. Two were released because they were just kids. Two others were dismissed by the judge because of lack of evidence, but that was wrong. The six others, three men and three women, were held for trial. They all ultimately plead guilty and were given two years probation. They have all turned against the strike, at least the women have and I think the men too. They were all Mexicans and they found the strike leaders didn't care anything about them and left them in jail though their bonds were only $500, while they raised $10,000 to get out Pat Chambers, the white leader. (Interview with district attorney)*

In Fresno County—

*Five or six were arrested on vagrancy charges, all plead guilty and were given floaters except one who got sixty days and then was given a floater. (Interview with deputy district attorney)*

Federal immigration authorities arrested one union leader, Leroy Gordon, suspected of being illegally in the country.

The total of fifty-six arrests noted above from interviews with officials in four counties does not agree with the total of 101 arrests of strikers reported by the *Western Worker* (November 20), or of 113 reported by the *Hanford Journal:*

*As the strike crisis appeared past, yesterday, it was learned that 113 persons have been arrested in connection with the strike, forty in Tulare County, twenty-eight in Kings County, twenty-two in Kern County, seventeen in Fresno County, and five in Madera County. (October 28)*

The discrepancy between the various figures may be explained partly by the number of arrests on charges such as vagrancy when strikers were held for perhaps only a few hours and never brought before a court. For example, the following arrests by a ranch superintendent deputy appear not to have entered the sheriff's enumeration at the close of the strike:

*Eleven men have been arrested in the Shafter-Wasco district in connection with alleged cotton strike agitations, according to the sheriff's office which is not patrolling the county's cotton areas to... inhibit any serious trouble in connection with labor. The arrests were made last night by Charles Ellwood, deputy sheriff and superintendent of the Hoover Ranch, according to Undersheriff Charles Rankin. (Californian, October 3)*

The Cannery and Agricultural Workers' Industrial Union sought to maintain its organization and membership in the San Joaquin Valley. Headquarters in Tulare were continued for the remainder of the year, and the union sought to maintain contact with the migrants through ranch committees:

*Now that all of the comrades will be going into the fields to work, we must make certain that we lose contact with not a single union member. The best method in this respect is the setting up of ranch committees on every ranch. (Cecil McKiddy, section secretary, Instructions to Central Strike Committee members. October 29, 1933)*

Mass meetings, defense committees on behalf of arrested strikers, and speaking tours by Pat Chambers and Caroline Decker also were employed to sustain the interest of the pickers.

Union leaders also sought to win the support of local small farmers by securing signatures to contracts to employ workers through the union, and by urging farmers to become members of Communist-sponsored groups. However, work among small farmers met with little success, and the pickers rapidly discontinued union activity after they returned to work and the strike no longer served as a focus for their attention. Contact with the locals also was weakened by migration from ranch to ranch in the cotton area and then into other sections of the state.

Occasional union meetings were still being held by the Bakersfield, Shafter, Wasco, Tulare, Corcoran, and a few other locals by the middle of November. Locals at Delano, McFarland, Pixley, Visalia, Dinuba, Hanford, Fresno, Kingsburg, and elsewhere had practically ceased to function by that time. By the middle of December only the Tulare headquarters were still open and only occasional meetings were being called in other sections of the valley. No more than a skeleton organization remained.

Members of at least one local, at Wasco, deserted the Communist leadership and requested acceptance by the American Federation of Labor. (Interview, editor of *Kern County Labor Journal*) Miss Decker charged the AFofL with:

*. . . trying to organize in the San Joaquin and Imperial valleys and. . . paying organizers ten dollars a day. They are trying to lure leaders away by promising to pay, but they haven't been able to do it. (Speech on November 27. There is no evidence that this was true.)*

*They are trying to bring in the red scare, to stir up race prejudice, and use every method to disrupt.—Together with the AFofL is the Mexican consulate and its fake Mexican union. They too are sending disruptive organizers into the fields in an effort to divide the workers and organize a Mexican union. (Western Worker, December 11)*

Disintegration of union organization did not mean that union leaders did not still hold the allegiance of the workers. A few local leaders remained actively loyal, and there was a general apprehension that, as one peace officer expressed it, "They could call a strike in five minutes if they wanted to." However, the union never resumed much activity, and finally disappeared when its parent, the Trade Union Unity League, was abolished by the Communist party in favor of the tactics of working within other trade unions, instead of organizing their own.

## ATTITUDES

The alignment of groups according to interests and attitudes lies back of the pressures which produce violations of civil liberties during the clash between employers and employees. In the southern San Joaquin Valley, the vocal elements of the community, save for the strikers themselves, generally sympathized with the growers. Valley newspapers encouraged this partisanship:

*The people of the valley must not forget, either, that failure to harvest the $90,000,000 cotton crop in the south San Joaquin Valley must inevitably result in hardship to citizens and government for the care of men and families deprived of an opportunity to earn at least a portion of their living in the cotton fields. (Times-Delta, October 13)*

The growers were called "our people," in contrast to the largely foreign migratory cotton pickers. The following excerpt from an editorial entitled "Looks as Though Our Cotton Farmer is the Forgotten Man," indicates the prevalent feeling:

*The farmers are our people, and it would appear that it was about time the government and our good American friends [referring to labor agitators, officials of the National League for the Defense of Political Prisoners, and university students with a communistic flair] gave at least a sidelong glance in their direction. They will remain with us after this unfortunate episode is a closed incident, while 90 percent of the strikers, about whom such a great ado is being made, will be moving on, many probably back to their own country where they belong.* (Times-Delta, *October 19)*

The *Tulare Advance-Register* requested absolute support by the citizenry of the growers:

*It behooves every business man, every citizen to support the farmers 100 percent in this crisis and see that he gets a square deal. Any compromise whatever with the strike agitators means bankruptcy for the farmer, the end of cotton raising as a major industry in this section, and the abandonment of approximately one-third of the farms before next year when there would be a much larger crop of radical troublemakers with a brand new set of impossible demands. (October 20)*

The *Hanford Journal* declared:

*The* Journal *believes that the growers are absolutely right in standing pat and refusing to pay unreasonable demands for $1 a hundred for cotton picking. The* Journal *is glad to see they are presenting a solid front. The very rightness of their stand has contributed to their anger over the situation. They are within their rights also to evict strikers who are occupying their cabins, burning their wood, using their water, burning their electricty, and refusing to work. The growers are justified also in guarding their ranches, in keeping out trespassers, particularly agitators who go into ranches and try to get pickers to quit. (October 6)*

This acceptance by the rural press of the growers' position was made the basis of a request by the defense attorney for change of venue in the Chambers trial for criminal syndicalism.

*He asserted that because of its large circulation in this community, the* Times-Delta *had influenced and molded public opinion to such an extent that it would be impossible to secure a fair and impartial trial here.*

*Wirin made similar assertions concerning the* Tulare Times, *declaring that both it and the* Times-Delta *consistently supported the side of the ranchers in the controversy. That the ranchers realized this was evidenced by a resolution passed by the Tulare County Farm Bureau thanking the two newspapers for their stand on the strike, Wirin charged. (*Times-Delta, *November 13)*

The San Francisco metropolitan press, particularly the *Chronicle* and *News,* presented strike news in a manner much more friendly to the strikers than the valley press, and were bitterly attacked for doing so. For example:

*Tulare County is getting a lot of undesirable notoriety from the cotton strike.* The situation is bad enough without having the San Francisco Chronicle *print the following in boldface type on its front page:*

*"Meanwhile, a plan to 'starve the strikers out' was mapped at a meeting of Tulare County planters, supervisors, the district attorney, the sheriff, and the Visalia chief of police."*

*Such a statement is absolutely untrue and viciously damaging. As a matter of fact, Tulare County officials have leaned backward in trying to keep hands off, and allow the parties to the difficulty to get together and settle their differences amicably. (*Times-Delta, *October 12)*

On the other hand, the *Los Angeles Times* and its representative, Chapin Hall, who was antagonistic to the strikers, received the approval of the local editorial writers. (*Times-Delta,* October 25)

The *Western Worker* attacked even such newspapers as reported the news rather amply and accurately, declaring of one that its "hypocracy and slimyness [sic] would fill an encyclopaedia." (November 6) A few groups in the valley expressed themselves publicly on the strike. The Bakersfield Post of the American Legion attacked the communistic leadership of the strike, while the Ku Klux Klan was reported to be planning to enter the conflict. (*Chronicle,* October 27) One newspaper, although denying the truth of the report, nevertheless advocated such action editorially:

*... it might not be such a bad idea at that. The strikers do not appear to have stood much in awe of the legally constituted authorities, who, with the exception of sheriffs and the district attorney's office, from the fact-finding commission to the labor and food administrators, have petted, pampered, and fed the reds and their charges, while harvest moon and torrid sun glowed on cotton fields' thwarted harvest. Perhaps white-sheeted knights might throw the fear of the devil into those whom neither state nor federal authority was able to throw the fear of God. The mystery of what is under a sheet is sometimes a powerful influence. (*Times-Delta, *October 27)*

The fears of the community were played upon by comparing the actions of union agitators to those of gangsters like "George (Machinegun) Kelly. . . fomenting disorder, illegal interference. . . with right of private contract and preventing people from working through intimidation." (*Times-Delta,* October 7)

The Hanford Chamber of Commerce stated in an open letter to the Corcoran Chamber:

*May I assure you that directors of the Hanford Chamber of Commerce are in thorough accord with the attitude of your farmers. It has become a situation of county-wide concern and you may be certain that sober-minded citizens of this community will never approve any movement that makes it necessary for our farmers to be dictated to by communistic radicals. (*Journal, *October 10)*

Organized labor in the valley was generally sympathetic to the strikers but was very hostile to its Communist leadership. Labor papers published virtually no strike news, while the *Labor News* of Fresno even printed in the name of the "hosts of organized labor" a bitter attack on Communists near the conclusion. This statement may have been in answer to a virtual demand three days earlier by Ralph Taylor, secretary of the Agricultural Council of California:

*California farmers expect the conservative, thoughtful heads of labor to put down the "left wing" of the labor movement which has been responsible for this campaign of lawlessness and destruction.* (Times-Delta, *October 23)*

Organized labor in San Francisco, however, gave more support to the strikers. It depreciated "the prevalent idea that the economics problem of the farmer can be settled by resort to vigilante and Ku Klux Klan methods." (*Labor Clarion*, No. 3)

### California's Disgrace

*The strike in the agricultural districts of the state had grown to its present proportion not so much by reason of the fact of low wages and miserable working conditions, as because of brutal methods used to suppress it. Injustice and brutality are poor weapons for a rich and powerful state to countenance in the suppression of the weak and lowly element in its population, on whom California's fabulously rich agricultural and horticultural industries rely.*

*The agricultural workers, most of whom are illiterate foreigners induced to settle in the state by the growers under misleading promises, are just as much entitled to the protection of the state as are their oppressors.*

*The plight of these agricultural workers who toil endlessly in the terrible heat of California's interior valleys must arouse the sympathy of every right-minded citizen. Composed largely of Mexicans. . . who were actually imported by the landowners without regard to economic conditions, they are shifted from pillar to post in a nomadic life which precludes the possibility of enjoying the benefits of American culture and comforts. Paid a mere pittance, when seasonal employment is ended they find their way to the cities, to become a charge on the charitably disposed urbanites, or to fill public institutions provided by a benevolent state for indigents. Thus the men responsible for their being in the country escape taxation for their support and the burden is placed upon those who had no part in bringing them into the state and who received no benefit from their labor. (October 13)*

Within the valley, the temperate attitude of some members of the clergy was conspicuous. Six ministers from Visalia and Tulare investigated the Pixley shootings, reported favorably on the conduct of the strikers, and later appealed to their communities to donate food and clothing to the strikers. (*Times-Delta*, Oct. 12, 14) Similar interest by religious leaders of the Fresno District Council of the Methodist

127

*Documentary History of the Strike of the Cotton Pickers in California 1933*

Ministerial Union brought reproof from a valley newspaper for extending an invitation to speak to Caroline Decker, "whose keenness of mind and brilliance of expression is undeniable. . . ." (*Times-Delta,* November 20)

Examples of the bitter resentment expressed in the San Joaquin Valley on four subjects will serve further to indicate the inflamed state of mind produced by the strike:

State and federal investigation; alleged but uninvestigated responsibility of gins, finance companies, and electric power interests for the difficulties of the cotton farmers; leadership of the strike by outside agitators; and the conduct of a handful of University of California students in the strike area; and the actions of Professor Ira B. Cross as member of the governor's committee.

San Joaquin growers generally resented the actions of state and federal governments in the strike area, particularly the distribution of food to striking pickers, NRA Director Creel's assurance to the strikers that they had the legal right to picket, the conclusions of the state fact-finding committee, and even the very state police intervention which at one time they earnestly requested. State activity, on the other hand, had a strong exponent in certain other quarters, especially the *San Francisco Chronicle.* Prompted by the death of three strikers, the *Chronicle* strongly advocated state control in the area in an editorial entitled, "Governor's Duty To End This Bloody War," which said:

*It is the state's duty to step in and end the lawlessness. The local authorities have not prevented it and by their close relation to local feeling are handicapped in preventing further lawlessness. Why does the governor hesitate? (October 12)*

In a later editorial the same newspaper commented:

*The local authorities are not in a position to enforce the law evenly on both sides in such a strike as this. The votes that elected the district attorney and sheriff—supervisors as well— are all on one side of the dispute. The farmers can hire and fire the county officers; the cotton pickers, who are itinerant laborers, have no votes. And the strike is the one big issue in these counties with all the residents on one side. (October 13)*

In direct opposition, the local papers insisted first upon protection of the crops:

*One can readily see the ultimate result of the new state and federal welfare policy. The workers will hold out against employment as long as the government supports them. The effect upon industry is also patent. It is string-halted if not destroyed. (*Sentinel, *reprinted in* Times, *October 26)*

*One thing seems certain: the strikers have been encouraged by the policy and attitude of the state and national governments. (*Sentinel, *reprinted in* Times-Delta, *October 25)*

As the strike drew to a close and it appeared that state pressure was needed to urge acceptance of the proposed terms upon the strikers, certain valley interests shifted their position and requested state intervention. An editorial called "It's Up To Rolph" stated:

*The Polyanna, head-in-the-sand attitude of Governor Rolph and his order in connection with the cotton strike has become a public scandal.*

*Governor Rolph is on trial in the San Joaquin Valley. His is the responsibility for anything that happens in the strike zone now.*

*Local peace officers have done their part, citizens have done their part, growers have done their part. The rest is up to Rolph.* (Journal, October 27)

After the pressure had been successfully exerted to obtain acceptance by the strikers, the governor received general commendation:

*Happily for California, the obstacle raised by misguided agencies and which unquestionably delayed the harvesting of the cotton crop for several critical days, and at one time even threatened to create chaos in a great agricultural area, has largely been removed. Governor Rolph, though belatedly, having assumed direct charge of the menacing situation, having pledged himself to pursue a policy of firmness and sanity which promised an end to the intolerable situation due to coddling of reckless and communistic leadership.* (Californian, October 27)

Outside interference implied inability of the communities to govern themselves and was inimical to the interests of a substantial section of the resident voters. Therefore it was resented and opposed. A leading grower charged that the attitude of officials in protecting the rights of strikers had led them to believe:

*that the government wanted them to strike. Creel talked to them and said they might picket and Branion fed them. (Interview)*

*Undersheriff: We didn't want state help. We had things under control here. (Interview)*

*Sheriff: If the state and federal governments had let us alone we could have handled it. Everything was going fine until Creel came down and told them they could raise all the hell they wanted to. (Interview)*

*District attorney: The NRA seems to have been on the side of the strikers everyplace. It makes them think they have a right to strike whenever they want to. Then also the federal government came down here and definitely took the side of the strikers. They fed strikers who just wouldn't work, while they won't feed the poor unemployed who want to work. If it hadn't been for the federal and state food, the strike would have been broken a week sooner. Rolph was right on the side of the strikers, too. He's always been a labor union man. They made him mayor of San Francisco and then governor.*

*Creel made us plenty of trouble, too. The sheriff just had the strikers well in hand when he came down. The strikers were quieted down to where they didn't picket much and when they did picket they obeyed the sheriff, and moved on when he told them to. But Creel came down and told them they could do whatever the sheriff said they should not do; they said Creel said they had the right to do it. (Interview)*

*Sheriff: Creel came down here and he might just as well have told the Mexicans to go out and commit murder. He told them they could strike and picket and all the rest of that. Picketing is what caused all the trouble. That's what got the farmers sore.*

*I could have handled it if it hadn't been for Creel and the state highway patrol. I could have stopped the picketing. It isn't lawful to obstruct the highways whether to hold a church service or to picket. But Creel spent an hour and a half in the Corcoran camp and told them they could do plenty. Then he went to see Pat Chambers for an hour. After that he spent only twenty minutes with the growers. Then he went and told our district attorney the strikers were within their rights to picket.*

*Jimmie Rolph stole money, given by the federal government, to help the strike. It is the first time in the history of this country that they have done such a . . . thing. Branion came down here with a corps of assistants and gave food to everybody. That's all the Mexicans wanted. They would have stayed there all winter. (Interview)*

The gins, the finance companies, and the electric light and power companies were occasionally pointed to as the evil spirits behind the curtain. However, no investigation was made of the activities of these bodies. All three groups were accused of making exorbitant charges for the services they performed. An increase in ginning rates was the cause of protest by the farmers in at least one district:

*The West Side Land Owners' Association today was on record as protesting against the proposed ginning rate of 30 cents per 100 pounds of cotton this year, an increase of 100 percent over last year's rate. (Bee, October 12)*

The Visalia and Tulare ministers who made a public report following the Pixley affair suggested investigation of the companies:

*We discovered it to be a common opinion at Pixley that financial interests are largely to blame for this economic and industrial situation. The part played in this tragedy by finance corporations and their agents could wisely be investigated by proper state authorities. If they play no sinister part, that fact should be known. If they do play an evil part, they should be held responsible. (Times-Delta, October 12)*

A valley newspaper editorially declared:

*Should Investigate Cotton Finance Company Angles To Pickers' Strike. There is a third party in the cotton strike imbroglio, a silent partner, who has been referred to frequently, but who has not been brought out into the open—the cotton finance corporation. The crux of the problem lies there, and the only agency that can get at it is the federal government through the NRA or the AAA. For the most part the strikers and the growers are powerless to help each other.*

*A majority of the cotton growers are tenant farmers who seek financing from the inception of their operations. Banks cannot loan to them because they possess neither the personal nor property qualifications. There are scarcely any cotton loans in the local banks. The Federal Farm Loan Corporation does not advance money to farmers for cropping activities, and the Regional Agricultural Credit Corporation, another government setup, has offices only in Los Angeles and San Francisco, with very sketchy contacts in the San Joaquin Valley. The cotton growers are, therefore, forced into the clutches of the cotton finance companies, whose terms are onerous and whose supervision extends to every activity from seed to harvest, the farmer being budgeted as to his expenditures in each separate operation. If the finance company has allotted 60 cents per hundred pounds for picking, that is all the grower has to spend for that operation, without the consent of the company which is advancing the money.*

*It is stated that these companies, not the grower, reap the premium which attached to valley cotton because of its superior quality. Because the contracts are based on eastern cotton prices at the time of contract, price advances are, therefore, also reaped by the finance companies. Of course, the companies assume considerable risk in their transactions, for which they are entitled to compensation above the amount which would be earned in a normal banking transaction. The deal is the same as those of the methods of automobile, radio, and washing machine financing, in which interest rates in excess of 12 percent are not infrequently obtained.*

*All hands to this unfortunate controversy would be farther along had they united earlier in a demand that the federal government survey this phase of the problem and move for a correction which could solve the present situation. It may not be too late yet for government authority to arrange sufficient modification of contracts to permit growers to pay more than 60 cents per hundred for picking.* (Times-Delta, October 21)

Several independent growers also attacked the gin, finance, and power companies, and it was generally hinted that others would have done so were they not fearful that such action would mitigate against receiving future crop loans. M.B. Kearney testified before the governor's committee that:

*We will be glad to pay more to the poor slave who has to do the work. Under present conditions we cannot do it.*

*I do not think that either the large or small farmer, the way things are manipulated, could pay. If the finance companies and the San Joaquin Light and Power Company were put in their right places, we could pay so they could eat.* (Hearings)

The union also attacked the companies and sought to unite the small farmers in a joint attack upon them. The strikers' spokesman before the fact-finding board argued:

*We again call your attention to the startling condition where free American citizen cotton growers frankly tell cotton pickers that they can afford to pay 75 cents a hundred pounds, and that they want to pay 75 cents a hundred pounds to cotton pickers, but that they dare not pay 75 cents because if they do, they will be punished and ruined by the cotton gin operators and the financial interests who dominate the cotton industry.*

*We are informed that the cotton grower sends his cotton to the gin operators, who arbitrarily determine the quality and the price that is to be paid for the cotton. We are informed that independent California cotton growers have sent their cotton to cooperative gins where they get much higher prices for their cotton than is paid by the private monopoly gin operators of the district, who seem to control not only the cotton growers but also dominate the lives of the cotton pickers. This higher price is paid for cotton because the independent gin operators honestly measure the length of the cotton and inform the cotton growers that it is of better quality and longer length than do the operators of the private monopoly gins.*

*We call your attention to the fact that this year, the same as in previous years, the cotton gin operators and finance companies compel the growers to sell their cotton to them prior to its maturing, at a price that the cotton gin operators and financiers know would yield them a handsome profit because of the ascending market and the restrictions that the government was making possible by limiting output that would further stimulate prices, and also by the guarantee of the government of ten cents a pound to cotton growers.*

*We also insist that it is the absolute duty of your commission and of the federal government to make an investigation of the methods and profits of the cotton gin operators and the finance companies, so that their racketeering methods will be exposed.*

The readiness of peace officers and growers to blame the strike entirely on outside agitators, and their blindness to other causes, were marked:

*Sheriff: If the laws had teeth so we could catch about twenty rats the whole thing would be over. (Interview)*

*Clarence Morrill, chief of California's Bureau of Criminal Investigation, today blamed the San Joaquin Valley labor trouble on communism.*

*The state—for that matter, the whole Pacific Coast—is a hotbed of communism. I've been expecting this a long time.*

*"There have been robberies of guns from state armories several times lately," he said. "They have been preparing a long time."*
(Californian, *October 11)*

Local newspapers were unanimous in condeming the agitators. The *Fresno Bee,* for example, on October 6 printed an editorial:

*People Getting Weary of Communist Agitators. But our people are getting exceedingly weary of the activities of the professional communist leaders, mostly from New York, who are motivated by no honest desire to improve working conditions, but rather propose to feather their own nests while promoting the cause of social anarchy and red revolution.*

*And they are getting very tired of the spectacle of these unprincipled agitators, most of them of alien origin, and strangers to California, actually forbidding those who want to work from working, on threat of physical violence.*

*They do not work themselves except in stirring up strife and disorder.*

*They look to their dupes to supply them with food, clothing, shelter, and spending money.*

*They loaf between working seasons and then descend on the scene like vultures who have smelled carrion from afar.*

The papers also took the growers' position that the pickers should be represented by pickers, not by professional organizers:

*But one thing is certain: The strikers cannot accept communistic leadership and ideas and get anywhere in their dealing with patriotic Americans. If they will get rid of men whose chief purpose is to stir up trouble rather than to exact justice, they will have taken a long stride towards peace and prosperity.* (Times-Delta, October 12)

Editorial columns accepted the view that the agitators ruled by force and were not merely the instruments for expressing the pickers' desires:

*Consul Bravo is authority for the statement that his nationals are ready to return to work at the 60 cents per hundred pounds which the growers have been paying. Sheriff Buckner of Kings County, in arresting a leader today, asserted that the men in the concentration camp at Corcoran who are willing to work were being restrained through intimidation.* (Times-Delta, October 13)

The *Tulare Advance-Register* whipped up the popular emotions with an attack on the "reds":

*Out With The Agitators. Every day of the so-called cotton "strike" it is becoming more apparent that the strife is due almost solely to a program for promoting unrest and dissatisfaction among the laboring classes by professional "outside" agitators.*

*... the "strike" would vanish into thin air overnight if the outside agitators were rounded up en masse and escorted out of the country as they should be. And in the future, we should guard well against allowing them to get a new foothold for sowing the red seeds of radicalism among an otherwise happy and contented people.* (October 16)

In addition to these editorial comments, various valley newspapers reprinted communistic literature said to be widely distributed by the union among the workers. (e.g. *Times,* October 22, and *Times-Delta,* October 23)

To these charges against the agitators Miss Decker commented: "There was one thing that made this strike possible—it was the development of leadership from the ranks, coming from the bottom up." (Speech, November 27)

An attack on the University of California revealed the uncritical state of popular judgments in the valley at the close of the strike, and afforded an outlet for inflamed passions. It required to touch this off only the presence of one professor as member of the governor's committee, and the conduct of about seven students said to belong to the local affiliate of the National Students' League.

These seven students gave some publicity to their views, which were sympathetic to the strikers, and in addition participated in picketing excursions and resisted efforts of local officials who sought to curtail their activities. Two students testified before the fact-finding committee, charging that the sheriff's officers dealt summarily with the pickets, did not allow them to stop their cars, threatened the use of tear-gas bombs, and acted in an unlawful manner. (Hearings)

Their presence in the affected area as partisans led to a demand for an investigation of the university by the chairman of the Tulare County Board of Supervisors, heralded in the headlines of a local paper as follows:

*A.J. Elliott asks probe of U.C. radicals. Supervisor raps university students for entering local dispute. Found among pickets. Says taxpayers furnish money to educate young radicals.* (Times, *October 28)*

The manager of the University of California News Service replied:

*I understand there is some bitterness down there toward the university because of the activities of these people, most of whom are not students here at all. It is not fair to judge the institution by them even if they are all students. Twelve thousand young men and women mind their own business and work as we believe they should. Half a dozen become involved in something like this strike and are observed where the workers are not: the university is judged by the half dozen and not by the twelve thousand.* (Times-Delta, *October 30)*

The basic misunderstanding of the nature of a university which made it possible for valley opinion to propose laying violent hands on education is plain from the following:

*The chairman of the Board of Supervisors of Tulare County makes a timely suggestion. It is common knowledge in this county that students from the University of California actively participated as agitators in the so-called cotton strike, some of them becoming particulary obnoxious in their activities as pickets. . . . But we are wondering whether the censure runs rightly to the students. It has long been a matter of concern that the colleges of the nation house many instructors whose preachment is a direct encouragement to communism, who find in Russia's government policies that which commands their admiration.*

*One does not have to guess as to the opinions of these instructors. We have heard them on the lecture platform; we have heard them outrage American audiences by declarations alleging that the country is on the road to communism, that the signboard on the highway points directly to Moscow, that reverence for our own institutions has faded, and all in all, painting a picture calculated to impress the unthinking and the immature.*

*With such preachments in the lecture halls of our universities, what else can we expect than that youth shall be attracted by communistic leadership which seeks to destroy industry and finds its highest inspiration in misdirecting the activities of the thoughtless and uninformed? What ought to attract the attention of the public, particularly, is not that university students should have taken part in unseemly demonstrations on the highways of the state, but that institutions of learning should employ men to teach the youth of the land who can only see, in a most serious and menacing situation, that a communistic leadership is being denied civil rights, and outrageously calling upon the authorities to protect it against the defensive attitude of those such leadership would destroy.*

*Meantime, not only a good many farmers, but a good many citizens are reaching the conclusion that if our universities are to become the centers of communistic teaching, society will be better served by such employment as will eliminate those who find inspiration in Moscow instead of in Washington. (Californian, October 30)*

The lengths to which even university alumni could go in their failure correctly to judge the situation is indicated by the statement of a large grower:

*I am an old California man. I graduated there. I have followed the football teams and have supported the university in every way possible. There are a lot of old California men around here that feel the same way about it. The university is losing a lot of support. I cannot talk freely with you. I cannot help but think that you are a Communist, too, and will use any information I might give you against the growers. (Interview)*

A sheriff also was caught in the hysteria:

*I don't want to support a university that teaches the students to be socialists, to wave the red flag and destroy America. (Interview)*

The *Pacific Rural Press* even demanded in an editorial that the College of Agriculture and Gianinni Foundation of the State University "must be for the farmer first and everyone else second...." (See Appendix)

Following the cotton strike vigilante action flared up in Imperial Valley. Shortly, a statewide organization of growers arose, sponsored by the Farm Bureau and the Agricultural Committee of the State

Chamber of Commerce. This organization, now known as the Associated Farmers, represents predominantly the viewpoint of the larger growers as to labor policy.

At no time since 1933 has a strike of agricultural workers in California been accompanied by such complete documentation of its course and such clear delineation of the alignment of groups within the community. Nor has any other strike given such impetus to organization of agricultural employers. This organization now seems established on a permanent basis and is making efforts to spread into the Pacific Northwest and the Middlewest. This study, therefore, has seized upon an opportunity which rarely is so fully available to contemporary historians. By use of documents and observations made in the field during and after the strike, it has portrayed the conditions out of which present alignments have developed, and the characteristics which were so clearly revealed at their genesis.

## APPENDIX

(A number of significant documents are included here, partly because they would unduly have burdened the continuity of the textual account of the cotton strike, partly because most of them appeared after the strike ended. They are necessary, however, to adequate presentation of the attitudes which developed out of the agricultural strikes of 1933.)

### I. SOME POINTS OF VIEW

Out With The Agitators. Every day of the so-called cotton "strike" it is becoming more apparent that the strife is due almost solely to a program of promoting unrest and dissatisfaction among the laboring classes by professional "outside" agitators.

The very fact that caravans are continually organized to "picket" fields in an effort to intimidate pickers at work is sufficient proof that the "strike" is in fact an artificial one, and would fall of its own weight if the agitators were rounded up and the laborers allowed to return to the fields or not, as they chose, free from fear of interference or threats.

All of which is ample evidence that the "strike" would vanish into thin air overnight if the outside agitators were rounded up en masse and escorted out of the country as they should be. And in the future we should guard well against allowing them to get a new foothold, or sowing the red seeds of radicalism among an otherwise happy and contented class of working people. (*Advance-Register*, October 16, 1933)

The Farm Labor Strike Racket. Promotion of so-called agricultural workers' "union" in California within the past two months and consequent "strikes" launched in various localities give evidence of a new type of racket which is being vigorously promoted within our borders.

A variety of attempts similar to the local cotton "strike," all organized in the same manner and bearing the earmarks of the same group of racketeers directing them, have been launched at opportune times in various parts of the state.

Among these was an attempt to form such a "union" among Imperial Valley farm workers. Prompt action of officials in escorting the racketeers out of the district thwarted the "strike." Undaunted, the organizers moved to Ventura where they succeeded in getting a larger total of dues from "members" but failed to win out in the strike when authorities stepped in and prevented violence in picketing. No time was lost in jumping to Tulare where the Tagus strike was launched. More dues were collected from workers and with little official opposition a settlement was exacted.

Flushed with partial victory, and visions of a vast sum in dues from a growing membership, the organizers rushed plans for a grape-picking strike in the Fresno and Lodi districts and polished up details of the cotton "strike" to be launched here, followed by an orange-picking strike when the harvest in eastern Tulare County opens.

The Fresno and Lodi strikers were "called" by the racketeers, but once more they found the forces of law and order too powerful. Repulsed, they returned again to Tulare where a more fertile field of memberships and dues was to be found in the cotton harvest and the forthcoming orange crop. The results of this campaign are too well known to be repeated here.

It is sufficient to state that a membership of some 4,000 pickers is claimed, which with an initiation fee of 50 cents a head, would total several thousand dollars for the coffers of the racketeers, with additional sums to be paid from time to time in dues—should the "strike" succeed.

That is the story of the farm labor strike racket in California within the past few months. And it contains two clear-cut conclusions.

First, that the various strikes are one in purpose, promoted by a central group presumably principally interested in dues and in advancing the cause of communism.

Second, that wherever the force of law and order has quickly exerted a restraining influence on attempts to coerce workers in fields, the strike racketeers have failed. Also, that in almost every case the worker—the "comrade"—has paid the bill. He is the real victim of the strike racketeer. (*Advance-Register*, October 17, 1933)

Looks As Though Our Cotton Farmer Is The "Forgotten Man"

The strike situation has not been helped any by the influx of labor agitators, officials of the National League for the Defense of Political Prisoners, and university economic students with a communistic flair. The wires to Washington have been burdened with protest in behalf of the strikers, most of whom are Mexican nationals, while not a single voice is raised in behalf of the cotton-growing farmers who face ruin unless the pickers resume work before the crop is destroyed by inclement weather which may come now at any time.

The farmers are our people, and it would appear that it is about time the government and our good American friends gave at least a sidelong glance in their direction. They will remain with us after this unfortunate episode is a closed incident, while 90 percent of the strikers, about whom such a great ado is being made, will be moving on, many probably back to their own country where they belong.

Americans are reputed to be fond of justice, and there are certainly two sides to this situation. If the farmers lose their crops, there will be no one to help them. If the pickers do not go back to work, the government has guaranteed that they will be given food, clothing, and shelter.

On the eve of the appearance of a fact-finding commission, which has been appointed by the federal and state governments to find a right solution of the difficulty, it is foolish, almost suicidal, to encourage the strikers to believe that they are being unfairly treated by the peace officers and courts, that the right to picket extends to the right to invade property and defy officers, and that no matter what they do, alien or citizen, they will be fed and cared for in idleness. (*Times-Delta,* October 19, 1933)

An observer of the labor trouble at Lodi says that some of the state representatives who came to arbitrate "were as bad as the Communists."

Perhaps he was dramatizing his story by the customary and conventional hyperbole, but criticism of the state's efforts in agricultural labor disputes has come from other sections and it is understandable why farmers do not care to leave it to Rolph's men.

For instance, men like Tim Reardon. Tim is a San Francisco political labor leader. Need more be said?

As an advocate and battler for labor he is doubtless a whiz, but as a calm, judicial arbiter, looking at both sides dispassionately and making decisions broadly, he is probably overpriced at a dime a dozen. (*Pacific Rural Press,* October 21, 1933)

---

Telegram to George Creel, NRA administrator, San Francisco, Calif.: "The cotton strike in the San Joaquin Valley is directed by well-known Communists with California headquarters in San Jose, California, with Russian Communist connections, and these facts are well known by county, state, and federal authorities. The strikers are composed of approximately 90 percent itinerants, Mexicans easily led and intimidated. Price being paid pickers 60 cents per hundred weight, cabins, light, fuel, and water furnished free. Due to heavy yield and large bolls the average picker can pick three hundred pounds per day.

This exceeds the average going wages paid American farm labor in other agricultural crops as well as cotton in this valley this season. With few exceptions Americans working and satisfied with this price. Believe your investigations will disclose price being paid in Texas for best picking ranges from 40 to 60 cents and in Lower California where price is being set by Mexican government for its own nationals, 49 cents American money and no accommodations furnished at either place. Communist leaders have organized large unsanitary concentration camps of these strikers, and strikers are held in these camps practically prisoners through intimidation by leaders. Caravans of strikers are sent out from these camps for the express purpose of intimidating the community and satisfied pickers. Immediately adjoining the city limits of Corcoran one of these camps is estimated to contain 3,780 strikers and the population of the city of Corcoran is estimated at less than 2,000 persons. The trustees of the city of Corcoran and all the civic organizations of the city of Corcoran have publicly passed resolutions that the camp is a menace to the health and safety of the city and have appealed to the local authorities and the governor of this state for removal of same but have obtained no relief. The food for these camps is being furnished from the Federal Emergency Relief Fund. Upon authority of sheriff of Kings County and backed by proof that is indisputable, federal relief workers have gone to the workers in the cotton fields in Kings County and tried to induce satisfied workers to quit work and accept federal relief on scale of $5.00 per week for man and wife. The farmers who have worked these crops through the year with heat ranging as high as 118 degrees and who at the present price of cotton and the picking scale of 60 cents per hundred have practically nothing left for their efforts are wondering if in combating the communist influence they are going to have the Communists supported by the federal government in form of food and money. Federal Labor Commissioner Folin of Los Angeles has stated that if the intimidation of workers was stopped and he could be authorized by Washington, he could furnish 5,000 laborers out of the 2,000 now on federal relief in Los Angeles for picking the cotton at 60 cents. The local authorities seem powerless to combat this situation and the governor of this state has been appealed to without relief. We respectfully refer you to Edward Fitzgerald, federal conciliator, Los Angeles, who investigated these conditions and advised strikers to return to work at price of 60 cents pending further hearings, but Communist leaders influenced strikers to ignore his advice. We also respectfully refer you to Federal Attorney Pierson Hall of Los Angeles, familiar with conditions here, and George Creel, administrator NRA, San Francisco, who are thoroughly familiar with conditions here and know the menace existing to life and property in this valley. We are now appealing to you as a last resort to correct this situation." [From] L.D. Ellett, chairman, Corcoran Cotton Growers' Association Committee, Corcoran, Calif., October 21, 1933.

Growers Post-Strike Proposals to Governor Rolph. Growers say granting of the following requests is necessary to end bitter "labor difficulty":
1. All concentration camps to be closed immediately and occupants ordered to go to work or move out of the San Joaquin Valley.
2. Closing, permanently, of agitators' offices in every town in the valley.
3. Prevention of nightly meeting of reds and agitators in valley.
4. Refusal of free food to able-bodied workers. Handling emergency relief administration funds by local organizations familiar with situation, instead of by state authorities.
5. Distinction to be made between industrial and agricultural labor commission. Welfare departments to be reorganized and to handle these two phases separately.
6. An official study of the personnel of these two departments with a view to eliminating undesirable officials and employees. (*Bakersfield Californian,* October 28, 1933)

The Valley Tells Gov. Rolph. . . . *The Chronicle* of October 27 carries a great banner saying: "Ku Klux Klan's Blazing Crosses Warn Strikers." Just another pipe dream of a *Chronicle* reporter, comments a *Visalia Times-Delta* editorial.

And as you burrow into the fine type of the *Chronicle* article under the blazing head you discover that the cross was "figuratively set ablaze" by a secret order of Klan officials promising cooperation of citrus growers.

Meanwhile a big delegation of valley leaders call upon Governor Rolph. They tell him that they were promised protection from the radical agitators if the growers would pay 75 cents for cotton picking. It seems that George Creel, federal NRA representative, promised such protection, and asked who would furnish it, replied that Governor Rolph would. The governor says it is up to the sheriffs. And the sheriff says they are under bond and they have got to be careful about creating an army of Tom, Dick, and Harry deputies to handle the situation.

Thus the hot plate is handed around the circle. Meanwhile many growers feel they were sold out. They cannot afford to pay 75 cents for cotton picking and it makes them wild to see agitators bellowing for more.

Growers want that promised protection, and if they do not get it, they will probably provide some of their own. These are red-blooded Americans and not the big city type of human doormats.

A number of demands were made of the governor. One was that the strikers be ousted from their camps if they do not go to work. Another was that federal relief be shut off from able-bodied idlers. The distribution of food through federal plans has been a scandal. Let the regular welfare agencies do it, was demanded.

Also they want Governor Rolph to keep Labor Commissioner Frank C. MacDonald out of the valley and the state welfare department.

Whether the governor was really listening is always difficult to determine.

One member of the delegation, asked what was accomplished by visiting the governor replied: "We all got our pictures taken."

Frequently that is all such delegations get—their pictures in the paper. (*Pacific Rural Press*, November 4, 1933)

The workers know that they won by defeating not only the finance companies and rich ranchers, the local sheriffs and their deputies, but the entire capitalistic government including the state police, the U.S. state and federal so-called mediation boards, and the treacherous Mexican consul. (*Western Worker*, November 6)

---

Box 406 Bakersfield, California
*November 10th, 1933*
Mr. R.C. Branion
*Federal State Welfare Administrator, San Francisco, California*
Dear Sir: At a meeting of the board of directors of this association, Wednesday, November 8th, the following resolution was passed unanimously:

"WHEREAS the distribution of welfare aid has a direct effect on the harvesting of agricultural crops, and

"WHEREAS in the recent labor disturbances in the cotton harvest in the San Joaquin Valley, one of the most disturbing influences in the settling of this trouble was the distribution of welfare aid to those voluntarily idle, and

"WHEREAS charity which encourages labor to remain idle is un-American and dangerous to our institutions of government,

"THEREFORE BE IT RESOLVED that the directors of the California Cotton Cooperative Association request the federal and state welfare agencies to define or revise their policies to the effect that aid will be refused able-bodied workers who refuse to work when work is available."
Yours very truly,

California Cotton Cooperative Association, Ltd.
C.C. Seeden, *Secretary and General Manager*

---

Those Philanthropists, the Ginners. Our recent suggestions that increased pay for cotton pickers should be taken out of the ginners instead of the growers leads to some interesting investigation and to even more interesting results.

For instance, it is found that ginners have a code pending in Washington which would increase ginning fees 100 percent and would put a special penalty of 5 cents additional on the ginning of all cotton over 1½ inches staple.

It is the plea of the ginners to Washington that present ginning rates are not compensatory. That remains to be demonstrated. We do not observe ginners getting in line at the bank along with cotton growers.

And whaddaya mean ginning fees?

If you refer only to the running of the cotton through the gin, the price in the San Joaquin Valley has been 15 cents, and it is now proposed to increase it to 30 cents, with the Anderson-Clayton crowd, who handle about 50 percent of the cotton of the state, seeking to reduce it to 25 cents.

"Yea, so you can squeeze the little gins out," retorted the critics of this big, powerful, nationwide crowd.

But, however that may be, the fees which gins charge are not limited to the mere running of cotton through the gin.

It is commonly reported that they make their big money out of the cotton seed, and that is not all.

The California gins sell bagging to the farmers and ties and insurance with storage space, and sell seed and credit.

They charge the farmer $3 a ton commission to sell his cottonseed to an oil mill, and if investigation does not prove that it is often a case of a gin merely turning the seed over to one of its subsidiary brothers-in-law, then we owe an apology for what we are thinking.

It is a known fact that the ginning companies own most of the cotton because they have financed its production for a rate of interest which surely nets them an additional profit.

So, it would seem as if growers might well look a bit deeper into this matter. They are certainly interested in what gins may do by way of a code and if a 100 percent increase in ginning charges is made, the gins should be forced to show their books and demonstrate that they are losing money. *(Pacific Rural Press, November 11, 1933)*

---

Council Backs Up Police Chief in Action Against Cotton Strike Leaders. "Union's" Demands Rejected. A list of demands made to the city council last night by a delegation from the Cannery and Agricultural Workers' Union and the International Labor Defense were flatly rejected, and in addition Mayor Hahesy informed the delegation that businessmen and representative citizens of Tulare had decided at a meeting the night before to get the organization headquarters out of town. Mayor Hahesy said that Tulare was getting a name throughout the state as a "hot-bed" for harboring the headquarters of strike leaders, and that was the reason the businessmen had decided at their meeting to see that the headquarters left town. *(Tulare Advance-Register, January 4, 1934)*

Red Flag "Unions." First it was the peach pickers' strike, then grapes, garment workers, lettuce, beans, and cotton. Now it is a milkers' strike. Why?...

Fortunately, these questions are easily answered. The San Joaquin Valley now knows them from experience and is not likely to be taken in a second time....

They are primarily designed to gain membership for the Communists. Practically none has resulted in any benefit to the real worker, who is only a pawn and at the best a source of revenue to further the Bolshevik plots against American government.

The campaign is much like that of the IWW a few years ago, except that it is more ruthless and aims principally at ultimate revolution and overthrow of the government. The traitorous attack is doomed to failure, but that does not mean that its leaders are to be excused. On the contrary, they should be taught the folly of hoisting the red flag or any other over the stars and stripes on American soil. (*Tulare Advance-Register*, January 8, 1934)

Send Them Back to Russia. It is high time that the agitators were rounded up and sent back to Russia where they can actually practice what they preach. (*Tulare Advance-Register*, January 11, 1934)

Valley Expresses Self. Sentiment in Imperial Valley today approves action taken in Brawley and El Centro Tuesday night when vigilantes ordered leaders in agitation which has been ripe for the past two weeks to leave the county and took somewhat radical steps to see that they did leave. (*Imperial Valley Press*, quoted in *Brawley News*, January 25, 1934)

Not Mob Violence, But Valley Spirit. Mob rule is a thing to be avoided above all others, but it was not mob rule nor mob violence that removed from Imperial Valley Tuesday night the menace of active agitation among the valley's lettuce workers, content if left to themselves to continue peaceably in the fields. It was not mob violence—it was a studied, organized movement of citizens seeking the only way out of difficulties threatening the community's peace, when the hands of the law had been tied by the law itself.

The names of the men who took part in the move against strike agitators are not known, but the service they rendered their community is an outstanding one.

"Imperial Valley is not San Joaquin Valley. Stay out!" This, in effect, was the message delivered to agitators—and they took it to heart. (*Morning Farmer*, quoted in *Brawley News*, January 26, 1934)

Vigilantes Organizing Over Valley. Visalia, January 31 (UP). San Joaquin Valley farmers are organizing quietly into vigilante committees, determined to prevent recurrence of agricultural strikes which paralyzed harvests in the valley last summer, it was reported here today.

The farmers reportedly have hired trained investigators to check on the records of known Communist organizers and to watch their movements. It was understood the orgranization planned to stop at their inception any attempts to foment strikes during the coming harvest seasons. (*Tulare Advance-Register*, January 31, 1934)

Free Speech and Criminal Speech. Free speech is not meant, nor does it give anyone the right to promote plans for destruction of life, property, or the government. . . . Free speech and criminal speech are two different things. . . . The more drastic the action against those who make criminally traitorous utterances against the government, the safer will be the right of free speech in America. (*Tulare Advance-Register*, February 2, 1934)

A Real Public Service. The Reverend Charles Woessner, who is resigning this week as pastor of the First Baptist Church of Tulare, will have the best wishes of many Tulareans in whatever future endeavor he undertakes. Besides serving the community through church activities, he performed a distinctly meritorious civic service in invading the headquarters of the Communist organization, masquerading as a labor union [sic] and exposing it for what it really was—a drive for "red" revolutionists. It was he who secured the incriminating literature published in this and other newspapers which first called attention of the entire state to the real agitators and motives behind local and other labor troubles. The community owes him a debt of gratitude for this service. (*Advance-Register*, February 9, 1934)

Peace officers of five San Joaquin Valley counties prepared today to organize into a solidly knit organization to prevent communist-fostered farm labor troubles. . . uniform legislation against picketing and plans to combat [sic]. . . troublemaking by Communists. . . . (*Advance-Register*, February 13, 1934)

Colleges of Agriculture Should Represent Agriculture. Are agricultural colleges supposed to represent agriculture and be advocates of that basic industry, or are they neutral fact-finding courts rendering decisions for or against agriculture as cold logic may decide?. . . In other words, for whom is the Gianinni Foundation working?

The above questions are blunt, but not unfriendly.

They are asked with the understanding that many college professors believe they represent pure science and no person or class. . . .

But these are new days, with imperative new needs, and the suggestion is offered pointedly and specifically:

That the college of agriculture must be for the farmer first and everyone else second, and unless it is it cannot expect to hold the farmer's support in these tax-tight days.

We all know that agriculture is our biggest and most basic industry; that it creates most of the wealth which supports the college; that agriculture must prosper if the state is to be sound; so why shouldn't the college of agriculture be the active, partisan friend and representative of agriculture? This does not mean subserviently. A real friend is frank. Taking off the moth-eaten halo of the past and putting on serviceable work clothes is no cause for losing self-respect. (*Pacific Rural Press,* March 25, 1934)

(Apropos of the lynching of two kidnapper-murderers at San Jose):

The more fuss the Civil Liberties Union, Mooney Defense League, and other communistic brotherhoods make over the San Jose lynching, the more we are inclined to believe that the jury of 15,000 citizens returned the right verdict. (*Tulare Advance-Register,* January 3, 1934)

## II. TACTICS

(The following statement purports to be a Communist manual of agricultural strike tactics. It was reprinted in the *Tulare Advance-Register,* April 4, 1934, under the headline "Details of red plot are exposed").

Resolution on the manner of organizing strike struggles in the agricultural field. As drawn from the experiences of the 1933 strike movement, convention March 17-18 District No. 13.

### I. Introduction

The convention meets at a moment of our greatest opportunity for developing a struggle movement for higher wages and better conditions in practically every industry of our district. This movement, will, however, materialize only if our (Communist) party organizations give the proper leadership to the union and in the development of the struggles. This leadership must not be in the form of issuing direction and orders to other comrades. We too often have the experience that when we call some leading comrade to account for failure in his assigned field of work, the comrade excuses himself by saying "It is the fault of the membership, or the comrades of the lower organizations. I told them what to do, and they didn't do it." Leaders who at this stage of the game confine themselves to telling others what to do, instead of devoting the bulk of their own time to leading by participating in the struggles directly, are foredoomed to failure, and should be immediately replaced. Also we must eliminate either this practice of leading comrades, or, if necessary, the leading comrades themselves who are simply administrators inside the organizations and do not directly enter into the practical work in the field of organizing workers. The third category of comrades who, though well intentioned, follow the practice of running from town to town, and from field to field, without accomplishing anything in any one place, must either be corrected in their manner of work, or eliminated from work, because their whole achievement is to run up expense, and discourage the local workers, who see in such activity much wind, but little practical achievement.

Danger of spontaneity. Because of these bad practices and because of our frequent negligence and lack of contact with large sections of the working class, spontaneous strikes have developed by workers who tire of waiting for us to give them proper leadership, and who go out and strike, unprepared though they may be. The movement of organized strikes in comparison to the movement of spontaneous strikes must be continually increased if the strike movement of the workers is to result in substantial gains in hours, wages, and conditions, and not result in futility and discouragement. It therefore is important for us to study our experiences of the previous year and understand wherein lie our shortcomings in order to accomplish more during this coming year.

School. As a first step in that direction, the school organized for March and April, 1934, is a good step forward. This school should not be lost in general theorizing by the students and teachers, but should concretely examine our practice in strikes during the past year and test and amend our theory concerning these strikes in the light of that practice. With the experiences of this school, we must subsequently systematically organize schools throughout the district all the year round in order to train as rapidly as possible a large corps of efficient and experienced organizers who understand the objectives of the work and by what methods to carry it through.

## II. Preparing to Strike

Surveying the territory. The most important thing in the leadership of a struggle is to know the territory, the condition of the industry, and the relation of forces. Probably the outstanding shortcoming of the leadership of the 1933 struggles was that too large a part of the leadership consisted of comrades who were not native to the situation that existed, and did not know the territorial conditions of the industry, or the relation of the contending forces. To learn these things, it is of minor value to study the statistics concerning a particular territory as reported by the government. Also, it is a wrong practice to issue lengthy questionnaires to the workers, or the lower functionaries, to have filled out in order to learn the territory. There is only one way to become a complete master of all knowledge concerning a particular locality, and that way is to have thorough discussions with all the workers, the poor farmers, and others who might be factors in a coming struggle. For this, the best comrades must not sit in the offices of the union or (Communist) party, but must go into the fields, and only a handful of comrades stay in the various centers for purposes of coordination. Official statistics and such information should be gathered but should always be regarded as secondary sources of authority. The chief source which guides us in our decisions along any lines at all must be the information that we gather from workers, poor growers and whatever we can learn from whatever contacts we may have with the richer growers or their agents.

Setting the demands. Having a thorough knowledge of the territory, the next thing to do is set demands around which the struggle is to be fought. The most effective struggles are fought where the fewest demands are raised. However, for this, these few demands must really be important to every worker in the industry who would be so seriously affected by them that he or she is willing to get out and struggle and sacrifice for winning them. In order that such demands are really set, they should not be announced until a representative of the workers themselves decides upon them without being influenced by outside comrades against their own will. Unless the workers themselves are ready and willing to fight for these demands, it is useless and wasteful to enter the struggle.

Setting the time to strike. The next important thing is to choose the proper moment to strike. Here again it is of paramount importance that the workers determine at which moment to strike. They, best of all, know the conditions of the industry, and when the boss needs them most. The time to strike should be determined by exactly that [sic] when the boss needs the workers most.

The first apparatus. Organizers should not begin to organize in a territory by calling general mass meetings and general conferences of the workers. It is first important to go into the towns where the workers are hired, or into the camps or on the ranches and there hold first informal meetings, and then formal meetings with the workers, until in at least a large number of places, especially those from which the strategic and big ranches draw their workers, are reasonably well organized, have at least a committee functioning, and are somewhat prepared for a greater step. Then the next step is to call a wage conference of delegates from those camps to agree on demands and to broaden our organizational forces. This conference should be as broad as possible, being certain that it is not so broad that it exposes itself to the police and the growers. The delegates to these conferences should be assigned to establish organizational connections where we have none yet in the strike area.

Leaflets. We want to call to the attention of the comrades that, up till now, we have said very little about distributing leaflets or issuing such agitational material. This is not an omission, but is because up to this point the issuance of leaflets frequently hinders the struggle rather than helps it. First, because it sets demands which the workers may not be prepared to fight for. Even if it puts these demands in a temporary optional way, "Final decision to be made later," it has a tendency to make the workers feel that they can join the movement only conditionally upon their acceptance of these demands. For this reason, it is personal contact and mouth-to-mouth talk with the workers that will be decisive to the success of our preliminary organization work. If leaflets have to be issued, that should only be done up to this stage under extremely important circumstances, and should not be relied upon as a major organizational weapon.

### III. Setting Up Machinery—No Promise

The next important thing to consider is to set up a thorough and efficient machinery in order to mobilize every possible force for winning the strike. In this connection one thing is of especially outstanding importance. The organizers must make no promises to the workers. We must not promise them a strike nor success in a strike, nor induce them to go on strike on the basis that we will surely supply them with large amounts of relief, defense funds, money for picketing caravans, etc. On the contrary, it must be impressed on the workers that everything depends on what they themselves do. The whole strike is in their hands. If they are ready to strike for better conditions we (Communists) will give them leadership, help them contact working class organizations in other parts for funds, food, etc., and we will help them to coordinate their strike movement with workers in other parts of the state in the same industry. But even here, we should create this contact not by sending the outside organizers to other parts of the state, but rather sending delegations of the workers themselves to other parts to spread the strike movement. Our approach must be that we want to help workers organize, and we will give them the best of our experienced leadership and support to help them win, but at every step, through democratic elections, through the speeches that we make, and the agitational material we issue, we must impress on the workers that the struggle is in their own hands, and that they must learn how to become experienced leaders, and not to depend only on the outside organizers.

The central strike committee. As a first measure to create this initiative from the workers themselves, it is important to set up the central organization committee, which should be elected at the preliminary wage conferences. Unless we have already an organizational guarantee that we will absolutely be able to call a strike, this committee should not be called a central strike committee, but a central organization committee. The composition of this central organization committee should be delegates from the various camps and ranches. The function of the organization committee should be to consider the one or two, or at the most, three major questions which most profoundly affect the strike at a particular moment. This committee should not become a theater, whereby every mass organization has its representatives make big speeches about the importance of building their own organization. At all times the committee must limit itself to only the main questions.

In organizing our leading committees in such a situation, we must be extremely careful to bring the rank and file into the leadership, and especially to bring them into those posts which are decisive for making decisions as to the course of their strike. For this purpose, the qualifications for leading comrades in a strike shall not be their abilities in the office or on committees, but rather, their abilities as workers in the field. In other words, their abilities to lead other workers in the actual course of the struggle. Union card delegates should be chosen on the same basis. The windy gas-hounds should be kept out of leadership, and instead, the practical devoted comrades who understand the importance of detailed organization work should be given every leading post, and the comrades who make the speeches should be put under the control of such leading committees. As near as possible, good speakers and good organizers should be the same people, but where that is not possible, we must be careful that our leading committees don't begin to consist of comrades who have the most wind.

The auxiliaries to the strike. Each helping organization to the strike must perform its own function. Thus, as a regular army cannot very well win battles without the aid of its supply trains, hospital corps, etc., so strikes cannot be fought without the aid of auxiliary organizations.

1. Among these are a relief organization to consist of strikers organized into committees to gather and distribute relief and cooperating with the WIR.

2. Similar defense committees cooperating with the ILD. The policy to guide the workers at trials should be carefully worked out. No worker should be allowed to go to trial without help from the defense committee. The strike organizers must not become panicky if there are not enough lawyers to handle the cases, but union representatives should be brought in and trained to become responsible to help for defense cases. This will especially be necessary where the number of arrests reaches large numbers. Bail, defense, prisoners' relief can only be carried through if the greatest initiative is developed among the workers themselves.

3. It is necessary to have a negotiations committee, whose function should be to reach the poor farmers immediately and try to split them away from the big grower and gain settlements to cooperate with the United Farmers League for this purpose, and to draw up a very simple agreement which the growers are asked to sign. This agreement shall not have much legal verbage, but shall be so simple and in so few words that every farmer can understand its contents, and that no loophole be left for gymnastics.

4. A press committee must be organized. The purposes of the press committee should be: a. To publish a bulletin as often as possible for the strikers themselves, giving them constant information on the progress of the strike, and keeping the workers informed as fully as possible. This bulletin should be very brief, but published in every language which the strikers themselves use.

b. The press committee must also arrange to issue constant releases to the capitalist press answering the slanders against the strike and presenting the workers' side of the struggle. This must be done even if the capitalist press does not print our bulletins because eventually our press releases will have the effect of weakening the lies spread against us.

5. A financial committee must be established with possibly one expert so far as accounting is concerned, but chiefly consisting of workers themselves who shall control the receipt and disbursement of all funds, and who shall be responsible to the mass of the workers. The type of worker to be chosen for such a committee should be such that no worker will question the integrity of the handling of these finances.

Just prior to the strike vote, delegates to the conference should be instructed to hold elections in their respective localities for representatives to central strike committees.

All committees must be responsible to the central strike committee, but at every meeting of the central strike committee it shall not be necessary that every committee shall report, but only those committees shall report whose questions are being handled at that particular central strike committee meeting.

It is important to mobilize all the women, youth, and children in the struggle. In addition to the picket lines, the women can be organized, especially in the relief apparatus and to work with the children. The children should be organized to play games based on the strikes. Instead of "cops and robbers" they should play "workers against growers," and in the course of the play the lessons of the strikes and their simple but profound political significance can be taught to the children. The children should also be organized into picket lines and demonstrations in support of the strike, especially in the towns, to organize the sentiment of the rest of the people. As in most agricultural areas, the youth predominate in canneries. It should therefore be especially the job of the YCL and the youth sections of the union to take hold of the job of organizing the canneries and bringing them into solidarity with the workers; every effort must be to mobilize these backward workers in support of the strike. For this purpose, mass delegations of the strikers themselves should be sent to the packinghouse workers over the heads of whatever unions and existing machinery there might be, and appeal to the packinghouse workers both on the basis of solidarity as well as for gaining improvements for themselves for united action against the growers. This should be done preliminary to the strike actually breaking out, as well as after the strike has broken out in the fields if the packing shed and cannery workers have not yet come out.

Technical preparation. Before, in the setting up of the machinery, it is of paramount importance that all technical equipment shall be prepared, including a mimeograph and typewriter, dues stamps, and due books, and strike cards for all workers, so that the relief distribution should be controlled.

The union centers. During the time of the strike, it must be remembered that if the workers are really to retain with themselves any lasting lessons from the strike, the importance of the entire militant movement, and especially the district center of the C&AWIU, as well as the leadership of the TUUL, must be constantly brought before them not merely in speeches but in practical actions. For example, when there are disputed points, our comrades should propose to consult and get advice from the C&AWIU or the TUUL, and send in reports on all preparations and strike developments. The granting of charters to new locals should be made an occasion for impressive ceremony.

Defense squads. And finally, already before the strike, defense squads should be organized which should later be enlarged to become guerrilla picketing squads, both for the purpose of defending the camps against attackers, and for the purpose of pulling those ranches, canneries or packing sheds, where access by a mass picketing line is more difficult. These defense squads should be chosen very carefully so that no stoolpigeons get into them, and the bravest workers put into them, and the best manner of defense should be discussed and decided upon by the workers themselves.

The strike call. Now we are ready to issue the strike call. This strike call should be extremely simple. It should be first read and approved by the central organization or strike committee. It should be translated into every language the workers who are being appealed to, read, and above all, it must be very precise and to the point. When we are ready to issue the central strike call, we must assume that the call itself will not win the workers for the strike, because that agitation had already been prepared, but we must issue the call in order to most sharply and pointedly put the one, two, or at the most, three demands to be fought for, the date of the strike, and what to do the minute after the walkout occurs.

Conduct of the strike. The main weapon for conducting the strike is of course the picket line. The purpose of these is to keep scabs out, to pull out the more backward workers, and to keep a solid organization for defense against vigilante attacks. Every picket line should be led by responsible and courageous leaders. They should be of two general characters: guerrilla picket line and mass picket line. Both must be utilized together and to supplement one another. In other words, even while the mass picket lines are parading up and down the highway and calling upon the workers to strike, the guerilla picket lines must find other entrances to the ranches and help take the workers off. When the terror breaks loose on a large scale, it will be found that more and more we will have to rely on the guerilla picket lines. For this purpose, the guerilla picket lines must be efficient. They should not be too large, but consist of at the most from one to two carloads of workers, and they must be able to move very swiftly.

Headquarters. There should be an open headquarters wherever possible. The purpose of these headquarters shall only be for contact. In other words, we are not to keep mimeographs, typewriters, or other such strike machinery in these headquarters. Not even all strike leaders should come to the headquarters, but many leading comrades should be held in reserve. There should also be reserve strike headquarters where comrades can gather in case the open headquarters are attacked. Sometimes it is wise not to have a separate union headquarters, but to use the feeding kitchens or one of the shacks in the camps for contact purposes. All the issuance of leaflets, bulletins, and records should be kept at other places, known only to the special comrades assigned to that work, and should be kept as secret as possible so that they are not attacked.

Leaders. The leading comrades should be divided into those who must become known generally because they are the open speakers, or members of the negotiations committee; and to supplement these, a whole series of leading comrades must not be known except by the workers through their mingling among the workers, or through their participation in the leading councils of the strike apparatus. Leaders must be chosen very carefully. They should not be the type of comrades who get easily enthusiastic and who despair just as easily. We should especially beware of such leaders who spread the theory that strikes can be won in twenty-four hours. While the enthusiasm of the masses is at its height it is the duty of the leaders to utilize that enthusiasm to its full extent, but themselves, to keep a sober realization of all factors involved, and to make decisions on such a realistic basis. At the first sign that a leader is getting discouraged and pessimistic, he should either be corrected or removed. Above all we must have leaders who do not easily get discouraged or pessimistic when difficulties arise.

The Communist Party & YCL. How should the Communist Party and YCL be brought before the workers in the strike? We should distinguish the party from the union on a political basis. In other words, we must show the role of the union so far as getting economic improvements is concerned, but utilize every incident in the strike to prove that the government is on the side of the bosses and that we must also have a party that will bring the government on the side of the workers. We must explain to them that such a party is the Communist Party, and that the government by its nature is on the side of the growers, and we must establish a workers and farmers government if we want the government to be on the side of the workers. Also, in our manner of recruiting, should the party and the union be distinguished. For the union there should be mass recruiting from the platform, and through leaflets, but for the party there should be recruiting person to person. The best workers should be chosen, but this should not mean one or two best workers. "Western Workers,"

"Lucha Obreras," "Why Communism," and other such literature which will bring the workers close to the Communist movement should be systematically distributed.

The menace of disruption. Above all, we must watch for those comrades who continually prate against "party interference." These comrades represent the capitalist influence in our ranks who try to split the Communist Party from its active leadership of the workers' struggles. The workers themselves rarely demand the elimination of the Communist party except where the party comrades, through opportunist errors, bring such a condition into being. We must not wait for the bosses to raise the "red scare." On the contrary we must continually warn the workers both in the preparations for the strike, and during the strike itself, that the manner of the bosses' breaking up the strike will be chiefly through trying to split the ranks of the workers, and then through terror. The workers will easily understand that they must fight against terror, but they will not easily recognize the tactics the bosses use to split their ranks. We must warn the workers in advance that the bosses will use such tactics as religious issues, race issues, political issues, issues of nationality. We must warn the workers that this strike in their union should be carried forward primarily on the basis of united action to win their demands, and no differences as to political or religious or national or racial distinctions should be allowed to enter into it at all, and that anyone who tries to split the ranks of the workers on the basis of these issues should be considered an enemy. The workers should all be asked at certain times to rise and solemnly pledge to such a platform. This will impress itself on the minds of the workers so that when the agitation of the growers comes out with their slimy talk to split the ranks, the workers will be prepared for it, and will drive them out. Only where our comrades under opportunist influence try to hide the red issue, or cover up the fact that Communists are taking a leading part in the strike, only in such cases, does the red issue in the hands of the bosses become effective. If we are the first to come to the workers to warn them against these issues, such methods will not be effective. During the entire strike, we must especially watch for any AFofL, Socialist party, or other social-facist or facist influences entering the strike. We must warn the workers against those who pretend a "free interest in the strike" but who talk for the elimination of this or that militant leader. Especially for those like the Socialist party who raise a few dollars for relief, and then try to use that as a wedge to go among the workers and split their ranks by telling them it is unfortunate they have "Communist leadership" and that "they stand a better chance of winning if they rid themselves of the Communist leadership." We must warn the workers of this even before the AFofL and Socialist party or other social-fascist splitters come among these strikers and make as the only test for leadership those who fight the hardest on picket lines, and other strike activity against the bosses, the growers, and their uniformed or plain-clothes agents. Finally, we must be prepared to answer quickly in our strike bulletins any maneuvers to introduce arbitration boards by investigations conducted by the labor commission, federal government, or liberal agencies.

## V. The Settlement

It must be remembered that strikes are won and lost not only with the vanguard of the workers, but also with its most backward sections. In other words, we must not allow only the most militant workers to decide whether to accept a settlement, but all workers must share in the decision. The bosses will maneuver with offers of settlement against us. Their objective will be to split the ranks of the workers with such offers, and create indecision and wavering among them so as to make impossible unified action of the strike. We must meet every such maneuver chiefly by letting the workers themselves decide the questions in as democratic a fashion as possible, and by the leaders always keeping alert to see not only how the most militant sections of the strikers receive the offers of the growers, but also how the most backward sections receive these offers. It is most important to watch that we do not become influenced solely by the most militant sections, but while encouraging and strengthening the leadership of these most militant and best workers in the strike, we must also take into consideration at all times the moods of all sections of the strikers.

In the process, and after the settlement of the strike, an intense organizational drive must be begun to consolidate the gains of the strike organizationally and idealogically through popularizing the achievements through discussion and explaining the shortcomings so that workers will know how to fight better next time, and through drawing the best workers into the Communist party, TUUL, and other parts of the revolutionary movement.

## STRIKE STRATEGY IN THE AGRICULTURAL FIELDS
Issued by the District Committee of The Cannery & Agricultural Workers' Industrial Union
District Headquarters, 81 Post Street, San Jose, California

Since the coming of the Cannery and Agricultural Workers' Industrial Union into the fields, thousands of workers have been organized and have taken part in struggles for better living and working conditions. Considerable experience in revolutionary struggle and in strike strategy has been developed. With greater and greater masses of workers constantly being drawn into struggle, the time has now come to take stock of the various methods and tactics used in preparing, calling, and conducting strikes of field workers. This is necessary so that all class-conscious workers may benefit by the experience of the past.

In general, three methods of calling strikes have been used. These methods are: (1) The method of holding mass meetings, which may be called the public or "open" method. (2) The method of calling secret preliminary conferences of worker-delegates, or the "quiet" method. (3) The use of both the open and quiet methods. The advantages and disadvantages of these three methods were explained and discussed at the last district committee meeting of the C&AWIU.

### I. The Open Method

Many of the recent strikes have been called by the public or open method. That is, the union, by leaflet, advertisement, or other means, calls a public mass meeting of workers to consider the question of calling a strike. If the sentiment of the majority is in favor of striking, the strike call is issued, a strike committee elected from the floor, and general instructions issued in regards to picketing, etc.

Some of the advantages of the open method are: This may be the only way to break into a new territory or a district in which the union is very weak. This method often results in new and valuable recruits into the union. The open method is perhaps the quickest way to call a strike, and sometimes upon the quickness by which a strike is called hinges the question of victory or defeat. This method has proved comparatively successful in a number of instances.

The disadvantages of the open method are: (1) The results of a public mass meeting with little or no preliminary work are too uncertain. It is hard to anticipate and be prepared for everything that may come up. (2) Secondly, a public meeting will expose those workers who take a forward or bold stand, and these workers will likely be fired from their jobs or perhaps be arrested by the police. The workers know what is likely to happen and many class-conscious workers will stand back rather than take a bold stand. (3) The open meeting gives the bosses warning to mobilize strikebreakers and gives the police time to deputize thugs and gather new armed forces of suppression. (4) Such a method will increase the danger of bringing stool pigeons into the general and central strike committees. (5) It is difficult at such a general assembly to make the necessary preliminary preparations or to draw the rank and file of the workers into a free discussion of the conditions and problems that are faced. (6) There is no assurance that at such a meeting there will be a wide, truly representative assembly of workers. (7) Calling a strike of workers when they are off the job increases the difficulty of getting the workers onto the picket lines.

### II. The Quiet Or Delegated Conference Method

This method involves the calling of preliminary conferences of worker-delegates representing as many ranches as possible, especially the larger ranches. The workers can be summoned to the conference by union men who are working on the ranches, or by unemployed union men who can make contacts in the early morning and while looking for work. Much can be done by both employed and unemployed during the noon hour to secure delegates.

This method of calling secret or "quiet" conferences of worker-delegates from the various ranches before the calling of the strike has a number of important advantages: (1) The main advantage is that the identity of the workers is kept from the bosses—there is no exposure of the leading, most active workers. (2) The bosses and the police are kept in the dark about the strike, and although they may hear rumors of strike, they cannot be sure, and when the strike is called, it comes as a surprise to the bosses and police. (3) This quiet method of calling preliminary conferences enables full and detailed discussion by the workers of their conditions, wages, strike sentiment of fellow workers, when best to call the strike, the demands, and the ranches most important to bring out on strike. The conferences will bring out on which ranches the union is strong and those on which the union is weak. Certain comrades thus can be assigned in time to get work on or obtain delegates from the ranches in which the union is weakly represented. Whenever possible, union men should be working on the ranches, as much more effective work can be done from the "inside" than from the "outside." (4) These preliminary conferences make it possible to set up the entire strike apparatus prior to the calling of the strike, such as, the relief committee, the leaflet committee, the publicity committee, the central strike committee, etc. The entire conference may be turned into the general strike committee. (5) At the conference, opportunity is had to explain the role and functioning of the union, and new members can be signed into the union. There is also opportunity to give detailed information to worker-delegates on the method of conducting a strike and particularly about the importance of establishing and maintaining a picket line.

The disadvantage of the conference method comes mainly when the union is weak—when there are few union men working in the ranches or when there are but few contacts established. Another disadvantage of the quiet method is that it sometimes turns out to be too quiet, that is, the workers themselves don't know a strike is being prepared and will be as much surprised as the bosses when the strike is called. To avoid this, care must be taken that during the preparatory work of the conferences, a general agitation for strike is carried on among the workers on the ranches. This will assure a readiness on the part of the workers to walk out when they receive the strike call.

*III. Combination "Open" and "Quiet" Method*

The third method of preparing and calling a strike is a combination of the other two. Conferences of worker-delegates are held prior to the calling of a strike, but the open mass meeting is held on the eve of the strike as well. This is a very common method, perhaps the most common.

The chief advantage over the quiet conference method is that it assures a more widespread knowledge of the strike among the masses of the workers.

The disadvantages are again those of exposing the leading comrades, of giving the bosses a chance to send in strikebreakers, and giving the police the opportunity to mobilize their armed thugs. Thus we can see advantages and disadvantages in each of the three methods. In choosing their method, the comrades will have to be guided by the circumstances of the particular situation they face. As the union grows and our experiences broaden, these methods will be improved and new and better ways found to increase the standard of living of the workers—and finally to bring about the establishment of the workers' own government which will once and for all bring an end to exploitation and give all workers a decent standard of living.

No matter which method is used the following should receive special attention if successful strikes are to be led:

(1) Preliminary Preparations: Of utmost importance is to have a well-functioning local and section apparatus. The section and various local committees should meet regularly. Full information should be possessed about the area in which the strike is to be called—the number of workers, the important ranches, the various roads to the ranches, strategic points for establishing picket lines, etc. Contact should be secured with at least each large ranch.

(2) Strike Committees: General and central strike committees should keep in touch with ranch committees at all times. The ranch committees must maintain contact with growers. Meetings of the various strike committees must be held at least daily in order to receive reports and to meet the changing developments with a change of tactics.

(3) Relief: Strikes are usually won or lost over the question of relief. Relief machinery should be prepared prior to the strike and in operation from the first day of the strike. A committee under the leadership of a competent person should be set up to handle relief. Liberals and sympathizers can often be brought into this work.

(4) Publicity: Publicity in the form of mass meetings, news releases, leaflets, etc., should be conducted constantly during the strike. Liberals and sympathizers can also be utilized in the committee set up to handle the publicity. Assign someone to take pictures of the picket line, mass meetings, and, in particular, to photo any attacks by the police.

(5) Picket Lines: Picket lines must be established and maintained from the first day. It is particularly important that the picket line be formed early in the morning to prevent strikebreakers from being brought to work. Experience seems to show that it is better to mobilize the workers right on the picket line rather than mobilizing them somewhere else first and then going in mass to picket.

(6)Educational Work: In order to keep alive the militant spirit on the picket line, the leading and politically advanced comrades or any comrades who address the workers must not only deliver agitational and political speeches, but it is even more vital that they instruct the workers as to the role of the union and how it functions. Since a large portion of our membership consists of migratory workers, it is particularly important to stress the duty of these workers to act AS UNION MEN NO MATTER WHERE THEY ARE OR IN WHAT CROP THEY ARE WORKING. This must be done not only on the picket line, but in all the mass meetings as well.

(7) Recruiting: The question of recruiting and building the union is of equal importance to winning the strike. A recruiting committee should be in possession of sufficient books and stamps to enable recruiting at all times, whether on the picket line, at the mass meetings, or in committee meetings. The recruiting committee should be under the control of and instructed by the dues secretary.

(8) Defense: The usual method of the bosses to break a strike is to arrest the leading comrades. This is done in order to behead the strike and intimidate the workers. To meet this danger two preparations should be made: (a) Defense squads should be formed from the first day of the strike. These squads should prowl around and protect speakers and act as the bodyguard of the comrades. The defense squads should set the example by their militancy against police terror. (b) The best elements among the workers should be taught the duties of each functionary. Thus when something happens to the leading comrades there will be someone prepared to take their places.

(9) Leading Comrades: It is necessary that leading comrades receive a minimum amount of rest and sleep during the strike so that they will be sufficiently alert mentally to meet the new developments from day to day and from hour to hour. Instances are known where strikes have been lost merely because all the leading comrades exhausted themselves in the first few days of the strikes. All comrades can get the needed amount of rest if there is organization of and division of work.

(10) Developing Leadership: In every strike, in every struggle, the comrades will witness new workers cropping up into leadership, playing an active, militant role in the struggle. These workers must be drawn into the leading strike committees during the strike!

(11) The District Office: Full information, from the beginning of the strike activity to the end, should be sent to the district office of the union. Only through the constant cooperation of the various sections of the union through the district center can we hope to build a strong, powerful union.

Small Farmer, Worker Unite in Struggle. The strike of the California cotton pickers is of great significance because it is the first in the industry for a long period and involves a great mass of the most exploited workers in the state. But the feature that should attract the widest attention from the agricultural workers and small farmers is the fact that it shows in actual practice how the workers and small farmers are united in struggle. The theories of the IWW or such as the Socialist Labor Party, and similar sects, that all farmers belong to the exploiting class, are shattered completely by such living experiences.

For weeks in preparation for the strike, the United Farmers League, an organization of the small farmers in the district, cooperated with the workers because one of the chief strike demands is that the finance companies who have already contracted for the purchase of the cotton crop shall raise the price to the farmers. The small farmer realizes that his position is similar to that of the worker. In face of the cost of living rising, he must turn over the crop for a price that was already set, which will not leave him anything for even an existence. Both he and the agricultural worker face the common exploiter, the finance companies, who reap the profits.

The small farmers immediately declared their willingness to accept the demands of the workers, for $1 per hundred and recognition of the union.

The action taken in the cotton fields should serve as an example for all similar situations. In this manner, struggles will serve as a means for uniting the two giant forces against capitalism.

In this manner the attempts of the large growers to organize the mass of small farmers into their terror squads against strikers will fail!

(*Western Worker*, October 9, 1933)

III. STATISTICS OF STRIKERS RECEIVING RELIEF

Analysis of 3,006 cases of cotton strikers (10,602 persons) which received relief from the California Emergency Relief Administration, 1933:

Of 2,426 cases for which data are available, 48.6 percent were Mexicans, 44.9 percent were American whites, and 6.5 percent were Negroes. This certainly underrepresents Mexicans among the whole body of strikers.

Of 8,556 persons whose age was ascertained, 18.7 percent were under school age (1-5); 33.1 percent were of school age (6-17); and 48.2 percent were over school age. 35.6 percent were between the ages of 18 and 44 years, inclusive. Only 12.6 percent were 45 years of age or over. Only 4.7 percent were 55 or over.

Single persons comprised 31.1 percent of the 3,006 cases, but only 8.8 percent of all persons receiving relief.

Of the 2,070 families, 20.6 percent were comprised of 2 persons; 35.4 percent of 3 or 4 persons; 44 percent of 5 or more persons; and 13.3 percent of 8 or more.

# UPRISINGS ON THE FARMS

The agricultural proletariat of America is struggling for a place in the sun. From New Jersey to California its shrill and insistent cries are rising to a pitch that will be heard. Strikes and picketing, which we had assumed to be a distinctive accompaniment of industry, are spreading to the countryside. Only last July, pickets battled with police and firemen on truck farms in southern New Jersey, and vigilante farmers banished the leader of the strike. In southern Ohio the weeders of "the world's largest onion patch"—"mostly barefoot, illiterate farm hands imported from the Kentucky hills"—demanded 35 cents an hour and an eight-hour day; their pickets matched "knives and slingshots" against clubs and a threatening machine gun of the deputies, and guarded their leader, bruised and beaten by strikebreakers, from the fury of a lynch mob. The Sheep Shearers' Union (AFofL) reached down into west Texas to include Mexican shearers, and the shearers of New Mexico went on strike. On the Pacific Coast more than forty rural strikes have occurred since December 1932; sometimes two and three have been in progress simultaneously. In July in the San Joaquin Valley of California, "the largest peach and apricot ranch in the world," remembering the previous year's strike and warned by "grapevine" of a repetition of 1933, was reported to be rushing toward completion a "moat" three feet deep and four feet wide, behind which hand-picked employees were to be admitted through guarded entrances. Grape pickers struck in July, and white (AFofL) packers and Filipino laborers harvesting lettuce in the Salinas Valley struck in August. In September, 200 "vigilantes. . . riddled a Filipino labor camp with bullets and set it afire."

Evidently, the generalized picture of the farm laborer rising rapidly through tenancy to ownership is no longer valid. What then has laid the background for the explosions which we are now witnessing? Is it the Communists, who are active in many parts of the United States among the rural population? Frequently they are the organizers of dissension, but they did not make the setting. For forty years we have been building, and are continuing to build, dams at high cost to bring more lands under irrigation. Today we know that this "creation" of land has often been uneconomic for the public and for the farmer, and we are just beginning to discern that, particularly in the Southwest and West, it has entailed the establishment in our midst of a numerous and racially alien proletariat. The problems of this group—largely Mexican and Oriental, but including southern poor whites and Negroes—are now pressing dramatically and insistently upon our attention. The delicate issues of race segregation in residence, school, and even work are being overshadowed by the more conspicuous, widespread, bitter, and almost continuous labor conflict. Truck crops—onions, lettuce, cantaloupes, fruit—all of them favored by postwar shifts in the national diet, require large numbers of laborers. The demand is generally seasonal, women and children frequently work, workers are usually migratory and practically propertyless. The rise of intensive agriculture has given us, almost unnoticed, a rural proletariat. And is it a matter for surprise that proletarians strike?

Uprisings of agricultural laborers in the United States are not without precedent. Twenty years ago the Wheatland hop pickers rioted in California; the government investigated, and the State Commission of Immigration and Housing was established. During the war, strikes broke out in the citrus belt, some of them, like the Wheatland strike, led by the IWW. In the Middlewest the "wobblies" established themselves among the migratory harvest hands of the wheat belt before the war. But shortly thereafter their influence among rural workers declined, then practically ceased. Increasing use of the combine harvester sharply reduced the demand of grain for migratory harvest laborers and contributed to the decline.

On the Pacific Coast the expanding labor demands of intensive agriculture were met increasingly by immigrants from Mexico and the Orient. Migratory families of Mexicans and mobile gangs of youthful Filipinos came to outnumber the whites in the principal valleys of California and Arizona, and Japanese and Hindustani tenants became predominant as truck growers in certain areas. Faced by this situation, white American laborers sought first to stop the influx of aliens. Then, when depression began to pinch, they turned to violence—threatening, shooting, and bombing Filipinos, and sending employers anonymous warnings under the sign of the death's head: "Work no Filipinos or we'll destroy your crop and you too." In May 1934 a white packing shed worker in Imperial Valley protested: "It doesn't matter to me if any member of the dark race is American-born or otherwise. This is white man's country and a white man is entitled to live first." Antelope Valley, northeast of Los Angeles, resists introduction of Mexican pear pickers with mob violence and takes pride in remaining the last "white man's valley" of the region.

But in the meantime, incipient labor organization was springing up among the Mexicans. In view of the widespread belief that Communists make all the trouble, it is well to recall that as early as 1928 Mexicans organized a union in Imperial Valley, California. They were promptly repressed by vigorous action of growers and local officials, who raised the then unfounded cry of "reds" and refused to negotiate. In the same year a union of Mexican sugarbeet workers sprang up in Colorado and endured for a couple of seasons. By 1933, white Americans in California, increasingly pushed down into itinerant rural employment, were uniting with Mexicans and Negroes to direct their attack against employers; and within a year they were cooperating with organized Filipinos. By mid-1934, in addition to the Communist-led Cannery and Agricultural Workers' Industrial Union, there existed some forty unions of agricultural workers in the United States affiliated with the AFofL.

The setting for labor agitation then plainly exists: distress, a proletariat showing restlessness, incipient organization, and frequently a racial cleavage added to the traditional separation of employer and employee. And the Communists, more than the conservative trade unionists, have sought to capitalize on the situation by furnishing organizers, strategy, tactics, and widespread contacts in order to win the allegiance of large masses of rural workers to their leadership. The Communists plan, and the attempts to work out their plans can be seen in the truck gardens of New Jersey, on the fruit ranches of California, the drought-striken farms of North Dakota, and the cotton plantations of Mississippi. Their aims are not essentially secret; even their tactics soon become public. The basic features of their plans may be read by any who take the trouble to inspect their "literature"; they need not be repeated here. Eventually, of course, they hope to establish communism; immediately they seek to build unions of rural workers who from experience will have confidence in Communist leaders. Under the title, "The Farmers Are Getting Ready for Revolutionary Struggles," a Communist writer declares hopefully: "Comrades, there are hundreds of thousands of agricultural workers all over the country who could easily be reached by us." Rural organizations are to coordinate their activities with urban labor. With the general strike impending last fall, apricot pickers left an orchard near Hayward as a gesture of sympathy for the longshoremen of San Francisco Bay.

The organization of rural workers proceeds principally in two quarters: among the sharetenants, largely Negro, of the "Old South," and among the "stoop" laborers—largely alien, but including whites and Negroes—who tend the fruit, truck, and cotton crops of the Southwest and Far West.

The plight of the sharecropper of the "Old South" has been long familiar: the expansion of cotton culture westward to lands where lower costs prevail, the competition of Middlewestern lands released from feed production by the tractor, the absence of an outlet through migration such as relieved the lot of the New England farmers after the Civil War. And now depression augments distress. To quote Dr. Calvin B. Hoover:

> *During the past four or five years, the number of former tenant farmers who are without means of livelihood has been steadily increasing... these families formerly were able to obtain a crop to tend but are now unable to do so. Many of them are living in tumble-down tenant houses and tobacco barns and any sort of shack which they can find. Their standard of living is appalling and is even much below the*

Farmers sheltering in ambush directly across the street from strikers' headquarters, Pixley, 1933. *Photo: Courtesy of the Bancroft Library, University of California.*

*customary low standard of living of tenant farmers who are engaged in production. The rehabilitation of these "squatter" families is demanded by every consideration of national responsibility.*

The cotton-limitation program designed to resuscitate agriculture has as a necessary effect a reduction in the number of people employed in producing cotton, and a clear tendency to weigh more heavily on the tenant than on the owner. And were this not enough, there impends the cotton-picking machine, which, if and when it arrives, will pull another main prop from under the economic structure of the South by eliminating dependence on huge local labor supplies. The Mississippi Delta Experiment Station has stated that it:

*expects commercial production of successful mechanical cotton pickers within the near future, followed by the use of much less hand labor in production as well as harvesting. Two or three cotton pickers are rapidly approaching practical, mechanical, usable perfection. (Bulletin 298, June 1932)*

In October 1934, the official in charge of the Delta Station is reported to have said to the inventors of a mechanical picker:

*Your machine should be placed on the market without delay. . . . There is no question but that it works and works well. The fact that you picked five bales in less than a day in cotton ranging from 36 to 72 inches tall is enough to convince the most skeptical.*

A momentus event if true. Yet coolly, with bare mention of the portentous problems which it raises, and with specific disavowal of any responsibility on the part of the "American farm," the authors of the bulletin declared what, under present conditions, may be true for those who will *remain* on the farm:

*Reduction of the farm-labor population 30 to 50 percent is essential to "decent" living standards on the farm. . . true enough, up-to-date farm equipment reduces the manpower necessary. So does all modern machinery. But Americans will not go backward. It is not up to American farms to absorb, even at pauper wages, either the labor released from modernized industry or nonessential farm labor replaced by the economical use of adapted farm machines. American genius must find other fields for replaced labor both from modernized farms and industry if peasantry is to be avoided.*

Among the victims of this situation, particularly the Negroes, organization work has started. A Communist states that:

*A highly important feature of our farm work is the definite organization of 7,000 to 8,000 Negro farmers into the Share Croppers' Union of the South, under the leadership of the party. . . . The party must begin to carry on agitation on the question of the seizure of the land by the sharecroppers. The result will be the recruiting of great sections of the toiling agrarian sections of the South, especially Negro sharecroppers, into the revolutionary struggles. (The Communist, June 1934, p. 577)*

The effects of this program have not yet come to the surface, but the editor of the Jackson, Mississippi, *Daily News* advised his readers on June 1:

*Listen, folks! The Negroes of Mississippi cannot be converted to socialism or communism, but dangerous agitators are moving about among them, and the situation is such that the best thought of both races should be concentrated on the subject. An overwhelming majority of our Negroes are law abiding, but they need sane leadership.*

It is in the other principal theater of left-wing activity, particularly in California, that the organization of rural laborers has reached mammoth proportions. In late 1932, a strike occurred among the orchard pruners of Vacaville, and the spring of 1933 ushered in a whole series of strikes which affected most of the important harvests of California. They began in the pea harvest in the Santa Clara Valley and in the berry crops near El Monte, east of Los Angeles, continued with the sugar beet, apricot, peach, lettuce, and grape harvests and reached a climax in the cotton harvest. In that strike, the area of intensive activity blanketed Kern, Kings, and Tulare counties, the major cotton-producing counties of the state, directly involved about 10,000 pickers, and lasted more than three weeks.

The strike of the San Joaquin Valley cotton pickers in October 1933 stirred emotions in rural California as never before, and succeeding strikes in Imperial and other valleys have but intensified them. As the fault of the earth exposes the strata which reveal its structure, so these agricultural labor disturbances have thrown into bold relief the alignments of groups—growers, Communists and strikers, and officials—their opinions, and behavior under stress. Let us sketch each briefly, necessarily somewhat inadequately, with the highlights which reveal the clash.

## THE GROWERS

Many are in financial distress; prices have been low; they face loss of their farms; improving prices mean but a chance to recoup some of their losses. The harvest upon which all depends is rudely interrupted by the strike. Said a grower in jail, charged with murder of cotton strikers at Pixley, "Every dime I have in the world is in that crop!" Another added: "They were picking until the strike pickets came; since 2:30 Friday afternoon, not a bale has been picked!" One day the strikers invaded a field, trespassed. Armed growers guarded the trespassers until the deputies could arrest them and take them to town. The caravan of pickets returned to town; the armed growers followed. A Communist leader delivered a flaming speech; the growers closed in as the strikers started for their hall. A scuffle, and the growers' guns roared, leaving two dead and several wounded strikers. For those interested in the factors underlying social conflict, and in possible solutions, dispute over personal guilt, or which party made the first aggressive gesture at the scene of the clash, is as futile as to discuss which child hit the other first, or, after a war has started, which country made the first warlike move.

The farmers often furnish shelter, rent free, to pickers. But when these would not pick, they were evicted; they should not accept the farmer's hospitality if they would not do his work. But the growers had not foreseen that the evicted strikers would concentrate at Corcoran, build a fence about their camp, station guards and keep out signs, hold strike meetings inside, and start their caravans of pickets at the gate.

The growers near Woodville appeared at a strikers' meeting, and after a scuffle, read:

*Notice to the public at large: We the undersigned agricultural producers and businessmen... do hereby... declare ourselves to be in a frame of mind to protect ourselves from present strike agitators and strikers... with intention to [legally] disburse [sic] all strike agitators and strikers from our locality. Our motto: Strikers work peacefully or leave the state of California.*

In Tulare, the resentment of growers against merchants who extended aid to strikers provoked the advertisement:

*Notice! To the citizens of Tulare. We the farmers of your community, whom you depend upon for support, feel that you have nursed too long the Viper that is at our door. These Communist agitators must be driven from town by you, and your harboring them further will prove to us your noncooperation with us, and make it necessary for us to give our support and trade to another town that will support and cooperate with us. Farmers' Protective Association.*

## THE STRIKERS

Largely they were Mexicans, but with them were many Negroes and poor whites from the South, migratory, living on wages reduced heavily by depression. A few were former cotton growers "gone broke." General Glassford in Imperial Valley has described this type of (Mexican) worker:

*The standard of living of Mexican field workers, at the present time, is based upon an average annual income of less than $400. With intermittent periods of employment, and the necessity for automobile transportation to seek work at the widely scattered ranches, very few Mexican families of agricultural workers are able to maintain a decent existence. Although it is boasted that melon pickers are able to earn $5 or more a day (occasionally as much as $12), the number of days when such earnings are possible are comparatively few, and melon pickers represent a small percentage of the field workers employed throughout the year. On one ranch where melon pickers were employed during a period of 15 days, I found that their average daily earnings amounted to less than $1.50 a day. It may be true that alien Mexicans receive higher wages and live better in Imperial Valley than they do in their own country, but this cannot constitute an excuse for countenancing poverty and squalor in the United States.*

*This is the kind of people whose lowly standard of living evoked from growers the statements: "Picking cotton, that's their lot." "They come from nowhere; they go nowhere. They do the country no good. It doesn't make any difference whether you pay them 15 or 35 cents an hour. Their women wear shoes only when someone will see them. They buy Buicks and don't know how to spend their money intelligently. They're stupid." And an official farmers' representative declared: "I do not object to the laboring man having conveniences, but I do object to the state stepping in and demanding that the employer, who has no responsibility for the laborer, provide them with convenience and facilities which they do not want." Eastern readers will recognize the parallel story of the European immigrants who didn't want bathtubs, "preferring" to use them as coal bins. But the strikers' own view of their standard of living appears from their declaration that they "would as soon be shot as starved to death working."*

With the strike three weeks old and strikebreakers still at work, they invaded the Guiberson Ranch, beat the pickers, and cut their sacks and auto casings. Upon another occasion they clubbed growers with grape stakes in a general mélée. But most of the laborers neither understand nor profess to favor communism, and do not even pay dues to the union whose leaders they follow on strike.

## THE OFFICIALS

Their position is difficult. Many try to enforce the laws equitably, and go to great lengths to curb "hot heads" on both sides. For example, according to an editorial in the *Merced Sun-Star* entitled "Blood on the Lettuce," Sheriff White:

*steadfastly refused the demands of extremists who wanted him to recruit and arm great bands of special officers, men who, however sincere, would have to be those completely untrained in the work of law enforcement. Thus he refused to create in Merced County exactly such a situation as later brought "blood on the cotton."... The violence of Pixley did more to advance a revolutionary thought in America in five minutes than all the "agitators" in the state could accomplish, unaided by such terrorism, in five years.*

But even this sheriff was forced by the farmers in late July to purchase submachine guns, extra pistols, and tear gas guns to arm the "minutemen" for the emergency which they expected.

Under the instructions to "keep the highways open and take no side," the state highway patrol officers in the same county did their work:

*without prejudice, without favor as to race, creed or economic position. The non-English-speaking laborer in a 1920 Ford laden with work-worn kids had the same consideration as did the driver of a V-12 car.... To the result that the criticism—just or unjust—which some patrol officers have brought down on them during the recent Imperial Valley disturbance, and in other sections, was completely absent here.*

But naturally the officers are under heavier pressure from the side of the growers than from the side of the laborers, most of whom are aliens, or migratories without vote in the community. One deputy acknowledged the pressure, saying,:

*We protect our farmers here. They are our best people. They are always with us. They keep this country going. They put us in here and they can put us out again, so we serve them. . . . Mexicans are trash. They have no standard of living.*

The economy of the rural communities is founded on their crops; so a district attorney says: "The crops must be harvested. Tulare County can no longer permit the Communists and radical agitators to move about our agriculture unmolested."

The rural situation in California grows increasingly tense. General Glassford said of Imperial Valley, where vigilantes successfully terrorized outside "agitators," including a party of Los Angeles clergymen, into leaving or keeping out of the valley:

*After more than two months of observation and investigation in Imperial Valley, it is my conviction that a group of growers have exploited a "Communist" hysteria for the advancement of their own interests; that they have welcomed labor agitation, which they could brand as "red," as a means of sustaining supremacy by mob rule, thereby preserving what is so essential to their profits—cheap labor; that they have succeeded in drawing into their conspiracy certain county officials who have become the principal tools of their machine. . . . One active vigilante remarked: "I'd like to be out of this mess, but what can I do? If I don't line up, my business will be ruined."*

But a valley newspaper declared that: "It was not mob violence— it was a studied, organized movement of citizens seeking the only way out of difficulties threatening the community's peace. . . . Perhaps the professional agitators have learned a lesson." And a cotton-gin foreman in the San Joaquin Valley said of a member of the governor's fact-finding committee, the recommendation of which was the basis of the cotton-strike settlement: "It won't be healthy for him if he comes down into the valley; the respectable citizens will take care of him."

The report of a federal investigating committee on Imperial Valley was answered by another committee, appointed at the request of the California State Board of Agriculture, Farm Bureau Federation, and state chamber of commerce, which declared that, "Technically, the committee does not find that there is a 'strike' in the Imperial Valley, nor that there is any 'strike' imminent in the Imperial Valley," and *inter alia* recommended, curiously (in view of the legal code of ethics and the practice of providing public defenders for persons accused of crime), that the state bar "investigate the activities of attorneys employed to defend persons who advocate the overthrow of the present government. . . ."

To many, the problem of rural labor is no longer a *labor* problem. In the words of a San Jose newspaper, "It is a crime problem." A sheriff believes that, "If only our laws had teeth in them, we could get fifty 'rats' and there would be no more trouble." A cotton-finance company man expresses a general conviction when he states that strict enforcement of the laws will solve the problem; and the committee representing the three state bodies by clear inference supports the view that the "suppressive activities on the part of the police" retard the plans of the communistic union. County after county passes strict rural anti-picketing ordinances, determined not "to let our industry become the football of irresponsible agitators who have no interest in it." Yet the farmers raise wages, too, remembering strikes.

Simon Lubin, founder of the California Commission of Immigration and Housing, speaking the view of liberals before the Commonwealth Club in San Francisco, said:

*We have little or nothing to fear from the "radicals" and "agitators." But there is genuine ground for fear—great fear—in the greed and selfishness, the intellectual sterility, the social injustice, the economic blindness, the lack of political sagacity and leadership, and the the mock heroics and hooliganism we observe within our state today....*

*It is a fact that we do need a socioeconomic housecleaning. Are we going to encourage the "reds," the "radicals," the "Communists," the "outside agitators" to do the job for us? Or are we ourselves going to do it?*

But the farmers are not impressed; they prefer to rely on vigilantes, ordinances, and other similar methods of solving the problem. As an attorney for the California Farm Bureau Federation replied confidently: "If the professional sobbers will stop lending aid and encouragement to agitators who spit upon our Constitution and our flag, peace and quiet can more easily be maintained and the situation will soon clear up."

The farmers are in control of their communities. Strikes are suppressed. "There are no agitators in the valley," says a farmer, and an official adds significantly, "except in jail." But what, besides keeping the "agitators" out, will they do to eliminate the causes of unrest? Some, but not all, seem curiously to forget their traditional hostility to conservative trade unionism: in Imperial Valley growers encouraged and dealt with a Mexican laborers' union fostered by the consul; at Marysville, the farmers tried to establish an AFofL fruit-pickers' union which they could dominate. A few growers are using the opportunity to work toward better housing, better employment methods, and so on. But will the farmers generally and the government see and grasp their opportunity to use power intelligently and deal with causes?

# 4

# PRELIMINARY REPORT ON DROUTH SITUATION OF NORTH DAKOTA
## Based upon field reconnaissance of the northwest quarter of the state, June 11-15, 1934.

I

This region faces the basic problems common to the semi-arid strip from the Rio Grande to the Canadian border known as the Great Plains. The present drouth merely presents in acute form the fundamental unsuitabiity of the existing economy, which is attempting to exploit and to survive in this area. The program to meet the immediate drouth situation is already taking shape; it is focused upon problems of cattle, human subsistence, and work projects. This preliminary report, however, is concerned only with those aspects of immediate relief which seem to contribute to permanent rehabilitation.

The drouth, while general, has borne very unequally on different portions of the broad region affected. This may be illustrated by type situations. Within the area reconnoitered, the situation of Minot is materially better than that of the northwestern strip of counties, particularly of Burke and Divide counties. The position of the Minot community can be strengthened by a variety of measures ranging from adoption by the farmers of cultivation by terracing to construction of small dams providing irrigation for growing of truck crops and the support of subsistence homesteaders. Of course, the usual measures of immediate relief are required, though in lesser degree than elsewhere.

In Burke and Divide counties, on the contrary, the essential unfitness of the present land utilization stands out starkly, despite the deceptively good buildings which favorable years of wheat have erected upon land and in the towns. The immediate situation also is most acute there. The farmers of these counties are forced to sell a very high proportion of their livestock, and they require food for the remainder and food for themselves. In Burke County it is estimated that 17,000 head of cattle out of 27,000 will be sold. The farmers are now receiving seed for forage crops, but the prospects for even these are very poor. The grasshopper menace is already so great that in this area, as in many others, the effort to exterminate them is like trying to bail out the ocean. Communist agitation is in progress among these farmers who are the worst hit.

II

Practically all classes of persons in the drouth area are severely affected:

A. Urban. In small towns, the merchants and businessmen, who naturally depend upon the prosperity of the agricultural community, are suffering severely. They are supported almost entirely by the relief funds which are distributed to other elements in the community, and then find their way to them through trade channels. Lawyers find support from the legal work attendant upon cattle buying. Physicians eke out a livelihood principally by fees from the county. The result is poorly supported physicians and poorly served communities. A good many businessmen are already broken, or are on the road to bankruptcy. Clerks, skilled laborers, and unskilled laborers, alike, find little or no employment. Relatively large groups of these persons are on, or are coming onto relief rolls. Twenty, forty, or 100 of these families, varying from town to town, are on the relief rolls and numbers have been on the rolls for two, three, and even four years. They may be classified in large measure as stranded population with no prospect under present conditions.

Transients are numerous at Minot and Bismark. Some 300 at Minot engage in work projects. Almost no other employment is available. Mr. Scatterday of the transient bureau states that North Dakota farmer boys have been coming to him since the drouth began at the rate of about one a day.

B. Rural. The largest element in the population consists of farmers, together with some cattlemen. Farmers in the worst areas are heavily in debt in respect to their land, livestock, and machinery. Much of their indebtedness is to the federal government, very little to the banks. They are currently working out on road projects, etc., their indebtedness for food and human relief. Farmers have been on relief to a greater or less degree almost continuously since 1931, when Red Cross relief was initiated.

III

Resumption of relief and rehabilitation: In the area worst affected no relief from relief is to be expected before the harvest of next year. In any case, therefore, population and unsold stock will need to be supported. In repayment of this relief, the people of the drouth area can do certain things to improve the position of the community permanently.

A. They can change the physical basis of their utilization of the land. The major project involved is the Missouri River Diversion Dam. This will not change North Dakota precipitation, as farmers, editors, and town officials hopefully imagine. Its permanent benefits will be found in improvement of the water supplies of North Dakota towns from the Missouri to the Red River, the improvement of sewage disposal conditions in these towns, flood control, the improvement of recreational facilities, particularly at Devils Lake where lake levels are forty feet below those of 1870, and the improvement of stock watering facilities for farmers with riparian rights along the James, Cheyenne, and Red rivers. The water table may be improved along these rivers for perhaps a mile on either side, but agriculture generally need expect neither increased precipitation nor creation of subsoil waters to improve their crops.

Numerous small dams may be constructed to improve water facilities and in some cases to irrigate tracts which will be suitable for production of truck crops. These will provide immediate work projects of permanent value.

B. Coupled with change in the physical basis of land utilization must come change in the economic basis of rural organization of western North Dakota. A "balanced" agriculture suited to Iowa is not suited to the Great Plains. Precipitation fluctuates greatly, and is even thought by some (state geologist, citing Kincer of U.S. Weather Bureau), to be on a secularly declining trend. In either case, probably only a sparser population, with tractor and combine harvester to produce wheat, operating either privately or under FERA direction, preferably the latter, can survive.

Unless the advantages of irrigation by dams, pumping, etc., to be established by work projects, are to go entirely to private individuals, the intensive agriculture made possible by its development must be used to support subsistence homestead colonies. Land levelling can be done as work projects. Those can be used first to rehabilitate the small-town stranded populations, the underemployed coal miners, etc.

Specifically, the Burlington subsistence homestead project to be made possible by a small dam will aid the coal miners near Minot. A much broader field for this activity lies in the valley of the Missouri River. Mr. Schollander of the Williston Experiment Station assured me that in various tracts in that vicinity, e.g., the Buford-Trenton, Williston, and Ruffland tracts, and many others, it will be possible to irrigate many thousands of acres by pumping from the Missouri River. More than a thousand acres have been irrigated in past years in this manner. The end of irrigation came for two reasons: the farmers of an earlier day found it more profitable to raise grain on dry land, and wheat rust increased because of irrigation. Neither of these objections hold against the use of irrigated land for truck crops. The presence of lignite in large quantities in both strip and underground mines makes power for pumping plants readily available.

In most cases, if not in all, the irrigated lands should be exploited by cooperative colonies which will combine the features of subsistence homesteads and the activities of self-help cooperatives in such matters as coal mining, canning, dress-making, etc. Material for construction of attractive log cabins is readily available on the Missouri bottoms. Houses can readily be placed on lands above the highest flood levels.

Unitary control of crop plantings, irrigation and harvesting is essential to avoid chaos. The individual homesteader cannot plant and irrigate at will without waste and confusion. Under proper administration the prospects of rehabilitating large numbers of stranded people are fairly bright.

C. Leading scientists and citizens of western North Dakota are naturally reluctant to admit the necessity for moving away any of their population, although they may concede their inability to solve the permanent problems of many who now are there. In the worst areas it is nevertheless true that an excessive overhead is being carried of costly county government, surplus animals, and too many people.

Submarginal land purchase is a first step toward relocation of population. Purchase of land for grazing reserves, while desirable, will not be the occasion for moving many people off submarginal land. At the top price of $10 an acre, fair amounts of land now cultivated could be purchased from farmers glad to sell, and whose departure would lighten the overload. These lands could either be taken out of cultivation, or operated by the government on the lines indicated, the wheat so produced to be distributed by FERA. An experiment of this character, concentrating on submarginal farms in two or three adjacent counties, might well be undertaken if and where politically feasible.

Purchase of lands from farmers, of course, will necessitate their relocation. Generally, this should be attempted only with great caution on lands on which others have failed to pay taxes. For some farmers, rehabilitation on irrigated subsistence homesteads in North Dakota is possible. Should important population movement be undertaken, the possibilities of relocation in lands to be brought under cultivation by the Boulder Dam, and by the Verde Dam of Arizona, should be investigated. While climatic and agricultural conditions are very different from those of North Dakota, it should be remembered that Mormons are colonized at Mesa, Arizona, and that middlewestern farmers pioneered Imperial Valley, California and other irrigated areas of the Southwest. The possibility of subsistence farming groups there should be investigated. Farming of such a type would have present political advantages in regions which are already trying to reduce crops which reach market.

IV

The drouth area may be divided into the eastern portion where the problem is truly temporary, and the western strip—the Great Plains—where the problem, based upon light, fluctuating, and possibly declining rainfall, is permanent. For the latter, I suggest the advisability of a consulting scientific committee on the Great Plains, including such persons as geographer, climatologist, geologist, agriculturist, and rural economist or sociologist or other social scientist. These can provide scientific research and advice on the rehabilitation of the region, concurrently with the administration of relief through the next year and more during which relief will be necessary. State agencies of administration and research should be encouraged, but the regional character of the problem of the western belt should be recognized and emphasized.

# 5

# THE MIGRANTS AND CALIFORNIA'S FUTURE
## The Trek to California and the Trek in California

A new common refrain has appeared in the headlines of our newspapers. We are told that California is menaced by an "influx of indigents," of "paupers," of "jobless." A Los Angeles "columnist" cries in alarm: "That 5,000 indigents are coming into southern California. . . leaves one appalled. This is the gravest problem before the United States. . . these tattered migrations." Lamenting our good roads he adds: "The Chinese, wiser than we, have delayed building a great system of highways for that very reason—to head off these dangerous migrations— indigent people stampeding from the farms into cities to live on charity." In June an aroused state assembly passed a bill to debar from California "indigents and persons likely to become public charges," but cooler counsel failed in the senate and the bill failed to become law.

Interested, but more aloof, the national magazines have taken up the story under the titles "California, here we come," and "Again the covered wagon." And they even ridicule us Californians, as does Walter Davenport in *Collier's*, that "All this migration of the unemployed" is "a part of [our] reward for all the milk-and-honey ballyhoo [we] had been broadcasting for years. Come live in southern California for the good of your soul, [we] used to sing. . . . In California, [we] once told them, you live life; elsewhere you merely spend it. . . . 'Even the tears one sheds in California are tears of gladness.' " So effectively have we "sold" our state that out of every five native white Americans now in California, three are literally "immigrants" to this state. Perhaps we Californians, native and "immigrant," can't complain too much that we are the Mecca of the nation, and that even the distressed have heard our praises and our appeals.

Stand today at the highway portals of California; particularly at the southeastern border. See the shiny cars of tourists, the huge trucks of slow-moving and conspicuous cars loaded with the refugees from drought and depression in other states. They travel in old automobiles and light trucks, some of them homemade, and frequently with trailers behind. All their worldly possessions are piled on the car and covered with old canvas or ragged bedding, with perhaps bedsprings atop, a small iron cook stove on the running board, a battered trunk, lantern, and galvanized iron washtub tied on behind. Children, aunts, grandmothers, and a dog are jammed into the car, stretching its capacity incredibly. A neighbor boy sprawls on top of the loaded trailer.

Most of the refugees are in obvious distress. Clothing is sometimes neat and in good condition, particularly if the emigrants left last fall, came via Arizona, and made a little money in the cotton harvest there. But sometimes it is literally in tatters. At worst, these people lack money even for a California auto license. Asked for the $3 fee, a mother with six children and only $3.40 replied, "That's food for my babies!" She was allowed to proceed without a license.

Are these people riff-raff? Are they the almost unmitigated "moochers" that some declare? Are they an "invading hoard of idle," as the newspapers call them? After having seen hundreds of them all the way from Yuma to Marysville, I cannot subscribe to this view. These people are victims of dust storms, of drought which preceded the dust, of protracted depression which preceded the drought. "It seems like God has forsaken us back there in Arkansas," said a former farm owner at a San Luis Obispo pea pickers' camp. "The cotton burned up," is their common story. They are largely farmers who have been carrying on agriculture on the family pattern which has been so long regarded as the great source of stability in our nation. One of them, recently picking fruit with his family in the Sacramento Valley, told succinctly this story of his decline from farmer to farm laborer: 1927—made $7,000 as a cotton farmer in Texas; 1928— broke even; 1929—went in the hole; 1930—deeper; 1931—lost everything; 1932—hit the road; 1935—serving the farmers of California as a "fruit tramp."

It is not only despair, but hope that draws the refugees to California, hope of finding work, of keeping off or getting off relief, of maintaining morale, of finding surcease of trouble; yes, and the climate, which even the poorest can share. "We haven't had to have no help yet. Lots of 'em have, but we haven't," said Oklahoma pea pickers on El Camino Real at Mission San Jose. "Relief? I wouldn't have it no way it was fixed." "All I want is a chance to make an honest living."—"When a person's able to work, what's the use of begging?" We ain't that kind of people," said elderly pea pickers near Calipatria.

Of course there are some persons who come to California simply as "touring transients" seeking more and better relief. The announced cessation of transient service relief and the program of the Works Progress Administration are intended to remove inducements to this type. But "transients" are not to be confused with "migrants." The great majority of those in distress who trek to our state avoid entirely or leave as soon as possible the "transient" class, i.e., persons on federal relief, with residence in another state. They join the "migrants" of California, i.e., persons who seek a living by work, following the crops. When relief is genuinely needed by these people to tide them over, there is usually genuine gratitude. "If it hadn't been for the relief groceries, what would we 'a' done? We think it's awful good in them to give us."

But their real temper was expressed by a southwestern refugee encamped as a migrant on a dreary field at Shafter: "So many give up and stayed; they just give up everything. This is a hard life to swallow, but we can't just sit there and look to somebody to feed us." White Americans predominate among the emigrants. Long, lanky Oklahomans with small heads, blue eyes, an Abe Lincoln cut to the thighs, and surrounded by tow-headed children; bronzed Texans with a drawl, clean-cut features and an aggressive spirit; men and women from Arizona, Arkansas, New Mexico, Missouri, and Kansas.

During the four months ending October 15, more than 30,500 men, women, and children—members of parties "in need of manual employment"—entered California in motor vehicles bearing out-of-state licenses, or probably about six percent of all persons entering in vehicles with out-of-state licenses. Largely they are refugees from drought and depression elsewhere. Thirty-five percent of them came from the three states of Texas, Oklahoma, and Arizona. Many refugees have already returned to the states whence they came; others will return. What the net permanent human deposit from this migration to our state will be, only the future can tell. Riff-raff? Probably no more than in every great migration. The weak are matched by the strong, the hardy, and the adventurous who seek in the West a new hold on life. Indigents? They are poor and in distress and many have had to take relief before they could obtain employment. When they arrive in our fertile valleys, without work or with insufficient work, they are the most ragged, half-starved, forgotten element in our population, needy, the butt of the jibes of those who look down on "pea pickers" and "fruit tramps," but with a surprising morale in the midst of misery, and a will to work. These people are not hand-picked failures. They are the human materials cruelly dislocated by the processes of social erosion. They have been scattered like the dust of their farms, literally blown out. And they trek into California, these American whites, at the end of a long immigrant line of Chinese, Japanese, Koreans, Negroes, Hindustanis, Mexicans, and Filipinos, to serve the crops and farmers of our state.

The catastrophic dislocation of people is always dramatic. It stirs our emotions and rightly so. We cannot remain unmoved while distress pours into our highways and byways. But in viewing the trek to California of the drought refugees, let us not lose this perspective. Rural migration, and the hardship and social instability which it entails, is not new to us, but old. For forty years or more laborers have been moving ceaselessly about our state with the seasons, following the crops. In 1927 the state Department of Education enumerated 37,000 migratory children alone. The best present estimates place the number of men, women, and children who migrate at some time during the year to work in the crops of California at from 150,000 to 200,000. Here lies the major, permanent, and almost unique rural labor problem of California. The drought refugees, merging with the much greater mass of milling hordes which continually moves up and down the valleys of our state, have taken the spotlight, but we Californians know that in the incessant movement of our own migrants center the problems which we must attack. To this perennial phenomenon of our state, I invite your attention for the remainder of this discussion.

Some aspects of the farm labor problem of California have been illuminated rather fully in the forums of our state. You have listened to discussions of the "embattled farmers" and the "Communists," and enquired whether the radicals can "capture the farms of California." I do not propose to discuss rural labor in the term of belligerency, of right and wrong, of law, or of patriotism, however defined. I intend rather to invite your consideration of some of the basic economic facts which underlie the agricultural structure and process in our state as they affect labor, and in affecting labor, affect us all.

The history of California agriculture can be written largely in terms of the shift from extensive crops to intensive crops. The dry farms, using mechanical methods of harvesting, which used to fill with grain the holds of sailing ships from all parts of the world, no longer predominate. With irrigation have come intensive crops with heavy demand for hand labor: citrus, grapes, fruit, vegetables, melons, cotton. In 1879 the value of intensive crops represented less than four percent of the total value of California agricultural production. In 1929, only a half-century later, intensive crops represented not four percent, but practically four-fifths of the total, or 78 percent. Here lies the real explanation of the great migrations of the past, which have given California its Oriental and Mexican labor population, and of the whiter migration of recent years and months.

Together with the rise of intensive crops is the large scale of the operations by which those crops are produced. The large farm is very prominent in our rural economy, and the large grower, as is well known, exercises great influence in the counsels of agricultural employers. More than one-third of all the large-scale farms in the entire country are located in California. Of all the farms in the United States whose product is valued at $30,000 or above, nearly 37 percent are found in our own state. California has within its borders 30 percent of the large-scale cotton farms of the country, 41 percent of the large-scale dairy farms, 44 percent of the large-scale general farms, 53 percent of the large-scale poultry farms, 60 percent of the large-scale truck farms, and 60 percent of the large-scale fruit farms of the United States.

Together with crop intensification and large-scale production organization have come commercialization of agriculture, higher capitalization, increased production for a cash market, and a high cash expenditure for wage labor. In Mississippi, typical of southern cotton culture, the average cash expenditure per farm for farm labor was only $137 in 1929. In Iowa, typical of the Middlewest, the average expenditure was $323. In the United States as a whole, the average was $363 per annum. In California, the average cash expenditure on farm labor, per farm reporting, was $1,438, the highest of any state in the Union, and almost four times the national average.

All these factors—the growth of intensive agriculture, highly capitalized, large-scale farming methods, concentrated ownership, and huge payments to farm labor—together have given us an industrialized agriculture, a system of open-air food factories, it might almost be called. Wage relations are highly developed; gang labor is employed, with foremen and sub-foremen. Elaborate piece rates are set up, with bonus payments. Farmers' agents recruit and distribute laborers. The state maintains labor commissioners who aid rural laborers to collect unpaid wages, just as they aid urban workers. Sporadic efforts are made at collective bargaining.

The rural wage-earning population so created, is, proportionately, the largest rural wage-earning class in any state of the Union. According to the census of 1930, barely 10 percent of all persons gainfully employed in agriculture in Mississippi were paid farm laborers. In the entire United States the percentage of farm laborers was 26 percent. In Iowa it was 27 percent. In California, paid farm laborers constituted 57 percent of all persons gainfully employed in agriculture. This was more than double the national average, and was the highest proportion of paid farm laborers in any state. In other words, of all persons gainfully engaged in agriculture—owners, tenants, managers, laborers—only one in ten were paid laborers in Mississippi, and one in four in the United States. But in California more than half were paid laborers.

By reason of the intensification of our agriculture, then, and the economic structure which developed it, we have built up in our midst a rural proletariat, if you will, largely of alien race, propertyless, and without ties, protective or otherwise, to the soil which they till. We have deviated far from the American homestead pattern of the family farm, which survives in many parts of the country and in our national ideals.

Not only is our agricultural labor class large; it is also highly mobile, living a large part of the year almost literally "on wheels." The automobiles of the laborers are not luxuries. To even the poorest they are vital necessities of life. And the cost of their operation and upkeep cuts a large figure in the family budget. The car must be fed gasoline and oil to make the next harvest, or to get to and from the fields, and its wheels must be kept shod more carefully than the feet of the children. "The way the world's on wheels now, you've got to have gas and eats, and we don't get no more," said migrants at Marysville.

From Imperial Valley, the migrants follow the harvest to the San Joaquin, Santa Clara, and Sacramento valleys, a distance of from 360 to 550 miles each way by air line, and much longer by road. Within each valley they move about, from camp to field, field to camp, and ranch to ranch. During August 1927, 11,500 Mexican laborers and their families, or a sustained daily average of 370, were counted moving north by motor vehicle over the Ridge Route to the San Joaquin Valley. Many more moved than were counted.

California migrants work also in other states: the Hood River and Yakima valleys of Oregon and Washington, the Arkansas Valley of Colorado, the Salt River Valley of Arizona. In August, Mexicans from California harvested the pea fields of Idaho. During the two months ending October 15, 7,600 California men, women, and children, migrants "in need of manual employment," returned to our state by motor vehicle. This number was almost one-fourth as great as the entries during the same period of needy workers and their families in cars bearing out-of-state licenses.

The life of the migrants is hard. It is not a succession of vacation camping trips. Employment is intermittent, jobs are often precarious, and annual incomes low. "We like to work and not just set around. I'd rather do anything but set around, but they just ain't no chance here in California, seems like," said a Kern County migrant last spring. "Livin'? It's kind of sorry. You work a while, then lay up a little, then go broke, and then move." "You wait for work two weeks," then "fight like flies for the work." "You eat it up faster than you can make it." A common estimate, among employers and observers, of the average annual earnings of migrants is between $350 and $400.

Incessant migration retards the education of children. A few American parents are beginning to complain that their children cannot write as good English as they. There is growing consciousness that for many of their kind the future portends not progress from generation to generation, but retrogression. "These days people can't raise children as good as themselves," said a fruit tramp at Winters. "My children ain't raised decent like I was raised by my father. There was no 'rag houses' then . . . but I can't make it," was the cry of a cherry picker.

The development of normal relationships between citizen and community, and between employer and employee, is not favored by constant movement. "My father was a track foreman at $1.25 a day, but we lived in a house and everybody knew us," said a fruit tramp. "This rancher has us for two or three weeks, and then he's through with me. He knows me till he's through with me." "Residenters" look askance at the nomads, and treat them as "outlanders." Children are stigmatized at school as "pea pickers."

Migrants are homeless, and at the mercy of whatever quarters may be available. In the increase of squatters' camps by the roadside, in the creek bottoms, or "no man's land," depression has dealt them a heavy blow. The California Division of Immigration and Housing describes these social pockmarks:

*"Groups of persons arrive at any given community and start a camp. No provision is made for sanitation, water supply, or even general camp cleanliness. Such housing accommodations as they may have are eked out by wood, tin, or such cast-off material as can be obtained in the vicinity. A sorry picture is presented of a condition that threatens to be a serious menace to those communities where squatter camps exist. Moving the occupants away simply spreads the condition and local authorities are loath to act against people who came there in the hope of securing some employment. The division's attention has been called to a number of these squatter camps during the last winter, but has no legal authority to take remedial steps. . . ."*

At a Sacramento Valley squatters' camp there were only two privies, both filthy, for 500 people, and the water supply was contaminated. At a camp in Kern County, water was obtained only from the nearest service station, at 5 cents a bucket. The United States Special Commission of Agricultural Labor Disturbances in Imperial Valley in its report dated February 11, 1934, stated:

*"Living and sanitary conditions are a serious and irritating factor in the unrest we found in the Imperial Valley. We visited the quarters of the cities where live Mexicans, Negroes, and others. We inspected the temporary camps of the pea pickers, and know that they are similar to the camps that will serve as places of abode for workers in the fields when melons are gathered. This report must state that we found filth, squalor, an entire absence of sanitation, and crowding of human beings into totally inadequate tents or crude structures built of boards, weeds, and anything that was found at hand to give a pitiful semblance of a home at its worst. Words cannot describe some of the conditions we saw. During the warm weather, when the temperature rises considerably above 100 degrees, the flies and insects become a pest, the children are fretful, the attitudes of some of the parents can be imagined, and innumerable inconveniences add to the general discomfort. In this environment there is bred a social sullenness that is to be deplored, but which can be understood by those who have viewed the scenes that violate all the recognized standards of living. . . It is horrible that children are reared in an environment as pitiable as that which we saw in more than one locality."*

For more than a score of years, the state camp inspectors of the Division of Immigration and Housing have done yeoman work. Struggling against the obstacles of public apathy, inadequate staffs, resistance of employers unwilling or unable to do better, reluctance of local officials to apply penalties to their neighbors for violation of state camp sanitation laws, they have sought ceaselessly to attain better conditions by enforcement and by education. Some ranchers,

Mexican workers on strike, 1933. *Photo: Resettlement Administration.*

notably larger farmers with long crop seasons, have been fully cognizant of the need, and have established good labor camps.

But even after all the efforts by enlightened and financially capable employers, and by state camp inspectors, the living conditions of scores of thousands of men, women, and children are actually growing worse, as the increase of squatters' camps plainly demonstrates. The situation has got beyond finding someone to blame. Smaller farmers are financially unable to provide for the numerous workers and their families whose services they require only two or three weeks a year. And the squatters' camps, not located on the land of the employer, are not subject to the jurisdiction of state inspectors. If inspectors bring too much pressure to raise ranch camp standards, the farmer may refuse to house his laborers at all. In that event, their only recourse is to a squatter's camp, worse even than the camp of the farmer. Then they have sunk to the bottom, where human deterioration is inevitable. As a squatter said, "Livin' a bum's life soon makes a bum out of you. You get started and you can't stop."

The hand of government should be extended to ameliorate the hardships of our largest agricultural group. Acting on this belief, the State Division of Rural Rehabilitation of the Federal Resettlement Administration, under direction of Harry Drobish, has engaged in study of the problem and has conferred with interested persons of all shades of opinion. The division is now conducting two experimental camps for migrants, one at Marysville, the other in Kern County. Both have been constructed with cooperation from the State Emergency Relief Administration, and upon express invitation from, and with generous financial cooperation of, the local authorities. The camps provide minimum decencies for migrants: healthful site, pure water supply, sanitary toilets and garbage disposal, shower baths with hot and cold water, and simple laundry facilities. Competent supervision will insure observance of reasonable regulations for maintenance of sanitation and order. It will provide leadership for recreational and cultural programs for adults and the children.

Friends of the effort to eliminate squatters' camps have felt some apprehension lest under the tension which prevails, large growers or vigilante groups might oppose establishment of decent public camps for migrants. To a very limited extent this may be true, but the attitude of the smaller farmers and many of the large growers is distinctly friendly. At the Marysville camp, large and small growers and townsfolk have alike welcomed the camp, declaring it a measure of public welfare and a boon to growers, to migrant workers, and to business.

Decent camps are not a palliative, for they are necessary to meet a permanent characteristic of California agriculture which demands mobile, seasonal labor. Nor do they induce excessive mobility. Migrant camps neither extend relief, nor will a chain of them alter the distribution of the relief load among counties. They simply make it possible for those who do migrate in search of work to move from one decent camp to another, instead of from one wretched camp to another.

The State Division of the Resettlement Administration is now considering the erection of from fifteen to twenty more camps with federal aid, and it welcomes public support. As a second step, the resettlement administration is considering a plan to establish selected laborers and farmers, who have lost their farms, on small plots of good land with decent homes, in order to provide greater stability and a chance to regain full economic independence. As part of a broader program of rehabilitation and resettlement, therefore, migrant camps have unique value. Not only do they contribute to the abolition of squatter camps; they serve also as reservoirs from which distressed farm people can be filtered upward and selectively re-established on part-time farms, as tenants, and even assisted back to the ranks of farm owners. Thus for some, camps will constitute a first rung in a reconstructed agricultural ladder, which they can ascend in traditional American fashion according to their abilities.

In the interest of laborers, growers, and the public, alike, it is imperative that measures be taken. It will not do to argue that the migrants are a low class, unworthy, and incapable of improvement, or that many are aliens. Without resorting to sound sociological generalizations, it is easy to see that large numbers of migrants have lived far better in the recent past than now. "We ain't the chasin' around kind. Never did this before," said migrants in the southern San Joaquin Valley. A federal conciliator points out: "It may be true that alien Mexicans . . . live better in Imperial Valley than they do in their own country, but this cannot constitute an excuse for countenancing poverty and squalor in the United States." At Marysville one hears, "Tain't hardly fair. They holler that we ain't citizens, but their fruit would rot if we didn't come."

# 6

*Survey Graphic*, September 1936

# FROM THE GROUND UP

A dispossessed Texas farmer last fall told his story succinctly:
"1927—made $7000 in cotton.
1928—broke even.
1929—went in the hole.
1930—still deeper.
1931—lost everything.
1932—hit the road."

In 1935 he was working with his family as a fruit tramp in the Sacramento Valley. His words epitomize the tragedy of thousands of the kind of people among whom I have worked during the past year. As regional labor adviser visiting projects of the resettlement administration in the Far West, I have seen whole populations which should never have settled where they are, fallen on relief; lands which should have been left in grass, ravaged by dust storms; farmers cruelly dislocated from their farms joining the migrants of the West Coast, squatting with them by the roadside, on garbage dumps, and on river bottoms; stricken people banding themselves together, seeking in simple cooperation to find a way out.

The resettlement administration was organized to meet the problems of rural folk such as these, who are in deepest distress, but whose rehabilitation is yet possible. Through its county and area rehabilitation supervisors it has been lending money to needy farmers who can be rehabilitated where they are, or elsewhere. It has been purchasing submarginal land, taking it out of cultivation and restoring it to beneficial public uses as grazing or forest reserves, recreational areas, or wild game refuges. It has been experimenting with removal of people from lands where their future is hopeless to others where a good life is possible. It has been aiding rural cooperatives where these offer better prospects for rehabilitation than do individual loans.

The people aided by the resettlement administration in largest numbers are, of course, rural rehabilitation clients rather than participants in projects. More than a quarter of a million of these clients, mostly families, are being restored to self-support by means of loans for poultry, bees, stock, teams, and equipment. Of $48 million loaned in this manner, approximately $10 million had already been repaid by clients from their earnings by April 15 of this year.

In all parts of the country, the effort has been made so to vary the program as to meet most effectively the problems peculiar to each region. This article describes some of the activities in the West with which I am personally familiar. Their significance lies not in the number of projects but in their value as demonstrations of means of rehabilitating people and lands.

In Taos County, New Mexico, numerous families took up homesteads on a remote plateau within the past decade or two. They built houses, grazed a few cattle, and planted small fields. But their lands could afford only the barest living in the most favorable years, and hardly any at all in others. Before long their crops failed, their cattle were gone, and they were reduced to cutting wood for a desperate living. Lacking water, which has been the solid support of the Taos Indian Pueblo for centuries, these newest white settlers were soon thrown on relief, permanently without prospects. An offer from the FERA to buy them out was accepted, and about seventy families were moved south of Albuquerque. There on the Bosque Farms, a significant experiment in resettlement of people en masse is in progress. These are people who failed on small dry farms. Can they succeed on good irrigated land? The settlers are building a community of small individual farms with auxiliary cooperative activities. Already they have harvested vegetables from community gardens for themselves, and hay and corn from community fields for their stock. The qualities of pioneers are needed, for methods are new, and there are hardships and discouragements even on publicly financed projects. As on the old frontier, women often supply the courage when the hearts of the men flag. "My husband was going to quit, but I talked to him and told him we were going to stay. On this project we'll be able to have more than we ever had before." Not all of the original homesteaders from Taos have the ability to succeed under new conditions, and these, when it is proved, are helped toward rehabilitation by other means. Those who remain are hard at work levelling land with Fresno scrapers, clearing fields of trees and brush, tearing down old ditch banks with bulldozers, and digging new ditches. Their temporary shelters of battened boards have been replaced by new adobe homes built in the style, and with material, native to the region. The children are in school, housed in a new adobe building erected by the resettlement administration. The mothers are meeting in their own PTA. And the vacated homesteads in Taos County to the north are closed to settlement, never again to be opened to other homesteaders who could only repeat the hardships of their predecessors.

In the West, the open range has long since disappeared. It was fenced by large stockmen in a great enclosure movement to protect private cattle and private grasslands. And it was encroached upon by settlers under homestead laws designed for farmers, not for stockmen. At Mills, in northern New Mexico, hopeful pioneers settled on the rolling plains and wealthy investors built a small town. But stock-raising could not yield a living on the limited acreage allowed each homesteader. So the sod was turned under, and the soil exposed. Wheat—good crops and high prices for a few years, then falling prices and falling yields, mortgages, drought, wind, dust. The square, unpainted houses are in bad repair or abandoned. The town mill, built too late even to be run, stands idle. The general store has shrunk to almost nothing. Only the government project office shows activity. About four-fifths of the inhabitants are being bought out and resettled nearby in a community of small irrigated farms similar to Bosque. Their lands will be leased for grazing only to the settlers who remain. These families can now succeed as stockmen with sufficient range.

In Utah the range was once good near Tooele. But a procession of flocks tended by men in covered sheepwagons have overgrazed it badly. What the sheepmen have not ruined, the farmers have. Their abandoned houses, their binders and harrows half buried in dust drifts tell the familiar story. Their vacant fields, covered with tumbleweeds, feed dust storms that still blow down the central valley. The government is purchasing 40,000 acres of submarginal land. There were no people to resettle, for they had long since departed. The range was gone, and with poetic justice the farmers who destroyed it were themselves in turn destroyed.

Today the range is being refenced, this time to restore and protect the very grasses. Cedar fence posts cut during the winter are assembled in huge piles. Old fences around wheat fields are torn down, and gangs of town laborers, small farmers, and sheepherders working on the Central Utah Dry Land Adjustment Project as relief workers are today putting up new fences. Grazing will be controlled, cultivation will be prohibited, and portions of the area will be used for experiments in methods of replanting and restoring the native grass.

More than one hundred miles from a railroad in a high valley near Bryce Canyon, Utah, lies the town of Widtsoe. Its history, too, is sheep, dry-farming, drought, relief. "This land used to raise forty bushels of wheat to the acre, but it won't now." "My father came here with $7,000, worked hard, and lost all," said a stalwart young man on work relief who could neither farm since the drought, nor dig coal since work in the mines had slackened. The government has taken options on practically the entire valley, including the town. A dozen families have been placed individually on farms elsewhere in Utah, in contrast to the method of community resettlement employed at Bosque. The remaining families are eagerly awaiting removal by the government from this bleak valley.

Two years ago the basis of the economy of Tropic, an isolated Mormon hamlet in southern Utah, was swept away by flood waters which tore out the spillway of Tropic Dam. The inhabitants were thrown on relief. Today crews of men from Tropic and nearby towns are working in shifts under resettlement, striving to rebuild and elevate the earthen dam in time to impound waters for next year's crops.

The housing needs of employed families with low incomes have also been the object of experimental thrusts in the West. At El Monte, east of Los Angeles, 100 families have been settled on fine suburban land, once a walnut grove. They are now living each on three quarters of an acre, in small, carefully planned homes. Their average income of $85 per month comes from steady private employment as garage mechanics, street car conductors, tire factory employees, hotel clerks, and so on, and will enable them to repay the government the cost of the land and houses. Enthusiastically, men, women, and children are planting intensive gardens to supplement cash earnings. "We couldn't have bought a home for ten years except for this project," said a young couple with their first baby. "At first we wished we could have built our own house, but now that we've lived here we know it was planned better than we could have done it," said another resident. In the San Fernando Valley forty families, and at Phoenix, Arizona, twenty-five families are settled on similar projects.

After the first impact of depression, small groups of newly destitute in many parts of the country began to attract national attention through primitive but heroic efforts to maintain themselves by salvaging surplus vegetables, cutting wood, and bartering labor for food and clothing. ["Whither Self-help?" *Survey Graphic*, July 1934, p. 328.] Congress authorized grants to these cooperatives from relief funds, with the aid of which a good many groups, especially in California, survived almost insuperable obstacles and demonstrated capacity to produce cooperatively on a small scale. To most members, self-help has meant in practice no more than a supplement to relief or to an inadequate private income. In the better units it has contributed to full-time members perhaps $15 to $25 per month. Now a number of the California cooperatives are applying for agricultural loans in order to achieve complete rehabilitation. The first loan by the resettlement administration to a self-help cooperative was completed in June to the Midway City Dairy Association near Santa Ana, a small unit with nine members. The mere prospects of rehabilitation fired morale. The plant was immediately renovated, and better equipment procured by trade. Bidding tactics of competitors were studied with all the zeal of poker experts, means of developing consumer cooperative markets were explained, and all plans laid to take full advantage of their new capital and condition as free producers in an open market. By means of this loan of approximately $7,000 it is expected that these nine men, most of whom were on work relief, can elevate themselves to economic independence and repay the loan with no further help. Other groups, beginning to see loans as a means of getting off relief and rising to full self-support at a decent level, are preparing budgets and applications.

The distress of the migratory farm laborers of the Pacific Coast was forcibly brought to the attention of the country by a series of strikes in 1933 in California and Arizona, most of them led by Communists. The laborers and their families migrate many hundreds of miles in a single season from Imperial Valley to the San Joaquin and Sacramento valleys and back, following the harvests. Numbers of them move in dilapidated cars from Arizona through California to Oregon and Washington, and even to Idaho and Colorado. Efforts to organize farm laborers are made from time to time. On June 6-7, a conference was held at Stockton at which it was decided to ask for harvest wages of $3 per day and abolition of piecework. The meetings were addressed not only by organizers and by the secretary of the State Federation of Labor, but by representatives of women's clubs, government agencies, the master of the California Grange, and large farmers. The executive council of the State Federation of Labor endorsed the move to organize fruit workers immediately. Farmers who have been leaders in efforts to improve housing urged that, "Instead of continued contests between farmers and workers, the two groups should work together for long-time results. Harvest workers are poorly paid and poorly housed because farmers are losing money. It is necessary to raise farm prices so the farmer can afford to pay decent wages."

The life of the migrants is hard. Employment is intermittent, jobs are precarious, and annual income is low. "We like to work and not just set around. I'd rather do anything but set around, but they just ain't no chance here in California, seems like," said a Kern County migrant. "Livin? It's kind of sorry. You work a while, then lay up a little, then go broke, and then move." "You wait for work two weeks," then "fight like flies for the work." A common estimate, among employers and observers, of the average annual earnings of migrant families is between $350 and $400.

The farmers, too, are under pressure. "Now we know that we ought to pay these people more wages to raise the standard of living, but the banks have got their foot on our necks." So there are disagreements over wages and conditions, and strikes have broken out in 1936 as in other years. Inevitably, the WPA, administering work relief for the unemployed, is drawn in as a third party.

California agricultural leaders [under auspices of the State Chamber of Commerce] voted unanimously to seek shutdown during harvest season of federal works projects employing men who otherwise would be available farm laborers.

"Starve them out!" was the advice of L.M. Meredeth of Santa Rosa. . . . Others present gave general approval of Meredeth's idea.

The state administrator of WPA asks assurance that a "reasonable wage" be paid before WPA workers are dispatched to farms, and holds that WPA "will be satisfied with the prevailing wage scale . . . even if this is considered in some circles to be notoriously low." On May 19, however, a district director of WPA took back workers who had rebelled against living conditions and low wages in the pea fields. He said:

*While it is against our policy to return a man to the work rolls*

Refugee families in the vicinity of Holtville in the Imperial Valley, March 1937. *Photo: Dorothea Lange.*

Migratory field workers home on the edge of a pea field, Imperial Valley, March 1937. The family lived here throughout the winter. *Photo: Dorothea Lange.*

*just because he doesn't like his job in private employment, there seems to be nothing else to do in these cases. We do not intend to have these workers become peons or slaves to the pea picking contractors.*

The cotton choppers' "strike" in the San Joaquin Valley in May 1936 reveals clearly the elements inherent in the situation. The organized cotton farmers, among whom the influence of the large growers predominated, set a rate of 75 cents per acre or 20 cents per hour. Fifty workers removed from WPA rolls refused this rate and "struck." Thirty members of the clergy— Protestant, Catholic, and Jewish—urged the growers to raise the rate, declaring that "underpaid workers offered a fertile field for agitators and radicalism." The directors of the San Joaquin Valley Agricultural Labor Bureau protested hotly that the clergy had "stepped out of their pulpits." "The farmers have worries enough without the well-meaning clergymen lining up on the side of the professional agitators." They asserted that choppers can earn the monthly security wage at 20 cents per hour by working ten hours a day for twenty-six days a month. This of course assumes steady work in an industry notoriously afflicted by irregularity. The growers ridiculed the eight-hour day, forty-four-hour week on farms, and stated that California choppers' wages are above those paid to cotton choppers anywhere in the world.

About the same time, organized small growers sided with the clergy and the laborers, and attacked both WPA and big growers for supporting low wages. Sensing the conflict of interest between small growers, whose income is in large part from wages because they too work in the field, and big growers, whose immediate interest is in low wages, the Weed Patch Grange resolved:

*Whereas, only through raising the level of farm commodity prices and the wages of workers will we overcome the depression, and*

*Whereas, the present effort to force unfortunate WPA workers to accept wages even lower than the subsistence allotment set by relief,*

*Therefore, be it resolved that Weed Patch Grange repudiates any self-appointed labor committee who only represent speculative interest in labor and soil. Those starvation wages set by said gentlemen who do not toil will foster class hatred and crime.*

*We protest the use of Kern County public funds and public officials by big landowners to intimidate by threat of starvation jobless citizens to work for wages insufficient to provide a decent living.*

Some growers voluntarily offered 25 cents instead of 20 cents. Many workers accepted 20 cents. Others held out for and obtained 25 cents, and yet others departed for the north in hopes of work at better wages in the orchards. A small group of men removed from WPA to compel acceptance of farm work adopted the method of the embittered. Told by their employer to chop cotton and "leave a clean field" behind them, they did so, leaving it clean not only of weeds, but of cotton. They were lodged in jail.

This shifting reservoir of human distress known as migratory labor, left to itself, can lead only to recurrent and bitter strife. But no program of rural rehabilitation can ignore it. Behind the tangled strife lie conditions of living which cannot be tolerated in the public interest, and which add fuel to the flames of conflict.

The United States Special Commission on Agricultural Labor Disturbances in Imperial Valley described conditions among migrant workers which unfortunately are not limited to that area:

*Living and sanitary conditions are a serious and irritating factor in the unrest we found in the Imperial Valley . . .we found filth, squalor, and an entire absence of sanitation and a crowding of human beings into totally inadequate tents or crude structures built of boards, weeds and anything that was found at hand to give a pitiful semblance of a home at its worst. . .In this environment there is bred a social sullenness that is to be deplored, but can be understood by those who have viewed the scenes that violate all the recognized standards of living.*

It is at this point that the resettlement administration attacks the problem of migrant labor. Two camps for migrants have been established, one in Kern County southeast of Bakersfield, the other at Marysville in the Peach Bowl. Eight more are being erected.

The very simplicity of the government camps shows the elementary character of the needs of the migrants. Pure water is piped through the camp to people who have had to buy it at 5 cents a bucket or get it from a service station a quarter of a mile away. Sanitary toilets adequate in number replace at Marysville two unscreened, open pit toilets which were supposed to serve a thousand people. Hot and cold showers are ready for the end of the day in lieu of a bucket of water or an occasional river.

In erecting ten migrant camps, the resettlement administration does not thereby assume responsibility for determination of wage rates for farm laborers. Nor are the camps adequate to accommodate all the laborers who now congregate to serve the farmers of the districts in which they are located. But they assist local and state health and camp inspectors to enforce the law, by providing decent places of refuge to which occupants of condemned squatters' and ranch camps can go. And since they are designed to demonstrate more decent living conditions, they will remove one of the most fruitful causes of unrest and strongest supports of agitation.

As a first measure of rehabilitation, then, the camps lift the migrants off the ground. But more must be done to meet needs which the migrants themselves express: "The trouble with us travellin' folk is we can't get no place to stay still." Making a living? "Yes, as good as draggin' around people can expect—if you call it a livin'!" As a second step, in order to provide some measure of stability for women and children at least, and to afford opportunity to supplement seasonal earnings, the resettlement administration is preparing part-time farms for several hundred agricultural laborers in California and Arizona.

Drought and depression, then, have exposed weak spots in our national economy. In many areas the dearth of water is so recurrent and so great as to be chronic. And to many people depression has brought collapse so complete and so protracted that they cannot rise by themselves to survive. The end of drought and the upturn of the business cycle will not solve the problems which have been so clearly revealed. The rains have come and prices have started to rise, but for hundreds of thousands a new and more stable future must yet be built from the ground up.

# 7

# LETTERS TO
# THOMAS C. BLAISDELL, JR.

Thomas C. Blaisdell, Jr.
Social Security Board
Washington, D.C.

Rawlins, Wyoming
August 16, 1937

Dear Tom:

1. At Rochelle, Illinois, the California Packing Corporation— Midwest Division—operates a plant packing peas and corn (other plants of California Packing at Arlington, Wisconsin; Sleepyeye, Minnesota; and DeKalb, Illinois). It operates in two ways—buys crops on contract with growers whom it finances (generally), *and* it raises crops on *its own* big farm. Most of the other packers in Midwest operate in first way only. California Packing is evidently doing at this plant what it, and the other packers, have done on a grand scale in California—i.e., go into large scale corporation farming. Something to watch!

Immediately adjacent, the Rochelle Farms Co. operates a group of large asparagus farms (on lease, I believe, rather than ownership basis).

California Packing, on its plants and farms (Rochelle and DeKalb combined), has a minimum of 213 employees, and a maximum of 1,871 employees (1936), the latter during sweet corn harvest (in August-September). The peak during pea harvest is approximately 1,200 employees. The pea harvest lasts from about June 10 to July 25.

Until about six or seven years ago the company simply ordered so many "he's" from the Chicago employment agencies. Then it began a campaign to get the farmers' wives and daughters to work in the plant, and local high school and college boys and girls, and even grammar and high school teachers. The manager claims this policy is highly successful. Emphasis is also placed on maximum development of local labor resources. Of this season's employees, 68 percent of the *plant and farm* employees come from within a radius of approximately forty miles, and 76 percent of the employees in the *plants* only.

Of those who migrate from a distance, a number come from southern Illinois around Mt. Vernon—350 miles away, some from Missouri, and a few from Tennessee and Arkansas.

This pattern is something to watch in the Middlewest. And these are the people who seek to be classed as farmers, to avoid wage-hour legislation—and social security next.

Suggestion: That the bureau of research itself, or through the state bodies in California, Florida, Arizona, and Illinois or Wisconsin, make a few sample studies from social security records now coming in, and other sources, to be ready in the next Congress. I know Mrs. Libman has done work on this—how about expanding it?

2. In Des Moines, Iowa, I talked with W.D. Kline of the State Employment Service. After telling me of the importance of Iowa crops, etc., almost his first words were: "But mechanization has taken away more and more of the work opportunities of the laborer." He illustrated with his own farm—"Up to six or seven years ago my father, brother, and I worked the farm (of 240 acres of Iowa land), with one hired man from March through September and two more during haying, and one during corn harvest in October and November. Now my brother does all the work with only the aid of an old man to do chores (not field work), and practically no hired labor. He does the work better than we used to and has plenty of leisure."—Reason: tractor and equipment, corn picker, etc.

The farmers complain that they can't get seasonal help, because of WPA, etc. But they offer only about three months' work; the men fear loss of place on WPA, or loss of a good, steady job in industry through the employment service which they might miss by taking the farm work.[1]

Displacement is proceeding slowly but steadily. It's given opportunity for some absorption on highway work, PWA jobs in mines and industries, etc. The laborers have "flocked to the cities and towns" where many are on WPA. And this in Iowa, too!

Of course, machinery isn't the only cause—there's drought and grasshoppers, and AAA crop program expanding acreage of grass crops, as well.

There's some migratory labor which comes in to pick corn, which is still largely husked by hand. It comes principally from Missouri, and is said to undercut Iowa prices. "They board themselves and sleep in their autos." Also, a few come from Nebraska, Arkansas, Kentucky, and Kansas, and a very few from Oklahoma. There is a little movement of Iowa labor to the Minnesota potato harvest.

3. In Colorado, I made inquiries concerning mechanization in sugar beets. E.M. Mervine (USDA at Ft. Collins), is confident that crosscultivation—which is now used *extensively* in Minnesota—will spread rapidly. Also that mechanical chopping along the row will do the work where planting practices made cross-blocking difficult (e.g., in California). He thinks the chief obstacle is inertia of growers, but even so expects five years to see it general.

Mervine thinks five to ten years will see mechanical beet harvesting general. He thinks the best harvester is already as far along as the cotton picker—or farther—but that cost of the machine, and inertia, and the inevitable delays of perfecting and "getting into production" will make adoption slower than with cross-blocking.

Successful cross-*blocking*, which Mervine thinks will become cross-*thinning*—much more effective in labor displacement, because it leaves almost nothing to hand labor—he thinks this will be achieved very soon. Mervine evidently works on these problems himself, and knows whereof he speaks.

A mechanical harvester he used in Colorado last year is to be tried near Sacramento, California, within the next week or two. So it goes. Partial mechanization in sugar beets means the end of the contract labor system, shorter seasonal employment, more mobility. Complete mechanization means wiping out the beet workers as such.

Had a fine talk with John Gross, Secretary of Colorado Federation of Labor, whom I've known for ten years. He's done a good deal to organize beet labor, but thinks the present moves in the Denver Convention under D. Henderson and his fellows are bad. Says they don't try to develop *trade unionism* among the beet laborers, but simply agitate them to make demands which are not genuine trade union demands, to build up their funds by "mooching off the politicians," asking them for a few dollars each to help the union. These give the money all right, but regard it as discharging their duty to the beet laborers. Also believes that H—and the others "get" the few who really try to develop trade unionism, by giving the authorities the information on the basis of which they are deported as aliens. Believes the agricultural workers are being "used" as pawns in the games of the sectarian leaders.—(I've seen evidence of this in California, too).—Gross is likely to rejoin Wagenet's staff soon. If he does, he's worth getting acquainted with in every way—and a fine fellow he is.

I'll be waiting word on the bureau publication of a report on my findings—and on Collier's attitude.

Cordially,
Paul S. Taylor

Memphis, Tennessee
June 30, 1938

Thomas C. Blaisdell, Jr.
Assistant Director
Bureau of Research and Statistics
Paul S. Taylor, Principal Consulting Economist


Migration to California

Last year we did not detect any well-defined movement of misplaced farm people from the Black Wax to California. This year it is clearly apparent. The district relief administration office in Waco, Texas, informed us that 60 percent of the requests for verification of residence are coming from California. It was estimated that these are now averaging one per month in each of the twenty-two counties in the district which cover the heart of the Black Wax and some territory west. The case workers say, "if California would leave us alone we could get our work done."

At Muskogee, Oklahoma, the county welfare director has stacks of letters and telegrams from California. The immigration from this eastern Oklahoma area continues, although crops are better this year. We saw a family from Joplin, Missouri, on the streets of Muskogee bound for Sanger, in the grape district of California. Several station attendants at Muskogee tell us that caravans of this type are a very common sight.

Near Webber Falls, Oklahoma, we passed a family from Paris, Arkansas. They are completely uprooted, say they will not return to Arkansas and said, "We are trying not to, but will be in California yet."

At Fort Smith, Arkansas, employment service men told us that the immigrants to California consist largely of rural unit, persons leaving submarginal land which the government has purchased north of Fort Smith, and persons encouraged to immigrate by travel bureaus. The attached clipping from the *Fort Smith Times Record,* June 27, 1938, is representative of ads which are run continuously in the newspapers. One of the employment service men said that he had personal knowledge these people encouraged Arkansas folk to go to California in order to get their fares. The price is about $15.00 one way.

At Atoka, in southeastern Oklahoma, we learned a good deal of the background of immigration to California, which has been heavy for some years.

The population of this quarter of the state has grown a great deal, perhaps even double, since 1930. Soil is poor, land is hilly, and woods abundant. During prosperity many people immigrated from this area to other places. When depression struck, they remembered the abundance of wood, the easy chance to squat practically rent free in the hills. But now the timber has been pretty well cut out, the market for railroad ties is poor, and owners are less ready to let choppers cut ties from what timber remains. Consequently, free water, cheap land for a shack and garden, and meager state relief and WPA are all that remain. So this population that went back to the poor land when the depression struck has steadily been oozing out again, this time westward to California. The advertisements of western cotton growers and the efforts of relief agencies to push off relief when cotton harvesting in Oklahoma, Texas, Arizona, and California was on had stimulated this immigration.

We have had no difficulty in finding local information on the migration to California from the valley between Fort Smith and Little Rock, Arkansas.

At Lonoke, Arkansas, in the Arkansas bottoms, we were told by the county case worker that requests for verification of residence come from California at the rate of about six a month.

The department of public welfare at Little Rock will furnish us with a county-by-county tabulation of verification requests from California and other states. I was informed by the statistician in that office that he is co-laboring with Woofter in the study of tractors in Arkansas. He is expanding the study to cover the entire state, not simply sample counties.

Paul S. Taylor
Enclosure

Memphis, Tennessee
June 30, 1938

Thomas C. Blaisdell, Jr.
Bureau of Research and Statistics
Paul S. Taylor, Principal Consulting Economist

Miscellaneous Field Observations

1. Fort Smith, Arkansas. Mr. Lee W. Caviness of USES, Fort Smith, estimated that 90 percent, or more, of the farm wage hands in the vicinity of Fort Smith, Arkansas, worked at sometime during the year in subject employment. This is because of the industrial development of Fort Smith and the fruit and vegetable packing in that area, which are partially covered under the present definition of agricultural labor. Caviness and another official who had experience in other parts of the state thought this percentage might prevail throughout the state. However, other officials, and I think probably they are correct, believe this percentage to be unduly high. The Fort Smith officials said that from 60 to 65 percent of the tenants and croppers also perform part-time work in covered employment and about 10 percent of the farm owners do the same. They estimated that the average duration of employment of the farm hands in subject employment was perhaps two months.

These officials told us that within the past fifteen months, the use of mobile agriculture has developed to the point where as high as 400 to 500 a day, in season, are daily hauled out of Fort Smith in trucks to the fields in Oklahoma or Arkansas. These people are returned to Fort Smith at night.

2. Menifee, Arkansas. At Menifee, Ark., in the valley northwest of Little Rock, we were told that agents for sugar beet companies had hauled Negroes in trucks to the sugar beet fields in Montana in 1937. Yesterday afternoon we were on the Lake Dick, Arkansas, Project of Farm Security. The project seems to be in excellent condition. Crops are satisfactory and morale is obviously high. The project manager made an extremely good impression. The comparison between his methods and the dictatorial methods of the efficient manager of Casa Grande will be well worth comparing. The project leaves a very good feeling with the observer.

Mr. John S. Roulhac of our Memphis, Tennessee office estimates that of the agricultural wage workers in this vicinity, including about twenty-five counties in western Tennessee and the Arkansas delta, 90 percent or more of the farm wage workers are employed in subject employment at some time of the year. This high percentage results, in part, because of employment in gins, but principally because of the accumulation of agricultural labor population in Memphis where industrial employment is sought in off seasons. A USES representative here thinks this figure is too high, but agrees that the interchange is nevertheless substantial.

Mr. Roulhac estimates that 50 percent or more of tenant farmers are also engaged part time in subject employment. His observations are based, in part, on his general knowledge of the people concerned, and partly on observation of the large number of these laborers who seek Social Security account numbers from the Memphis office. He believes that most of the agricultural wage workers in this region will earn the minimum of $2,000 in subject employment during their working life, even under present laws.

He believes that the stamp system of tax collection is far superior to the present method for agricultural labor.

We shall be in the office in Washington on Tuesday morning.

Paul S. Taylor

June 30, 1938

Thomas C. Blaisdell, Jr.
Bureau of Research and Statistics
Paul S. Taylor, Principal Consulting Economist

Displacement of Agricultural Labor by Tractors
I saw a manuscript at Texas A&M College by C.A. Bonnen of farm management division. It states that 15,260 farms are necessary to produce the cotton in five Texas high plains counties, if one-row, horse-drawn equipment is used. If four-row equipment with tractors is used the number falls to 3,346. While the minimum number may never be actually attained, there is no reason in topography or soil why the four-row equipment should not be used.

The following table shows percentages of from 126 to 141 farms studied using tractors each year from 1931 through 1937:

| Year | Percent |
|------|---------|
| 1931 | 25.5 |
| 1932 | 21.7 |
| 1933 | 20.5 |
| 1934 | 24.5 |
| 1935 | 46.4 |
| 1936 | 59.5 |
| 1937 | 78.6 |

The International Harvester sales manager at Dallas reported that tractor sales had fallen to about 50 percent of 1937. However, he emphasized that 1937 was such a banner year that this decline should be viewed in that light; also, that sales of other farm machinery to go with tractors already acquired was holding up very well. He said there is a strong demand for used, as well as new, tractors.

*Brazos Bottoms*

This area resembles the Mississippi Delta in every respect. Tractors have not swept this area yet, but are beginning to appear.

*Black Wax*

Use of tractors continues to expand in this area. Tenant displacement was heavy in the Black Wax even before 1933. Social Service Supervisor Carr of WPA in Waco, Texas, made the important observation that this year for the first time, none of her agricultural labor WPA workers left for cotton chopping. This is ascribed to the 1938 cotton acreage reduction.

*Arkansas Bottoms*

Use of tractors is insipient and spreading in this area southeast of Little Rock.

*Arkansas and Mississippi Deltas*

The U.S. Employment Service man in Memphis informs me that the use of tractors, labor displacement, and piling of displaced workers in Memphis and other cities continues this year.

Paul S. Taylor

# WHAT SHALL WE DO WITH THEM?
## Address before the
## Commonwealth Club of California

We call them "Dust Bowlers." Ever since the droughts of 1934 and 1936 they have been streaming westward from the Great Plains. A count at the California border records the entry to our state by automobile alone of 221,000 refugees between the middle of 1935 and the end of 1937. More than four-fifths of them came from the drought states. In vivid phrases they tell us the tragedy of nature: "Burned out, blowed out, eat out." What shall we do with them?

We call them "Dust Bowlers." But it is not only the parching of the plains and the blowing of the topsoil which expels these people. If that were all, the return of rain to the dust bowl would end the exodus. But the causes are more deep-seated and more enduring than the hostile fluctuations of weather. At the close of the war, prices of cotton and of wheat collapsed, and with them, many thousands of rural families were shaken from their positions on the agricultural ladder. Farm owners lost the equities in their farms and became tenants; tenants were reduced to laborers, and farm laborers did what they could. This process, begun in the depression of the early twenties, was accelerated by the depression of the early thirties. Then came drought and grasshoppers, and whole sections of the rural population already loosened by the accumulating forces of successive depressions were finally dislodged by a catastrophe of nature. Those not anchored by the farm program and the relief policies of the government are seeking refuge by flight.

Now the rains have come again to the Great Plains, yet the tide of refugees flowing westward scarcely slackens. The number of distressed migrants entering California during the last half of 1937 was 49,000, or only 12 percent below the number coming during the last half of 1936 when drought was severe. And more migrants have come to California during the first quarter of 1938 than came during the first quarter of 1937. Clearly, other expelling forces than drought are at work. The effects of depression and recession are still accumulating, and now mechanization of the cotton farms is an added factor in the expulsion of farmers and farm laborers from the Cotton Belt.

We have long recognized the future displacement of southern cotton workers when a mechanical cotton picker shall have been perfected. But the tractor has been scarcely noticed by the public or recognized by the government. Yet tenant farmers, sharecroppers and farm laborers—whites and Negroes alike—are being swept from the land and onto relief in some of the most important sections of the Cotton Belt. Planters are dispensing with their sharecroppers and tenants, retaining the few necessary to operate tractors and paying them by the day when they work. A cotton planter in the Mississippi Delta, to cite an outstanding example, had 160 sharecropper families. He purchased twenty-two tractors and thirteen four-row cultivators, let go 130 out of 160 of these families, and retained only thirty for day labor.

Where the tractors are appearing the rural landscape is strewn with abandoned houses. Residents in western Texas explain as they point:

*"There used to be two families out there. The tractor got both of them." "That farm has made a living for a family ever since the land was broke." "The tractors are keeping our families from making a living."*

Rural schools decline. Village merchants fail. Drought undermined them, and mechanized farming finishes them. Class bitterness is stirred, and even the government program intended to benefit the farmer becomes a focus of strife. A small town postmaster explained: "The landlords get the government crop reduction money and buy tractors with it, and it's putting the renters out. The landlords take all the reduction money. If the tenants don't give 'em all, they put 'em off." From those who already have been dispossessed from the land this story of the machine comes in bitterness and despair. From those who face the same fate the story comes in stark fear.

On a Sunday morning last June, I stopped at a tenant's house near the Texas panhandle. There I found seven sturdy young men gathered together for the morning. These Texans are all displaced tenant farmers, victims of mechanized farming. The oldest man in the group is 33. All are on WPA. They support an average of four persons each on $22.80 a month. All are married and have families except one, who supports his mother and father. These seven Texans represent and support twenty-nine persons. Native Americans all, none of them can vote, for Texas levies a poll tax of $3.50 on man and wife. These men, like hundreds of others, find nothing they can turn to on the plains where they were born. They search for 200 miles in every direction and find no places which they can rent. With mechanization, the size of farms is increasing, and little is left for the tenants but sub-marginal land, relief, or flight.

This process of sweeping farmers from the land is now under way in western Texas, southwestern Oklahoma, the Black Wax Prairie of Texas, the Arkansas and Mississippi deltas, and it is incipient in other areas. In 1930 the proportion of farm tractors in the United States which was found on farms of the ten southern cotton states was only 12 percent. By 1937 it had risen to 18 percent. In seven years the number of tractors in the cotton states has practically doubled.

The record of power farming in cutting cotton workers from the land is already impressive. Tenants, sharecroppers, and laborers are forced into the towns in large numbers and drawn back onto the farms for only short seasonal employment at chopping and picking time. A pattern of mobile cotton workers is spreading, with planters dependent on wage laborers imported seasonally from more and more distant towns and cities. On a Saturday morning last June, I watched from 1,000 to 1,500 cotton hoers crowded into huge trucks in Memphis, Tennessee, to be hauled to plantations as far as forty-three miles each way for the day's work. The trucks left between 5 and 5:30 in the morning, and returned as late as 8:30 in the evening. Mostly the laborers were former sharecroppers, going back to hoe cotton for $1 or $1.25 a day, cut from the land. The cotton worker's year thus is being divided into occasional employment by the day on the plantations between May and December, and virtual idleness in the towns from December to May. The burden grows of relief of unemployed farm laborers congregated in the towns and cities of the South.

As Californians, we have felt remote from the critical problems facing the population of the Cotton Belt. But our feeling is founded upon illusion, for the southern regional problem is national in its repercussions. California's stake in its solution is direct and immediate, for people in distress do not like to remain where they see no opportunity. Outlets will be sought wherever they seem to exist. Already from the western portion of the old Cotton Belt the victims of mechanized farming are moving west. Six weeks ago at a camp of migratory agricultural workers in the San Joaquin Valley, I talked with families expelled by mechanized farming from the three states of Texas, Oklahoma, and Arkansas. From 1935 to 1937 the common explanations of the refugees were "went broke" and "the cotton burned up." Now we are beginning to hear "tractored out."

What can these people do? Where can they go? They try relief in the towns, and seasonal labor in the cotton. They try to scratch out a living on the sandy and exhausted farms of their native states. They seek a precarious foothold on cut-over lands of the Pacific Northwest. They try for jobs in the shrinking labor markets of the industrial North. They join the migratory agricultural laborers of Arizona, Oregon, Washington, and California in the West, and of Florida in the Southeast. Most of those who leave the Cotton Belt come west. The time has certainly arrived when as a nation, as well as a state, we must ask the question, "What shall we do with them?"

First there is the problem of relief in California. We all know that refugee families are often destitute when they arrive, or commonly they become so during slack seasons. We all know that during recent weeks the farm security administration has been obliged against the wishes of state authorities to relieve the distress of more than 9,000 families who have been in our state less than one year. With prospects of more refugees to come, we are apprehensive and alarmed at the cost. We are harried by the fear that indigent refugees will acquire by a year's residence the legal right to continuing relief at our expense. In this state of mind, our California agencies have taken stern measures. The chief of police of Los Angeles tried illegally to blockade the border. Our state administration now denies relief from state funds, and also denies access to federal WPA funds to those in distress during their first year in California. If they apply for needed assistance, we give these transients only temporary relief while their residence in another state is being verified. Then we offer to pay their transportation back. If they refuse, we grant no further relief, and they must shift for themselves.

The states from which the refugee families depart increasingly are reluctant to accept the return of their distressed families, even at our expense. Authorities of Arkansas, for example, have recently advised the transient whose transportation back California is ready to pay, that relief funds in Arkansas are inadequate, that granting relief there usually involves delay, and that sometimes it is impossible to give any aid at all to persons in need. As a further deterrent this Arkansas citizen in distress in California is required to write back home "explaining . . . why you think that coming to Arkansas will be the best plan for you," before Arkansas authorities will decide whether or not they will authorize return. In a letter dated February 23, 1938, the welfare director of a county in South Dakota denies any responsibility at all for a family in distress in California which left his county only a few months ago. He writes to our authorities:

> . . . We wish to advise that Mr. Ford left South Dakota in the fall of 1937 for the purpose of establishing a home. Therefore he does not have a South Dakota state settlement and authorization for his return cannot be secured. We trust the above information will be of some assistance to you in planning for your client.

Other states impose similar obstructions.

Thus the states of emigration vie with us and with the other states of immigration in seeking to avoid responsibility for destitute farm families who have enough initiative to seek economic opportunity through migration.

The futility of our relief procedure is understood by the refugees themselves, who generally adopt one of two courses:

(1) If they want a temporary pleasure trip home from the coast, they accept California's offer to pay their transportation back. A letter dated February 2, 1938 from the county relief administrator of LeFlore County, Oklahoma, who figuratively throws up his hands at the whole proceeding, reveals the situation:

> . . . I wish to advise that it is humanly impossible for me to investigate and establish citizenship in this county of families desiring to return from California.

*In this department I have no case workers and the county being the third largest in the state, it is all I can possibly do to look after the people now in this county. In the past I have authorized the return of a goodly number of families from your state, and after they paid a short visit to their relatives and friends, they all returned to California, with one exception. In view of this fact I feel that it is an imposition upon your state as well as a burden on myself to investigate these cases and authorize return from which it seems, that in all cases, it is just for a visit.*

(2) If they do not accept their transportation home "for a visit," and the great majority do not, they simply tighten their belts, and with the aid of friends and intermittent work stick it out until a year's sojourn within the borders of California gives them the legal right to demand relief from our state.

We may as well face the fact that we cannot stem the tide by withholding relief from the destitute men, women, and children who are taking refuge within our borders. Our western growers and labor contractors invite and even aid some of them to come—both whites and Negroes. But they need no specific invitation, for we use them to harvest our crops and they are turning their backs on closing opportunities at home. However meager their existence as migrants on the Pacific Coast, it offers more than the prospect of indefinite dependence on relief at home. So long as this differential in opportunity exists, they will continue to come. As an attempt to check migration, therefore, our present relief policy is futile.

This is not to say that state administrators and state legislators are either perfidious or inhumane. Their failure to meet the distress of the migrants lies in the fact that the problem inherently transcends state powers and responsibilities. It cannot be left safely to the several states.

What shall we do? A California representative has introduced in Congress a bill providing federal reimbursement to the states for relief granted to transients, prescribing uniform state residence standards, and interposing a check to this growth of a population legally without income, by requiring that residence in one state shall not be lost until it is acquired in another.

Some Californians, our state relief administration and state chamber of commerce among them, believe that this bill introduced by Congressman Voorhis should specify state residence requirements more stringent than self-maintenance without relief during fourteen months out of twenty-four. But before pressing for serious modification of the terms of prospective federal aid we Californians will do well to remember two facts: first, we are asking forty-eight states to vote money which will go mainly to a half dozen states, and primarily to our own; second, if by insistence we jeopardize passage of a bill extending federal aid, the burden of relieving these people falls on us both legally and in fact, at the end of one year's residence in California. It seems plain, therefore, that not only common humanity but state economy as well, dictate that we urge the California delegation in Washington to demand passage of the Voorhis bill.

But relief of the distressed is not the only problem which centers about these people. Two and a half years ago in this forum I outlined a program for the abolition of squatters' camps in our state. I can report substantial progress in that direction. The farm security administration now maintains seven sanitary camps for migrants. Visit these camps as you drive through the southern San Joaquin Valley at Shafter or Arvin, at Indio in the Coachella Valley, at Brawley in the Imperial, or at Marysville in the Sacramento Valley. These camps are accomplishing what was promised of them, by promoting public health and sanitation and raising morale. In addition to the seven camps already in operation, three more are under construction.

But the task is not ended. Preventable disease still stalks the migrants and endangers the public health. In 1936, most of the typhoid cases in our state originated among the migrants. This year typhoid has again broken out on their trail. It started among the pea pickers at Calipatria in February, and promptly was carried to the San Joaquin Valley. Smallpox, too, has appeared. Prompt measures by the state department of public health, which has just administered 20,000 innoculations for typhoid and 56,000 vaccinations for smallpox, have checked the spread of these diseases. When the migrants need medical care and lack the money to pay for it, they face two alternatives. Either they are rejected by the county hospital authorities on the ground they are not residents, and so fail to receive treatment, suffer needlessly, and endanger the health of the community; or else they are accepted reluctantly, and the heavy cost of their care is imposed on the counties where they happen to be when they fall sick. Both alternatives are undesirable.

What, then, shall we do next about the problem of public health, sanitation, and medical care? First, the state division of immigration and housing, which is responsible for inspecting labor camps, has been crippled. We should strengthen it. Second, we should ask the federal government to share the costs of medical care of transients. These steps we should take for our own protection as well as for the protection of the agricultural workers.

And in addition, we should extend to agricultural workers the protection of social security laws, which, granted them in England and a dozen other countries, is still denied them in the United States.

Thus far I have answered your question, "What shall we do with them?" in these terms: We cannot stop them from coming by refusing to give them relief in California when they need it. They are forced from their own communities; directly and indirectly we invite them; we use their labor. Not only are they here by tens of thousands of families, but more are coming. These simple facts we must face. It follows as elementary, therefore, that whether we like them or not, we dare not tolerate in our midst their hunger and the malnutrition of their children, their unsanitary living conditions, and their disease. Neither the state of California nor the United States can postpone or avoid this responsibility.

But in your minds lie questions deeper than those which I have answered. You wish to know: Is there nothing we can do to check this stream of refugees which pours in upon us and threatens even to grow larger? Is there nothing we can do to so incorporate into our economic life those migrants whom we must receive, that the problems of relief, health, housing, and industrial strife which are now so pressing may not permanently afflict our agriculture? In brief, we face the question: What can we do to introduce some stability into a situation now marked by disintegration, chaos, misery, and conflict? It is to this fundamental issue that I now turn.

The Great Plains and the southern Cotton Belt, I have already pointed out, are suffering the dislodgment of their farm people because of various forces, among them drought and mechanization of the farms. Since we are receiving their dispossessed, it is logical and proper that we demand of those areas that they shall put their house in order, and provide the basis for maintaining at home the maximum number of their own people which those regions can support according to an American standard of living. In the Great Plains this means the fullest development of its potential water resources, the proper agricultural practices to conserve moisture, and the proper balance between crops and grass.

In the Cotton Belt more drastic and sustained measures are necessary. In from three to five generations our American ancestors, under the cotton plantation system, have mined the soil of its fertility and even destroyed the topography of its rolling surface. In the Piedmont especially the fields are badly gullied, and large sections of the country which were the most fertile are almost irretrievably lost to agricultural production. In many sections, the yield of cotton per acre is maintained only by the heavy use of costly chemical fertilizers. If the South is not to dislodge millions of her rural people, she must abandon the one-crop cotton complex, expand animal husbandry, develop a more diversified and self-sustaining agriculture, and undertake upon an even greater scale the conservation and restoration of her depleted soils.

In both the Great Plains and upon the better lands of the Cotton Belt the progress of mechanization is spreading the pattern of the large-scale industrialized farm with which we are so familiar in California. The progress of the machine cannot and should not be left to uncontrolled forces if human stability is to be achieved. I shall speak further of this problem shortly when I refer to our own rural structure.

What shall we say about the Great Plains and the Cotton Belt?

We should insist that they carry out the policies indicated in the reports of the committees on the Great Plains and on farm tenancy. The tenancy program, basic to stabilization in the South, has been held in Congress to a snail's pace. Because we receive those who are being dislodged in the South, and face the prospect of receiving more, California should insist that these agricultural reforms go forward. Our state should use its full influence in Washington to ensure adequate national support for the stabilization of the rural structures and peoples of the South and of the plains.

It may be that deterioration of the soil and overexpansion of agriculture have already gone so far that surplus populations in these regions must be squeezed out, even with a program of agricultural reform. Indeed, this is the view of our most careful students. If this be true, we should insist that the advantages of supporting surplus populations in those regions which produced them, on relief if necessary, be balanced against their opportunities for self-support elsewhere. They should not be cut adrift, or even encouraged to leave by shoddy relief policies at home.

This answer to the question "What can we do to check the stream of refugees?" will be unsatisfactory to Californians, but it seems in accord with the basic facts. If stabilization of the rural population in the South and Great Plains offers little hope of checking the flight of refugees immediately, at least it promises for the long run a balance between population and land which will not easily expel new waves of migrants in the future.

The final question remains: What can we do to so incorporate in the economic life of California those migrants whom we must receive, that the pressing problems of relief, health, housing, and incessant strife may not permanently afflict our agriculture?

Our first thought goes naturally to the land, and to the great reservoirs which the reclamation service is building in the West—Columbia Basin, the Central Valley project, Boulder Dam, and others. If new farms were rapidly being brought under irrigation in the years immediately ahead, a ready answer might be at hand. The Columbia Basin project alone will ultimately irrigate 1,200,000 acres of land, or half of the total of land to be irrigated by all twelve of the reclamation projects in the West. But the Columbia Basin will not be ready for any settlement within five years, and the last unit will not be ready for at least thirty years. The United States commissioner of reclamation, John C. Page, states of all these projects that "at no time in the next ten years will we be able to offer for settlement more than 150,000 acres in any one year." This implies that in no year during the next ten will new irrigation provide settlement for more than, say, 2,000 families. The commissioner dashed effectively the hope that new irrigation will resettle the refugees to the West when he said in January, 1938: "The Columbia Basin project, if it were finished at this time, would provide homes for less than half of the farm families already driven by drought from the Great Plains alone." The frontier is gone, and there are few new lands. If we are to solve our problem, we must solve it upon the lands which we now farm.

We are all familiar with the basic facts of farm organization in California, particularly the large-scale industrialized type which predominates in those areas to which the refugees are attracted. More than one-third of all the large-scale farms of the United States are concentrated in our state. Absentee and corporation ownership are common, hiring and firing practices follow the old industrial pattern, and a roving, landless proletariat provides the shifting peak labor supply upon which the crops depend. Our most acute rural problems are inseparable from this type of agriculture—destitute, restless workers, incipient labor organization, violent strikes, nervous and scarcely concealed vigilantism. It is the refugees and others now working in this type of agriculture that we mean when we say, "What shall we do with them?"

Our problem is how to introduce stability where there is none. As a first step we can stabilize many of the migrants on small garden plots of ground, adjacent to as much employment as possible, where they can raise a portion of their subsistence, living in a decent house, and keep the children in one school as long as possible. From this base the father and older sons can migrate when necessary. At Arvin in Kern County, twenty of these houses located each on two-thirds of an acre of land, are already occupied by farm laborers' families which rent them for $8.20 a month. The farm security administration has allocated funds for 150 more of these houses in California and has let contracts for eighty of them.

As a second step, we can select some families according to capacity, and stabilize them at a higher level by similarly locating and providing them with low-rental housing, and in addition, equipping them to supply themselves through a cooperative with dairy, poultry, and vegetable products. Units of this type have already been started in California and Arizona.

These two steps will stabilize and elevate the standard of living of the migrants as laborers. But we still hold in this country to the belief that there should be opportunity for those at the bottom to ascend the agricultural ladder. A third step we can take, therefore, is to establish landless farm families as operators on farms. Where land and other conditions are favorable, every advantage should be taken of the economies of machine methods and low overhead through large-scale operation. In the interest of consumer as well as producer, the economies of corporate farming so fully developed in the West should be retained. But instead of resident corporation managers on huge tracts employing hordes of landless laborers, could we not establish large corporate farms operated by resident farmers working cooperatively under competent management, and sharing the proceeds? The farm security administration is now operating a few farms of this type in the West and South. They are aimed not only to give opportunity to farmers who are landless. They are planned to establish a type of farm organization which will produce economically, prevent the deep divisions that now rend our countryside, and introduce stability among those who live from the land.

These measures are suited particularly to the portions of the old South and West, where mechanization and industrialization of agriculture are now producing the greatest human dislocation and turmoil. They should have a major place in the national farm program. The Department of Agriculture must face its full responsibilities.

*American Sociological Review,* vol. III, no. 2, April 1938

# MIGRATORY AGRICULTURAL WORKERS ON THE PACIFIC COAST

*Presented at joint meeting of* American Association for Labor Legislation *and the Social Work section of the* American Sociological Society *Atlantic City, 1937.*

Our social agencies, rooted in the traditions of England's parishes more than a century ago, are geared to care for *residents*. Our educational institutions, although they arose on a fast-moving frontier, were built for the children of *settlers*. In general, our laws look with favor on the freeholder, the taxpayer, the local citizen who is "part of the community." They were passed for the benefit and protection of neighbors. Migrants are tolerated or welcomed only when their work is needed or they have money to spend. When they become penniless and without visible means of support, they are given the social facilities of the community grudgingly or denied them entirely, and as "vagrants" they are urged, or even subsidized with enough gas and oil, to "get along" to the next community.

In the states on the western rim of the country, agricultural employers have long depended on mobile workers to harvest their crops. Since the Wheatland hop field riots twenty-five years ago and the studies of Carleton Parker, the problems of the itinerant worker have been brought home to the West, but they remain largely unsolved. Indeed, their complexity has grown, for race groups have multiplied and families have more and more entered the fields as migrants, bringing women and children where originally there were mainly roving single men. With expanding acreages under irrigation supporting ever more orchards, vegetables, and cotton with their heavy and highly seasonal demand for hand laborers, the dependence of far western agriculture on migratory labor has never been greater than now.

It is essential to the success of agriculture that the harvests shall proceed in peace, but in 1933 and 1934 the harvesting of crops was interrupted by more than fifty strikes. While there were few outbreaks in 1937, the growers report "agitators" in the field, are apprehensive, and are organized from Arizona to Washington. According to press reports, probably exaggerated, the associated farmers claim "35,000 militant farmers," 25,000 in California and 10,000 in Arizona, Oregon, and Washington, ready "to fight the subversive activities of the Communists and their allies," including the CIO.

The reasons for dependence on migratory labor, and for the peculiar labor relations which characterize irrigated agriculture in the Far West, are deep seated. As Adams, Landis, and Tetreau have shown, the demand for seasonal labor in California is three times as great at the peak as at the slack point; in Arizona it is six times as great; in the Yakima Valley of Washington, it is more than sixteen times the slack. These fluctuations produce both unemployment and continual movement following the harvests in order to dovetail employment.

Not only are existing conditions a product of the nature of the crops, but they are grounded also in the structure of agriculture which shows industrial characteristics to a marked degree. Of all large-scale farms in the United States, approximately 45 percent are located in the four far western states which stretch from Arizona to Washington. Wendzel has pointed out that while in the United States as a whole only 11 percent of the farms reporting hired labor employed three laborers or more, totalling about 39 percent of all the paid laborers, in the three Pacific Coast states, 20 percent of the farms employed three paid laborers or more, aggregating more than 60 percent of all the hired laborers. The extreme of contrast showing the industrialization of agricultural employment in the West appears from comparison of Minnesota and Arizona. In Minnesota, only 2.9 percent of the farms reporting hired laborers employed three or more; in Arizona, the proportion was ten times as great, or 29 percent. In Minnesota, these farms employed only 10 percent of the paid farm laborers of the state; in Arizona, they employed 82 percent.[1]

Not only is large-scale agriculture prevalent in the Far West and concentration of employment in relatively few hands, but wage relations are highly developed with gang labor typical, including piece rates, hourly rates, foremen, and labor contractors. Open-air food factories producing for a highly commercialized market predominate in many parts of these states and have stamped agriculture there with an industrial pattern.

To the migratory workers in Pacific Coast agriculture, this pattern means chronic irregular employment, frequent movement from job to job, often extending many hundreds of miles in a single seasonal cycle, and low incomes. Average earnings of migrant families applying for relief in December 1935, and January 1936, in California ranged from $381 in 1930 to $289 in 1935. Landis reports average family earnings of Yakima Valley migrants in 1935-36 as $276 among those who received relief and $425 among those who did not. By any American standard such incomes are low.

The condition of the far western migrants is not new, but it has been given national significance and rendered more complex by the tide of refugees from drought, depression, and farm mechanization. During the twenty-nine months ending November 15, 1937, some 210,000 migrants "in need of manual employment" entered California by motor vehicle. How many remain there is unknown, but the net accretion to the state and to its wandering agricultural labor supply is large. In lesser degree, the same influx is being felt in Arizona, Oregon, and Washington.

The pattern of the group whose problems we are to consider, then, is briefly this: The needs of intensive, industrialized agriculture are served by a large migratory labor supply. The total number of mobile people is unknown, but may well exceed 200,000. This group is unstable, subject to irregular employment, low earnings, and the social and political disabilities of nonresidents. In Washington and Oregon, the migrants are mainly white American families. In Arizona and California, there are also large numbers of Mexican families and some thousands of single Filipinos. In all these states, the number and proportion of native white American families from the Great Plains and other sections of the Southwest is increasing.

These migratory agricultural workers present important problems of labor legislation, social security, and social work. Five will be described:

1. *Child labor and education.* The principal evils of child labor in agriculture are avoided if laws for compulsory school attendance are well drawn and well enforced. Strict enforcement with eternal vigilance is the primary consideration. Whether or not this is achieved depends mainly on the attitude of the community. On the Pacific Coast, the attitudes of communities vary but in general they support enforcement. One pitfall in drafting legislation can be avoided. State funds should be allocated to counties and districts on the basis of actual attendance in school, not on the basis of mere presence of children in the school district, as in Oregon. The potential evils of this system are well known and have reached their fullest flower in the South.

The state of California encourages educational provision for migratory children by reimbursing counties for one-half the amounts which the counties allocate to elementary school districts "on account of special schools or classes for the children of migratory laborers," not to "exceed $75 per calendar year per teacher."

Avoidance of stigmatization of migratory children as "pea pickers," to be segregated for other than sound educational reasons, is hardly a matter for legislation but rests rather on a healthy community attitude and intelligent school administration.

2. *Health.* The bad conditions under which many of the migrant families live, strewn over the fields and by the roadside, cannot be described adequately; they must be seen. Of Imperial Valley a United States commission stated: "... we found filth, squalor, an entire absence of sanitation, and a crowding of human beings into totally inadequate tents or crude structures built of boards, weeds or anything that was found at hand to give pitiful semblance of a home at its worst." In 1937, a year of costly typhoid epidemics in California, approximately 90 percent of the reported cases occurred among agricultural migrants. A 1937 study of 1,000 children of California migratory agricultural laborers by Dr. Faverman reports that "migratory American children. . . were found to have medical and hygienic defects in 23 per-

cent more cases than resident American children examined in the rural areas of California during the same year." Also that, "Over 27 percent of the children have nutritional defects, many of which cannot be corrected because of the low family income."[2] It was found that only 10.5 percent of the children were getting daily the amount of milk "considered optimum for growth and development, while 15.8 percent were getting no milk."

Underhill, in a study of 132 families in California cotton camps, reports that "to the large group of people falling in the classifications of nonresident and 'state homeless,' medical care is not available except for emergency conditions. The group as a whole is unable to pay for private medical care because of low income, and those who do pay for it often deprive themselves of necessities by so doing. . . . Many of the group having definite or probable residence do not receive the medical care which they need. Their economic status does not permit their paying for this care."[3] Dr. Faverman found that 66 percent of the families which she studied had been in California less than the three years necessary to establish state "residence," and that 41 percent of the remainder have not been long enough in any county to establish county residence entitling them to care. The tragedy of the settlement laws is made only the more complete by the fact that of the 66 percent of families which had failed to establish California residence, "about 39 percent of these have lost their residence in their home states."

In order to raise the standard of labor camps in California, a state camp inspection division was created in 1912. This division was able to do effective work for many years but recently it has been stripped to the bone by the pressure of employers and by others seeking "economy." In the late twenties, a state law was passed authorizing establishment of tax districts to maintain local public camps for agricultural workers but it appears that the employers have never availed themselves of this statute.

At present, the Federal Farm Security Administration has assumed the initiative in stimulating improved sanitary conditions by establishing and operating a small demonstration chain of migratory labor camps. The future of this important and successful program will depend largely on congressional support.

Curiously, some of the militant employers maintain ill-concealed opposition to government camps. They fear that employees will unionize more readily in government camps than in those on their own land under their immediate control. They seem to feel that the hazard of unionization is more menacing than the hazard to public health, citizenship, and order which exists in the evil squatters' camps and bad private camps in which many thousands of families now live. Of course, many smaller farmers and even large growers approve the camps. Here is a new facet of the old issue of protective legislation.

The federal government is further promoting health among

For $10.00 per month, agricultural workers occupied this habitation, Brawley, November 1939. *Photo: Division of Immigration and Housing.*

The home of an agricultural laborer and his family in Hooverville, just outside Bakersfield. The house, constructed of palm leaves, pieces of tin scrap, and tree limbs, is on a lot purchased by the family for $125.00, $3.00 down and $3.00 per month. *Photo: Courtesy of the National Archives.*

western migrants by allocating funds from social security taxes for rural public health work. In California, the state department of public health has been enabled by these funds to assign physicians to migrants and to place nurses in the camps of the farm security administration. In the last session of Congress, H.R. 8225 was introduced by Congressman Voorhis to allocate more social security funds to states and counties for more adequate medical care to nonresidents and thus meet the aggravated conditions among western migrants previously described.

3. *Relief.* Statistics of relief incidence among migratory agricultural laborers are not available but it is undoubtedly heavy and would be heavier if settlement laws and other restrictions did not place so many obstacles in the way. There are about as many farm laborers as farm operators in the far western states, but in March 1935, there were on relief in these states approximately 10,800 farm operators and 29,500 farm laborers, or 2.7 times as many laborers as operators.[4]

Not only is the incidence of relief heavy among the laborers, but because of the steady influx of refugees to the coast, these states are apprehensive of mounting permanent relief liabilities. Counties and cities share the same fears as the states. The local measures adopted to meet this situation are sometimes desperate. A California county in 1934 voted $2,500 to subsidize the movement of pea pickers into the next county at the end of the harvest. Los Angeles police patrolled the borders of the state in what the press called a "bum blockade." The California Assembly passed a bill to bar at the border indigents liable to become public charges.

The issue between states and between counties of who shall bear the costs of relief is real but it is hardly a solution to leave the burden on the shoulders of the already distressed, nor to leave it entirely on the states and counties which happen to receive the distressed. Other states and the nation should share some of the responsibility.

Inequality of economic opportunity is not the only reason for emigration to the coast. Of the 210,000 migrants entering California, 50,000, or 24 percent, came from Oklahoma. In many counties of that state, the level of direct relief is only from $3 to $5 per family per month. Furthermore, when relief agencies of the western states offer to return indigents to Oklahoma, the county authorities in that state commonly acknowledge the residence of the indigent but decline to accept any responsibility. This is a particularly acute example of the interstate character of a relief problem which seriously afflicts the migratory workers. I am not familiar with any measures which have been taken to assess relative responsibilities of the states for their indigent people. However, in the last session of Congress, H.R. 8279 was introduced to reduce the burden on those states now receiving large numbers of poverty-stricken "transients" and to reduce the hardships suffered by these people because of inadequate state and local funds and the restrictive settlement laws. The bill provides federal funds for states which will expend them in relief to transients on the same basis as to its own needy citizens and which will agree that acceptance of such federally subsidized relief for less than fourteen months out of twenty-four shall not prevent acquisition of state and local "residence" rights by the recipient. The present volume of interstate distress migration and its probable continuance make imperative the adoption of some such plan.

The coming of the harvests produces regularly a cry of labor shortage from western growers. It is an old cry, for labor must always be moved to the fields, and the cry of "shortage" is another way of advertising "opportunity." To some extent, the growers' agents have always blamed relief agencies for withholding labor; since 1935, these criticisms have increased. Space does not permit weighing the issues between growers desiring abundant labor, clients clinging to the minimum security of relief, and agencies protecting clients from exposure to the hazards and hardships of migratory labor in the fields. It may be pointed out, however, that in California, in October 1936, when the index fell to 97, the crop reporting service for the first time in seven years or more reported less than 100 men available for the 100 jobs. In 1937, although growers continued to complain of the "cushion provided through relief agencies," their representatives reported the labor supply situation as "happy."

4. *Labor relations, wages and hours regulation, and social security.* The packing and processing of fruits and vegetables is commonly performed under industrialized conditions in the irrigated districts of the Far West, especially where the large-scale pattern of agriculture is most fully developed. Much of this work is performed by "fruit tramps" who migrate from crop to crop like the field workers. Under decisions by the Bureau of Internal Revenue and by state social security agencies, this work is held to constitute "industrial labor" when it is such in fact, and not to constitute "agricultural labor." By these rulings, the men and women who pack have been assured the protection of social security legislation, which exempts "agricultural labor."

Large processing employers oppose this recognition of processing as "industrial." They have sought, successfully in the Fair Labor Standards Bill which passed the Senate, to have considered as "agricultural" all labor performed "within the area of production" in "preparing, packing, or storing. . . fresh fruits or vegetables in their raw or natural state," no matter how industrialized the process. By focusing on the agricultural *product* in its "raw or natural state," attention has been diverted from the industrial conditions under which the product is processed.

The effort to expand the definition of "agricultural labor" at the expense of "industrial labor" is not limited to wages and hours regulation, nor to the processors of agricultural products. Fish canners, cotton ginners, turpentine and tobacco processors unite to exclude their laborers from protective legislation. If the definition of "agricultural labor" can be expanded, as the processors have already achieved in the Senate Labor Standards Bill, it is but a step to inclusion of the same definition in labor relations and social security legislation. Undoubtedly this is the intent.

The importance of the definition of "agricultural labor" is not underestimated by the large processors. Last year the conservative *San Francisco Chronicle* described, with the significant headline: "It DID happen in Salinas," the way in which private employing interests and local authorities handled the Salinas lettuce packers' strike. After the strike, the National Labor Relations Board held embarrassing hearings. Early this month (December 1937), the Associated Farmers of California protested against "usurpation" of power by the board in extending its jurisdiction to so-called "agricultural activities."

In the far western states, the administrative problem of extending social security to agricultural labor would be simpler than some of us have thought. If a social security law were to cover those farms which employ three or more hired laborers, practically two-thirds of the laborers would be protected, yet administration would need to reach only one farm in twenty.

5. *The structure of agriculture.* The grounding of many migratory labor problems in the industrialized structure of irrigated agriculture in the Far West was emphasized at the outset. It is pertinent, therefore, to invite the attention of students of social work, social security, and labor legislation to the agricultural labor program developed in the Far West by the Farm Security Administration. This program begins with the migrant labor camps described earlier. Its second stage, already started in the southern San Joaquin Valley, is provision of decent low rental housing for the more stable migrants. A third step proposes a combination of low rental housing with a small farm under unitary operation to provide the occupants with high-grade, low-cost dairy, poultry, and truck products, and some stabilizing equipment. A fourth stage of the program is establishment of large-scale corporate farms, with the work performed by the residents and the benefits paid to them, in lieu of corporate farms owned by absentees, operated by hired managers, and worked by hordes of migratory wage laborers.

This program represents an attempt to raise the standard of living of the migrants, to stabilize them, and so far as possible to give them a place on the land with the means for efficient and modern operation, so that they may be not only tillers of the soil but also resident owners. Though couched as a farm program, it is equally a labor program.

Social security, social work, and labor legislation thus appear in forms both old and new when they face the problems of migratory agricultural workers.

# REFUGEE LABOR MIGRATION TO CALIFORNIA, 1937

In the thirty-three months from July 1935 to March 1938, more than 200,000 migrants "in need of manual employment" streamed west from the drought states along the highways to California. The powerful impulse of droughts which reached catastrophic proportions in 1934 and 1936 has forced these and other thousands to emigrate in search of economic opportunity. But the dramatic, compelling, and pervasive power of nature should not be allowed to obscure the presence of other deep-seated causes of the dislocation of those whom we have been accustomed to call "drought refugees."

Among these other causes are the accumulated forces of years of agricultural depression, and now the beginning of mechanization in the Cotton Belt. As mechanization spreads, substituting machines for men, it bars the return of those expelled earlier by drought and by depression. It also dislodges more thousands of refugees.

This study carries through 1937 the statistical record and analysis of the refugee and labor migration to California described in previous articles. For over 2¾ years there has been available a fortnightly check on the number of migrants in need of manual employment entering California by motor vehicle. This border count, made available through the Bureau of Plant Quarantine, California Department of Agriculture, has been the only numerical index to the magnitude of the problem. A perspective of the movement covering a period of almost three years should afford some clue as to its future direction and stimulate thought directed toward coping with the problems following in its wake.

## NUMBER OF MIGRANTS

Between July 1, 1935, and March 31, 1938, 241,930 individuals (i.e., migrants in need of manual employment and members of their families), residents of other states, entered California. In addition, during the same period some 42,812 Californians of comparable economic status who had departed, reentered the state. In considering these figures there is an important question as to the extent to which they represent a net increase in the state's population. Returning Californians largely represent a shuttling movement of workers and their families into and out of the state. It is doubtful, however, that the same thing is true of the out-of-state immigrants; certainly it is not true to anything like the same degree. Even were it true, the implications are that the net migration is of a magnitude to compel the greatest attention. The tremendous surplus of agricultural labor now evident in the rural areas of the state, the numerically insignificant

## TABLE 1—Migrants "in Need of Manual Employment" Entering California by Motor Vehicle, by States, July 1, 1935-Mar. 31, 1938[1]

| State of Origin | Total, 33 months Number | Total, 33 months Percent | 1935 Last 6 months | 1936 | 1937 | 1938: First quarter |
|---|---|---|---|---|---|---|
| **All States excluding California:** | | | | | | |
| Number | 241,930 | 100 | 42,559 | 84,833 | 90,761 | 23,777 |
| Percent | 100.0 | ——— | 17.6 | 35.1 | 37.5 | 9.8 |
| Drought States | 205,477 | 84.9 | 32,185 | 73,187 | 78,332 | 21,773 |
| Oklahoma | 58,153 | 24.0 | 7,561 | 22,980 | 21,709 | 5,894 |
| Texas | 24,559 | 10.1 | 3,631 | 8,304 | 8,723 | 3,901 |
| Arizona | 25,018 | 10.3 | 3,097 | 7,329 | 10,613 | 3,979 |
| Arkansas | 19,204 | 7.9 | 2,866 | 6,890 | 7,232 | 2,216 |
| Missouri | 16,205 | 6.7 | 2,426 | 5,873 | 6,316 | 1,590 |
| Kansas | 11,128 | 4.6 | 2,238 | 3,900 | 4,484 | 506 |
| Colorado | 8,393 | 3.5 | 1,584 | 2,249 | 3,702 | 858 |
| New Mexico | 7,616 | 3.1 | 1,578 | 2,440 | 2,680 | 918 |
| Nebraska | 7,651 | 3.1 | 1,258 | 3,019 | 3,024 | 350 |
| Idaho | 5,258 | 2.1 | 1,193 | 1,733 | 2,012 | 320 |
| Montana | 3,038 | 1.3 | 834 | 969 | 1,102 | 133 |
| Utah | 3,027 | 1.3 | 678 | 1,069 | 1,063 | 217 |
| Iowa | 3,368 | 1.4 | 703 | 1,474 | 1,024 | 167 |
| Nevada | 2,342 | 1.0 | 502 | 614 | 923 | 303 |
| North Dakota | 2,346 | 1.0 | 532 | 912 | 834 | 68 |
| Minnesota | 2,086 | .9 | 487 | 825 | 707 | 67 |
| South Dakota | 2,824 | 1.2 | 468 | 1,067 | 1,164 | 125 |
| Wyoming | 1,836 | .8 | 337 | 738 | 659 | 102 |
| Wisconsin | 1,425 | .6 | 212 | 793 | 361 | 59 |
| Pacific States | 22,476 | 9.3 | 5,822 | 6,685 | 8,831 | 1,138 |
| Oregon | 14,305 | 5.9 | 3,629 | 4,384 | 5,592 | 700 |
| Washington | 8,171 | 3.4 | 2,193 | 2,301 | 3,239 | 438 |
| Industrial States | 8,891 | 3.7 | 3,106 | 3,261 | 2,091 | 433 |
| Illinois | 2,617 | 1.1 | 818 | 1,066 | 605 | 128 |
| Michigan | 2,068 | .9 | 658 | 827 | 456 | 127 |
| New York | 968 | .4 | 486 | 274 | 186 | 22 |
| Ohio | 1,260 | .5 | 436 | 468 | 259 | 97 |
| Indiana | 1,128 | .5 | 319 | 444 | 331 | 34 |
| Pennsylvania | 578 | .2 | 278 | 106 | 188 | 6 |
| New Jersey | 272 | .1 | 111 | 76 | 66 | 19 |
| Southern States | 4,492 | 1.9 | 1,205 | 1,516 | 1,346 | 425 |
| Tennessee | 1,084 | .4 | 298 | 371 | 294 | 121 |
| Georgia | 464 | .2 | 207 | 140 | 96 | 21 |
| Louisiana | 672 | .3 | 145 | 190 | 258 | 79 |
| Florida | 405 | .2 | 95 | 176 | 98 | 36 |
| Alabama | 457 | .2 | 120 | 153 | 137 | 47 |
| Kentucky | 421 | .2 | 101 | 152 | 137 | 31 |
| Mississippi | 358 | .1 | 71 | 143 | 101 | 43 |
| Virginia | 103 | (²) | 57 | 23 | 23 | ——— |
| West Virginia | 91 | (²) | 32 | 29 | 19 | 11 |
| Maryland | 109 | (²) | 29 | 50 | 24 | 6 |
| North Carolina | 194 | (²) | 15 | 58 | 109 | 12 |
| District of Columbia | 49 | (²) | 19 | 16 | 14 | ——— |
| South Carolina | 80 | (²) | 16 | 12 | 34 | 18 |
| Delaware | 5 | (²) | ——— | 3 | 2 | ——— |
| New England States | 594 | .2 | 241 | 184 | 161 | 8 |
| Massachusetts | 278 | .1 | 113 | 79 | 86 | ——— |
| Rhode Island | 58 | (²) | 31 | 10 | 17 | ——— |
| Maine | 43 | (²) | 40 | ——— | 3 | ——— |
| Connecticut | 151 | (²) | 36 | 67 | 40 | 8 |
| Vermont | 36 | (²) | 13 | 15 | 8 | ——— |
| New Hampshire | 28 | (²) | 8 | 13 | 7 | ——— |
| California | 42,812 | ——— | 9,901 | 12,839 | 14,215 | 5,857 |

[1]Data collected by border inspectors of Bureau of Plant Quarantine, California Department of Agriculture.
[2]Less than 1/10th of 1 percent.

results of the attempt of relief agencies to return out-of-state migrants to their places of former residence, the increasing burden of federal agencies equipped to care for nonresidents, and the steadiness with which the influx has been maintained all indicate that most of the migrants abandon, at the time of their departure, thoughts of return to their home states.

Recent developments in the state of Arizona give promise that similar border counts may soon be instituted there. Since Arizona is the principal channel of migration for this "refugee" labor, such a count will unquestionably shed light on the "net" migration to California and, in conjunction with the California count on the Arizona border, will aid in determining the extent to which Arizona is acquiring a residue of migrants. It has been authoritatively estimated that close to 30,000 out-of-state migrants entered Arizona during the past fall and winter for the purpose of harvesting cotton and other crops.

During the thirty-three-month period, roughly a quarter of a million persons entered California. As shown in table 1, some 42,000 immigrated in the last half of 1935, 85,000 in 1936, 90,000 in 1937, and 24,000 in the first quarter of 1938. The movement has been characterized by its steadiness throughout the period rather than by violent fluctuations. Momentarily disregarding the data for 1936 the extreme range in magnitude of quarterly migrations was not more than a third of the average quarterly migration. Excluding the year 1936, the minimum quarterly influx was 18,317 in the last quarter of 1935, and the maximum 25,110 in the last quarter of 1937. This range is 6,793, or about 400 less than one-third of the average quarterly influx of 21,993.

The returns for the year 1936 which show a considerably greater range, from 13,427 in the first quarter to 29,586 in the third quarter, must be regarded as reflecting in part the consequences of an ill-conceived attempt to curb immigration in the spring months of that year. The effect seems to have been to aggravate the usual seasonal decline in the spring and to delay entry into California until the control was removed, rather than to reduce the total entries to California during the year. Many, deterred from entering California, simply bided their time in Arizona or elsewhere. In all probability, the fluctuations in 1936 would have paralleled those of 1937 had not the statistically accidental factor of the "border patrol" interfered.

Practically 85 percent of the migrants come from states classed as "drought states" by the FERA in 1934. Oklahoma alone was the state of origin of 58,143, or 24 percent, and in combination with Texas, Arizona, and Arkansas accounted for over 50 percent of all out-of-state migrants. Less than 4 percent came from the industrial states, less than 2 percent from the southern states, and only 0.2 percent from New England. The remainder, 9.3 percent, came from the Pacific states of Washington and Oregon.

Certain revisions are required with respect to earlier observations as to the causes of the migrations. The coincidence that most of the migrants came from the so-called drought states led to the tentative conclusion that the drought itself was chiefly responsible. The unabated persistence of the influx throughout the year 1937 (table 2), a year during which the drought areas were greatly restricted, leads to the conclusion that, important though it was, drought was but a final straw added to fundamental changes that have been transpiring during the last decade and a half. The more plausible explanation of the movement now seems to be that it is the cumulative result of low cotton prices in the immediate postwar period and in 1932, the droughts of 1934 and 1936, and a growing use of mechanical apparatus, particularly the all-purpose tractor, in the areas of greatest emigration. These factors, in combination, reasonably account for a decline in economic status leading eventually to complete severance of all ties and to migration as a means of escape from a permanently constricted sphere of economic activity.[1]

Revision should also be made with respect to analysis of emigrations from Arizona. It was earlier believed that the Arizona migrants were chiefly participants in a seasonal interstate migration between California and Arizona. It is true that the winter lettuce season in Imperial Valley and the later spring lettuce harvest of the Salt River Valley in Arizona, that the early summer cantaloupe harvest in Imperial Valley and the fall cotton harvest in the Salt River Valley, Casa Grande area, and other parts of Arizona, provide the basis for a natural interstate flow of migrant agricultural workers. But, in addition, Arizona provides an ideal wintering place for migrants in route from states farther east. The cotton harvest, which lasts from September till as late as March, is a crop with which most of the migrants are familiar and which affords them an opportunity to replenish impoverished larders and to accumulate the means for continuing their travels. At the same time the winter climate in Arizona is extremely equable. Therefore many of the migrants recently dislodged from other states remain in Arizona past the turn of the year and consequently acquire Arizona license plates for their cars. The fact that April, May, June, and July are the months of greatest immigration from Arizona confirms this observation.

Table 2, showing the number of migrants entering the state of California by months throughout the year 1937, also indicates that seasonality probably is not so important as at first suspected. The sharp decline of the spring months in 1936 and the extreme peak in the fall of that same year are considerably leveled out in the case of 1937. Again it must be concluded that the 1936 tendencies were the result of artificial barriers rather than of a natural movement. Nevertheless, even in 1937 the movement in the fall months was somewhat greater than in the late winter months of January and February.

*Refugee Labor Migration to California, 1937*

*TABLE 2—Returning Californians and Out-of-State Migrants "in Need of Manual Employment" Entering California, by Months, June 16, 1935-Mar. 31, 1938[1]*

| Month | 1935 | | 1936 | | 1937 | | 1938 | |
|---|---|---|---|---|---|---|---|---|
| | Return-ing Califor-nians | Out-of-State mi-grants | Return-ing Califor-nians | Out-of-State mi-grants | Return-ing Califor-nians | Out-of-State mi-grants | Return-ing Califor-nians | Out-of-State mi-grants |
| Total............................ | 11,004 | 46,013 | 12,839 | 84,833 | 14,215 | 90,761 | 5,857 | 23,777 |
| January............................ | ———— | ———— | 2,663 | 6,774 | 1,053 | 4,949 | 2,903 | 8,724 |
| February............................ | ———— | ———— | 674 | 3,126 | 559 | 5,701 | 1,494 | 7,583 |
| March............................ | ———— | ———— | 625 | 3,527 | 387 | 7,752 | 1,460 | 7,740 |
| April............................ | ———— | ———— | 616 | 4,719 | 764 | 7,242 | ———— | ———— |
| May............................ | ———— | ———— | 629 | 4,895 | 999 | 8,299 | ———— | ———— |
| June............................ | [2] 1,103 | 3,454 | 816 | 6,079 | 999 | 7,908 | ———— | ———— |
| July............................ | 2,473 | 7,754 | 1,038 | 7,380 | 1,392 | 8,035 | ———— | ———— |
| August............................ | 1,713 | 8,773 | 957 | 9,657 | 1,551 | 8,156 | ———— | ———— |
| September............................ | 1,735 | 7,715 | 1,580 | 12,549 | 1,461 | 7,609 | ———— | ———— |
| October............................ | 1,238 | 5,730 | 1,441 | 11,848 | 1,724 | 8,302 | ———— | ———— |
| November............................ | 1,658 | 7,157 | 869 | 8,053 | 1,787 | 9,917 | ———— | ———— |
| December............................ | 1,084 | 5,430 | 931 | 6,226 | 1,539 | 6,891 | ———— | ———— |

[1]Data collected by border inspectors, Bureau of Plant Quarantine, California Department of Agriculture.
[2]One-half month only.

## FAMILY COMPOSITION AND RACE OF MIGRANTS

Border data, as arranged in table 3, show the predominantly family characteristic of the migrants. Of the 259,654 migrants who entered the state between June 16, 1935 and December 31, 1937, 42,449 traveled singly and 217,205 as members of family groups. During this period of 2½ years there was no marked change in the relative proportion of single individuals to families. However, it is probable that the number of single individuals entering the state is concealed by their attachment in some cases to family groups, and that the actual number of single persons was greater than shown.

There seems to be some slight tendency toward an increase in the number of passengers per car. In 1935 the average was 4.1, in 1936 it was 4.6, and in 1937 it rose to 4.7. Migrants from Oklahoma, Arkansas, and Missouri had an appreciably higher number of passengers per car than the travelers from the other states which are important sources of emigration.

The great majority of the migrants are of the white race, and observation confirms that they are of native American stock. Mexican migrants are principally returning Californians, Arizonans, Texans, and New Mexicans. They constitute, however, less than 4 percent of the migrants. The Filipinos rank immediately after the Mexicans in importance, and they travel characteristically as individuals. Negroes lag in numbers behind the Mexican and Filipino groups, but it is possible that the Negroes may play an increasingly important role in the future.

TABLE 3—Migrants "in Need of Manual Employment" Entering the State of California by Motor Vehicle via Border Stations, June 16, 1935-Mar. 31, 1938, Classified by Race and Family [1]

| Month | Total number of— | | White | | Colored | | Mexican | | Filipino | | Other | |
|---|---|---|---|---|---|---|---|---|---|---|---|---|
| | Cars | Pass-engers | Sin-gles | In family | Sin-gles | In family | Sin-gles | In family | Sin-gles | In family | Sin-gles | In family |
| Total.............. | 63,123 | 289,299 | 39,775 | 226,663 | 1,008 | 3,155 | 1,665 | 11,221 | 3,860 | 397 | 93 | 1,462 |
| 1935[2]................ | 13,676 | 57,017 | 9,297 | 41,702 | 181 | 520 | 451 | 3,135 | 1,122 | 161 | 72 | 376 |
| 1936................ | 21,378 | 97,672 | 12,729 | 77,200 | 396 | 1,045 | 533 | 3,313 | 1,642 | 151 | 13 | 650 |
| 1937................ | 22,167 | 104,976 | 14,232 | 83,505 | 284 | 1,192 | 521 | 3,788 | 979 | 77 | 8 | 300 |
| 1938[3]................ | 5,902 | 29,634 | 3,517 | 24,256 | 147 | 398 | 160 | 985 | 117 | 8 | ---- | 46 |

[1]Date collected by border inspectors, Bureau of Plant Quarantine, California Department of Agriculture.
[2]June 16 to Dec. 31.
[3]First quarter only.

## ROUTES OF ENTRY

Roughly, six of every ten migrants entering California do so via highways crossing the state of Arizona. The routes of entry of the remainder are divided almost equally between Oregon and Nevada. The preponderant use of Arizona as a route of entry is explained by the geographic origin of the great majority of the migrants and to the existence of greater work opportunities while enroute through Texas, New Mexico, and Arizona (particularly the last named), during the fall and winter months. To a lesser extent the volume of the flow across the Arizona border is also affected by seasonal exchanges of agricultural workers between California and Arizona.

Returning Californians weight materially the number of migrants entering the state via the Oregon border. For out-of-state migrants, Nevada is a more natural route than Oregon, and almost two such migrants come via Nevada for every one that enters via Oregon. In contrast, Californians returning across the Oregon border outnumber those returning through Nevada to such an extent as almost to wipe out the difference in out-of-state migrants and thus equalize the total flow of migrants across the borders of the two states.

## OCCUPATIONAL STATUS OF REFUGEES

The SRA of Imperial County, California, has tabulated the previous occupational status of the heads of the 320 transient families who requested relief between 1935 and the middle of 1937 and whose previous residence in another state was verified. The significance of this sample lies in the fact that Imperial County is the gateway through which a large part of the refugees enter California and the place where many of them find their first employment. However, since these families represent relief applicants only and are drawn from a single county, they obviously constitute a sample statistically inadequate to represent a migration to California which has numbered from 90,000-100,000 persons a year during the past three years. Generalizations based upon close numerical comparisons, therefore, should be avoided.

Nevertheless, the data reveal the occupational character of the migration in its broad outlines.

*TABLE 4—Origin and Previous Occupations of 320 Transient Families Requesting Relief in Imperial County, Calif., 1935-37[1]*

*[For explanation of numbers in Oklahoma, Texas, and Arkansas, see footnote 1, below]*

| State of origin | Total number of families | Occupational experience | | | | | Non-farm |
| | | Farm— | | | | | |
| | | Owner | Tenant | Share-cropper | Laborer | Total farm[2] | |
|---|---|---|---|---|---|---|---|
| All families | 320 | 5 | 41 | 37 | 105 | 175 | 170 |
| Drought States | 274 | 5 | 40 | 37 | 96 | 169 | 116 |
| Oklahoma | 123 | 2 | 28 | 31 | 38 | 94 | 47 |
| Eastern Oklahoma (No. 244) | 44 | 2 | 12 | 10 | 15 | 38 | 14 |
| Southwest Oklahoma (No. 213 and 214A) | 31 | ——— | 7 | 11 | 10 | 25 | 9 |
| Central Oklahoma (No. 242) | 15 | ——— | 2 | 1 | 3 | 6 | 10 |
| Southern Oklahoma (No. 247) | 5 | ——— | 1 | ——— | 3 | 4 | 1 |
| Other | 16 | ——— | 4 | 4 | 4 | 12 | 7 |
| Texas | 52 | 3 | 5 | 1 | 19 | 26 | 31 |
| Black Prairie (No. 252) | 14 | 1 | ——— | ——— | 5 | 6 | 9 |
| Plains (No. 215 and 216B) | 8 | ——— | 1 | 1 | 5 | 5 | 6 |
| Southwest Oklahoma-Texas (No. 213 and 214A) | 7 | ——— | 2 | ——— | 1 | 3 | 4 |
| North Central Texas (No. 217) | 3 | 1 | 1 | ——— | 1 | 3 | ——— |
| Lower Rio Grande (No. 224) | 3 | ——— | ——— | ——— | 2 | 2 | 1 |
| Corpus Christi (No. 223) | 2 | ——— | ——— | ——— | 1 | 1 | 1 |
| Other | 15 | 1 | 1 | 0 | 4 | 6 | 10 |
| Arizona | 14 | ——— | ——— | ——— | 7 | 7 | 8 |
| Arkansas | 35 | ——— | 3 | 4 | 17 | 21 | 16 |
| Black and Cache River Bottoms (No. 287 A-B) | 7 | ——— | ——— | ——— | 6 | 6 | 2 |
| Other | 28 | ——— | 3 | 4 | 11 | 15 | 14 |
| Missouri | 13 | ——— | 2 | ——— | 3 | 5 | 8 |
| New Mexico | 13 | ——— | ——— | ——— | 3 | 3 | 8 |
| Colorado | 6 | ——— | 1 | ——— | 2 | 3 | 3 |
| Nebraska | 5 | ——— | 1 | 1 | 3 | 3 | 2 |
| Iowa | 5 | ——— | ——— | ——— | 1 | 1 | 4 |
| Others | 8 | ——— | ——— | ——— | 3 | 3 | 5 |
| Pacific States | 8 | ——— | ——— | ——— | 3 | 3 | 6 |
| Industrial States | 17 | ——— | ——— | ——— | 1 | 1 | 16 |
| Southern States | 18 | ——— | ——— | 1 | 4 | 4 | 14 |
| New England States | 2 | ——— | ——— | ——— | 1 | 1 | 1 |
| Puerto Rico | 1 | ——— | ——— | ——— | ——— | ——— | 1 |

[1]*Data by courtesy of Robert S. Elliott, Mrs. Mildred Standler, and social-service staff of Imperial County, S.R.A. Data cover period 1935 to June 1937, with occasional figures from 1934, as indicated. County groupings and numbers in Oklahoma, Texas, and Arkansas follow the map "Type of farming areas in the United States, 1930" which accompanies "Types of Farming in the United States" (Bureau of the Census, 1933).*

[2]*The total farm figure may be less than the sum of persons with all types of farm experience, since some reported more than 1 type of previous farm experience.*

Previous farm experience was reported by 175 family heads. Five had been farm owners, forty-three had been tenants, thirty-eight had been sharecroppers, and 106 had been farm laborers (table 4). A few reported having worked in more than one farm status, probably in most instances representing descending steps on the agricultural ladder.

The proportion of persons with farm experience, including experiences in grades above laborer, is markedly higher among those from Oklahoma, Texas, and Arkansas, the principal sources of the migration, than among the refugees as a whole. Thus, all five of the former owners were from these states, as were also 38 of the 43 tenants, 37 of the 38 sharecroppers, and 75 of the 106 farm laborers, although only two-thirds of the transients included in the sample came from this source.

It is a common story among former farm owners who have joined the migrants in Imperial County that they lost their equities, when the price of cotton fell after the war, and became tenants or sharecroppers; that they became laborers and later migrants when cotton prices fell again in the early thirties and when this depression was followed by drought and by mechanization of the cotton farms.

It is noteworthy that 141 transients from Oklahoma, Texas, and Arkansas reported previous farm experience, and only ninety-four reported nonfarm experience. In the entire sample 175 reported farm experience and 170 nonfarm experience, a more nearly even balance. But twenty-five of those who reported nonfarm experience had also worked on farms. Some farm laborers were included among the refugees from every state or group of states.

Those who reported a nonfarm occupation had worked in miscellaneous business and industrial activities. Many of these were from rural towns and small cities dependent on the trade of the countryside. Adverse conditions on the farms dislodged them, too.

## SOURCES OF EMIGRATION

Light upon the sources of emigration is thrown by cross-tabulation of occupational status with areas of previous residence. Geographical concentration of origin, scattered origins forecasting potential migration from other important areas, and the dependence of emigration on agricultural conditions in particular areas stand clearly revealed.

The eastern Oklahoma cotton area, characterized by the census as "cotton, some livestock, dairy, self-sufficing," was the source of forty-four, or 14 percent, of the entire 320 transient families. Of these, thirty-eight came from farms; two had been owners, twelve tenants, ten sharecroppers, and fifteen farm laborers.

The southwest Oklahoma-Texas cotton area was the origin of thirty-eight of these families who requested relief in Imperial Valley. Of these, twenty-eight were from farms. Nine had been tenants, eleven sharecroppers, and eleven farm laborers. In both areas drought, depression, and recently power farming have been active factors in dislodgment of rural population.[2]

Among other areas of concentrated exodus are to be noted:

(1) Central Oklahoma (general farming, cotton, livestock, dairy, poultry), was the origin of fifteen transient families of whom two were tenants, one a sharecropper, and three farm laborers.

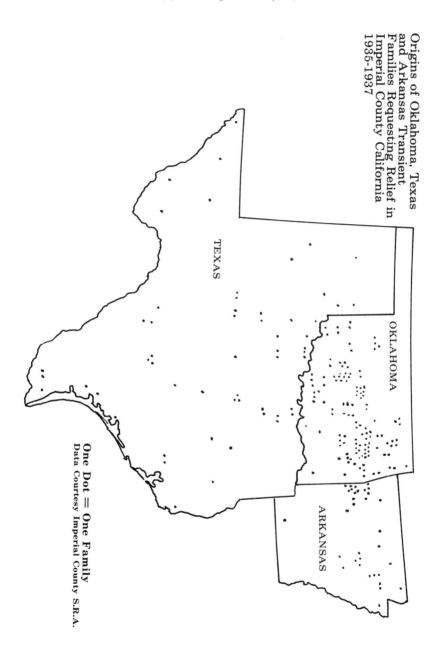

Origins of Oklahoma, Texas
and Arkansas Transient
Families Requesting Relief in
Imperial County California
1935-1937

One Dot = One Family
Data Courtesy Imperial County S.R.A.

(2) Northeast Oklahoma (general farming, livestock, dairy, poultry, self-sufficing), was the origin of twelve transients of whom two were tenants, five sharecroppers, and three farm laborers. Six emigrants reported nonfarm occupations. The entire eastern half of Oklahoma, together with adjoining counties in Kansas, Missouri, and northwestern Arkansas, have recently been characterized as "an outstanding problem area" of "low industrial stability, superimposed on submarginal agriculture."[3]

(3) Ouachita Mountains in western Arkansas and eastern Oklahoma where self-sufficing agriculture predominates, with some cotton and general farming, was the origin of sixteen transient families, of which two were tenants, two sharecroppers, and four farm laborers (one had status as both sharecropper and laborer).[4] Seven family heads previously engaged in occupations other than farming.

(4) Plains. From both high and low plains in west-central Texas where drought and mechanization are dislodging cotton farmers, many emigrants have come to California. Of the eight transient families reported from this area, the heads of five were farm laborers, two of whom had also been tenant and sharecropper.

The areas of scattering are important as well as those of concentration, for they indicate that emigrant contacts have already been established which will facilitate prompt movement if unsettled conditions should spread in those areas. Among the more important areas from this viewpoint of potential emigration are:

(1) Black Wax Prairie, the richest of the western cotton lands. This is represented on the map by the thin line of dots stretching north and south through central Texas from the Red River to San Antonio. Of fourteen transient families originating in this area, nine had nonfarm occupations, six had been farm laborers, and one had been a farm owner. If use of tractors continues to spread and dislodge farm families in the Black Wax, emigration from this area may develop volume.

(2) Lower Rio Grande Valley. From this area of intensive irrigated agriculture at the southern tip of Texas came three families, two of them farm laborers, one nonfarm.

(3) Corpus Christi. From this area came two families, one of them farm labor, the other nonfarm. The news sent back by emigrants to California could spread very fast and effectively in this great concentration point for migrant cotton pickers.

(4) Lonoke and White counties in the rice, cotton, and strawberry section of Arkansas already almost constitute an area of concentration. Failure of the berry crop because of drought and displacement of families by mechanization are factors. From these two counties came a transient sharecropper family, a farm labor family, one which had been both sharecropper and laborer, and two nonfarm families.

(5) The arrival in Imperial County of even a single destitute white tenant family from Mississippi County, Ark., stirs imagination of the

stream which might some day flow westward from the rich and densely populated delta lands where the tenant farmers are organizing and tractors are cutting white and Negro families from the land.

The areas of scattering have been described in detail in order to suggest the variety and expanse of the sources which may develop importance. The Negro is already beginning to appear among the emigrants, although the overwhelming majority are native American whites. In the Imperial Valley group of transients there were only eight Negro families from Oklahoma and three Mexican families from Texas and Arizona. Some day the racial aspects of this migration to the West may assume greater importance, as they already do in the migration of farm families of the Southeast into Florida.

The necessity, therefore, of close observation of these areas and factors, of the collection of more extensive migration data, and of their analysis by status of the migrants and by counties of origin, should be obvious. Only in this way can the problems which arise when more emigrants join the flooded agricultural labor markets of the West be anticipated and met.

*Land Policy Review,* vol. V, no. 1
(U.S. Department of Agriculture, Bureau of Agricultural Economics),
January 1942

# NONSTATISTICAL NOTES
# FROM THE FIELD

My method in the field is to observe, then to select. But some of my statistician friends demand numbers. When I tell them in detail what happened to a farm family I saw displaced in the Cotton Belt, they are likely to say, "What's that to us if you can't tell how many that has happened to?"

Perhaps I can't, and I answer, "By the time you statisticians know the numbers, what I'm trying to tell you about in advance will be history, and you'll be too late."

My statistician friends tell me gently that "observations are notoriously unreliable." Well, I say, that depends upon how well they are made, and what's behind them, and what's done with them—like figures on the value of products sold, traded, or used, or the number of farms on a cotton plantation. My statistician friends seem to love averages, and to be dissatisfied with my description if it doesn't strike them as "average" for the county, state, or perhaps the nation; if it isn't average it isn't typical, and it's only the typical that counts.

Average of what? I ask myself. Typical of what? Aren't there many averages and many types? And if the average reveals, doesn't it by the same token conceal? Besides, maybe I'm not interested for the moment in averages. Maybe I'm looking for trends, and don't want to cancel out the very item where I think I see the "future" foreshadowed by "history," by averaging it with another where the "future" has not yet struck.

One of my statistician friends tells me that if I want to reveal what farm houses or farm laborers are like, I must describe or photograph as they come, say, every fifth and tenth house or laborer. In that procedure, he says, he would have more confidence than in what I do. Can he be as right as he is logical? I think no curator of a museum would choose his specimens that way.

Except that these thoughts seem to cross the minds of some of my friends—sometimes they tell me—I wouldn't bring them up as introduction to a few notes from recent field work of Dorothea Lange and mine in the Middlewest. The argument seems about as fruitful as those consuming and endless debates over induction versus deduction, heredity versus environment, theory versus practice, but no more so. Anyway, I do not feel that I have been misled. The results I get from observation stimulate my own thoughts more than many columns figures; they have opened issues of significance; they fortify me in one of the ways of work that I like most. I have nothing against statistics.

## NOTHING FOR THEM

"It's a man's own fault if he goes broke—in America. He don't need to go broke if he uses his head for more than a hatrack. I started as a renter of 140 acres. Now I operate five farms. I hire six men during harvest, and have two big tractors, and run 1,620 acres." Our car, with its "foreign" license, was standing in the middle of a deserted block-and-a-half-long main street of western Nebraska. We paused to face the dead fronts of the Bonanza Hotel, the largest dance hall in the county, and the Angora State Bank. Obviously strangers shocked by the desolation, we needed to be put straight. So the big-shouldered, energetic farmer who walked by undertook to do it.

He continued: "When the drought was worst we got six or seven bushels to the acre and wondered if it was worth combining. This year we'll get thirty bushels of wheat. I made money all through—they've got the triple A, you know. Now I own the beer parlor, and all these town buildings for wheat storehouses."

As I passed the open door of the bank the voice of an old man, lying slumped in his clothing on an iron bed, called me to enter. All was junk and confusion within, but the solid square construction and iron vault confirmed the faded sign over the door. The old man was father of the farmer. He'd paid $500 for the building when the bank failed. He "came to that country when it was new, from Aberdeen, South Dakota, with $33,000." In 1919 he "paid income tax on $960 a month." One year he "went to the Holy Land with Aimee Semple McPherson and heard the Gospel twice a day." He gave his wife $54,000, but now she and the money were both gone.

Pointing south to a sturdy farmhouse surrounded by wheat, he went on: "Last year I bought that eighty and that house 36 by 36 with full basement, for $1,000 paid in hand. Now see the wheat! A third of them shocks are mine."

On the hill above town stood a white church, closed, wheat up to the door. "Where are the members?" we asked. "They all dried out." Everywhere wheat, and the signs of emptiness of people. The gas station man said, "Now they're hellin' around here for labor to harvest the wheat. Nine combines came by here today; 120 went through here last season. They travel on rubber from Texas, Oklahoma, and Kansas, and work to North Dakota and Montana."

Will the farmers and the townsmen who left come back now that there's wheat and rain? "No," the energetic farmer said, "they're not well-enough fixed to come back. There's nothing for them."

## ROSEBUD

Before 1909 the southern tier of counties west of the Missouri in central South Dakota was covered with grass. Sheep and cattle grazed upon it. It was known as the Rosebud Indian Reservation.

Beginning in 1909, blocks of it were opened to homesteaders in a series of land lotteries. I remember as a boy hearing people consider whether to keep their jobs in the city or to take up a homestead on the plains. I remember the talk when trainloads of landseekers went through Sioux City bound for the Rosebud when word came to the winners of the drawings, when trips were made to see the lands that were won, to decide finally whether or not to homestead the claims.

"Maladministration of the homestead laws," says a governmental report, "which was encouraged by predatory interests, led to the settlement of areas admittedly submarginal for farming purposes. During the war almost all the available land was broken for wheat, and excellent crops were raised when rainfall was normal and no pests appeared."

A generation after settlement, in the summer of 1941, came my first look at this Rosebud country. Almost the first sight after crossing the border from Nebraska was a vacant farmstead. A few miles farther brought us to an "inland town," a county seat. No rail or bus, a dozen telephones, few baths, and mostly outside toilets. But a cleaner, trimmer town than you imagine, and the people certainly are not shiftless. Between 1930 and 1940 the county lost one-third of its farmers.

"We've lost a lot of good men. They got discouraged and sold out. The state rural credit got the farms, sold the improvements off the place, leased the land to the big operators. The triple A wheat benefit goes with the land; they ought to limit the farmer's benefit to his own ten-year average.

"Half the businessmen in town are farmers. If a man's in one kind of business, it seems like he shouldn't go into competition with the man on the farm trying to make a living from it. But if it weren't for the triple A benefits there just wouldn't be a town here at all."

When you're in the field, don't expect people to agree on the triple A or on anything else. When they don't, maybe one of them is wrong. More often each is giving you another side of the truth, which has many. Accounts seldom divide simply into the true and the false.

Twenty miles east we talked with a crossroads merchant in a little town where many people left and went to Oregon.

Not all the people left, of course. Farmers' families are fewer, and it's tough on crossroads storekeepers. But the county seat in this belt of depopulation still grows. We had seen the same thing in northwestern Texas cotton counties during 1937. The census says this town grew from 720 population in 1930 to 1,013 in 1940. Farmers are the pawns of the game; they are moved about by greater forces. After years of drought and grasshoppers, they can't pay taxes.

"The land goes to the county and the county sells the houses cheap. The postmaster or anybody with money to invest buys the houses and moves them to town." Around the fringes of the county seat are twenty or more houses with sheet metal over the chimney hole in the roof, with new foundations, or with other fresh signs that they've been moved.

It's the same in the next county seat to the east: the people leave the farms to certify on WPA in the towns; the houses follow the people, hauled in, set down, stuccoed up, and rented out to them. Seventy of these was the count by local residents given to us in a town which reported 457 people to the census of 1940.

And in the next county seat beyond they say the number of farm houses moved in is about fifty. You can see them easily, out around the edges. They are the outward mark of what a rural sociologist labels, in professional jargon, "social-economic submergence in a plains state."

Maybe the housing shortage is worse because some people lacked foresight.

"A lot of people tore down the improvements on their farms to save taxes, and now wish they hadn't." Those houses could have earned rentals in town, or they could have stored free of charge the wheat crop of 1941.

## TOMBSTONES

Out in the country there are still empty staring windows to mark where farmers lived. There still are empty barns, silent windmills, and yards strewn with rusting iron and filled with overgrown weeds. Will the farmers ever return? It is more likely that these buildings are tombstones.

Nine miles east of Winner at a crossroad we pulled up short. In my brief case was an early report mimeographed by the Federal Emergency Relief Administration. On maps of 1935 the township where our car stood was shaded to denote "severe devastation" by "grasshopper infestation," "severe erosion" by wind, and was marked to indicate 52 percent of the farms already "abandoned." A photograph showed "grove and buildings covered by drifting soil," with those undulations and ripples on swollen soil banks so familiar from the pictures of dust bowls.

Now, six years later, we are standing on this same spot. Gleaming stubble of wheat rings closely what was the home acre. Underneath a cover of tickleweed is the soft and swelling line of soil drifts that choked to death the trees of the windbreak. Weeds and mounds mark the foundations of buildings. A lone tree in leaf shows perhaps where the well was put down—a spring of life on the grave of defeat of a farm family.

But this year the plains are covered with wheat. Out in the country the combines are running. Laundry hangs from the lines to mark those farmhouses where men and women have stuck it out. For some it is still tough. A farmer crosses the fence to our car, places his foot on the running board and says he's not finished yet, but he's "lived here twenty-five years too long."

For others who have taken over the lands of those who are gone, 1941 is a year of big reward. A sweating man in trousers and undershirt drives up to a service station, fills up, and drives away. "That man," says our host, "is running a combine night and day. This year he will clear $7,000."

"Science and invention," a local agricultural official explains, "are what makes it possible for a man owning 320 acres to run a 3,000-acre farm."

Thoughtfully in 1935 the supervisor of rural research in South Dakota for the Federal Emergency Relief Administration wrote these words: ". . . a return of favorable climatic conditions will unquestionably result in a new influx of farmers who will probably go through the same history as the earlier group. To prevent this, it is necessary that some measure of control be exercised over resettlement to provide intelligence for a rational depopulation of the county."

Framed as a question, the same thought was in our minds as we drove through the Rosebud six years later. Was this depopulation "rational"?

A homesteader gave us his perspective: "Thirty years ago the people got land for 75 cents and $1.25 an acre for homesteading. Now a man without money has no chance here. The big cattlemen and big wheat men got it sewed up."

Toward dusk that day we came upon a family in an old car with an Oklahoma license. The man had just shot a rabbit for supper, and was cleaning his rifle barrel. Yes, they work as migrants in the fields of California. Now they labor in the wheat harvest across the Dakotas. We did not ask, but the answer was in our minds: Yes, they'll be back in California, and in the cotton from Corpus Christi to Phoenix, and in the strawberries from east of Portland to north of Little Rock, and in the apple orchards of Yakima and north of Ogden, and in the potatoes near Kearney, and back in Oklahoma with the folks, and again next year in the wheat of the Dakotas where so many farmers have left.

## AGRICULTURAL LADDER

Northwest of Des Moines for 150 miles and more the barns are big, the barnyards trim, the houses four-square, the farmsteads bordered by trees. We pulled into one of these yards opposite a great red barn, with the owner's name and Plainview Farm lettered in white paint across its face. The farmer was broad, stocky, overalled, heavy-armed—the kind I had known as a boy, the kind made known the country over by Ding's cartoons of the Iowa farmer.

His story was success. He was the farm success legend of the middle border in the flesh. I grew up surrounded by the legend of which he is the epitome. That legend has enveloped the Mississippi Valley and permeated the minds of our best thinkers about our national agriculture. I say this without disparagement, for great values are embedded in the legend. But still it is a legend, part fact, part fancy, revealing with fidelity the strivings, ideals, and character of a people. This was the first good look I'd had at it since I was a boy, returning after long observation of industrialized farming in the West and some good looks at tenants and plantations in the South.

Hired man, 1901: "In 1901, my uncle hired me out to a farmer at $160 a year and board. I saved $100. I was seventeen years old and an orphan. I hired out twelve years, by the month, and made extra money threshing. The main object is the saving. I had saved $4,000 by 1913 when I got married. That year I bought equipment and farmed 160 acres on shares, two-fifths of the grain to the landlord and two-fifths of the corn. When I got off the rented place in 1918, I had $18,000 cash. With that I bought eighty acres at $225 an acre, and then another 80 acres at $150. In 1937 I bought forty acres for $100 an acre, making 200 acres.

"At one time—1919 it was—I was offered $500 an acre for my 160. If I had taken it, I would have bought some more land at high prices and then lost it all in the depression. So many here have done that. Now they're on relief, on the county. Many of them were well-to-do. Four families owned this farm before us. Not anyone who had it has anything now."

Hired man, 1941: The Plainview farmer continued: "My hired man's father owned a farm near here, also 200 acres. He had ten children. He said, 'We'll get more land for the children.' So he bought another section and mortgaged both farms to pay for it and lost both. The children are now working as hired help and WPA, all but one who is a renter.

"I pay my hired man $50 a month now. I give him a house, milk, eggs, garden, and electricity—and he's hard up, just as hard up one Saturday night as the next. His wife says they 'live only once and they're going to town a couple of nights a week if they want to. If the banks are going to go that way, we're going to spend the money before the banks go. Look at his dad. He worked hard and saved and owned 200 acres. See how he came out. We'll work hard till we're sixty-five and then live on a pension.' "

Turning tide: The successful hired man of 1901 was perplexed that his own hired man of 1941 failed to recognize that "the main object is the saving." But he had no ready answer. He was disturbed, too, by the lowered value of character as a business asset, and bothered by the doubtful social morality of consolidating land to make farms larger, which seems only in line with ideals long accepted, and with the sound economics of getting ahead.

"You couldn't find another man in the county that has followed in my footsteps," he went on. "You can't do it now without you got some backing. You can't get the credit; they used to place some value on a man's word. Now it seems they don't. Yes, it's profitable for a man to farm more land than we do; I'm buying another eighty. It's the best place I know to put my money. But it's not so good for the country. It puts the other fellow out; he'll go and live on Uncle Sam."

IOWA

About 1855, a German Protestant sect, the Community of True Inspiration, bought 26,000 acres of good land in eastern Iowa. The grandchildren, great-grandchildren, and even a few of the children are there today. Their forefathers pooled their goods when they went to the frontier before the Civil War and founded the seven villages of Amana. Their religion didn't command that, like early Christians, they should have all things in common, but it permitted it. At the time, it seemed to them the only way to ensure that their group would survive. The 26,000-acre farm was run as a unit, the society owned everything, no wages were paid, only small book credits at the society commissary. In time small factories were set up to balance agriculture and to employ the growing number of hands.

After three-quarters of a century, the people of Amana voted a change in 1932. Change, they realized at last, was necessary, inevitable. So they voted out communism in the form they had known it. No violent revolution, no throwing overboard old faiths, no jettisoning of the aged and the dissenters, no breach of the deep and pervading calm. Deliberately they chose private property in houses, and wages; private kitchens in every home, and no work, no eat. The 26,000-acre farm still belongs to the society of which all are members, and is still run as a unit. The woolen blanket mill, the refrigerator factory, the meat markets, stores, gas stations, and cabinet shop belong to the society. But the members now work for wages. Modified capitalism they call it—cooperative.

The society is very much alive today. I came upon one of the villages on U.S. 6—a charming French village pattern, inhabited by innately cultured and friendly German-Americans set down in the sea of isolated farmsteads and individualistic farmers that is the Middlewest. It is something out of a past strange to most of us. Its history is in the books but the society isn't embalmed between covers. It harks back to century-old dreams of Utopians, yet it was not built by idealists reforming the world. It was founded by realists seeking only survival. It is their success that today life pulses strongly through Amana.

What's the meaning of the great change of 1932? I asked a middle-aged man waiting for his meat at the butcher shop: how is it different now? His eyes began to twinkle and he spoke slowly, "Well, now the hayfever bucks work on the straw pile in the middle of the season."

Practical enough, I thought, for my own experience gave me comprehension, but I wanted to know more.

So I went on: "You didn't used to have poverty, did you?"

Well, each one of us had as much as the others."

I pressed the question: "Now that you have private property, and wages only if you work, have you poverty, too, like we have outside?"

"No," he said with understanding, and another twinkle, "No, but I think I can see signs of it coming."

At the moment I couldn't think of what to ask him next, so I left. But his replies have been pulling at me ever since to go back and find out more.

## ON A CAMPUS

Up the broadwalk came one of my own profession, a man justly recognized for a lifetime of work in his specialty. We paused and spoke.

"I, too," he said, "am writing. I am writing a history of agriculture."

Perhaps I can suggest a source or two that might aid you?" I volunteered, naming a good but little-known piece of research in local history of agricultural labor.

"Oh, but I'm writing the history of just agriculture," he explained.

"Yes?" I replied, "I've always held the hope that I could raise in men's minds the question, are farm laborers a part of agriculture?"

"Oh, certainly they are a part of agriculture," he said, ready to agree, "just as much a part of agriculture as—teams."

"Now you've proved the point of my question to the hilt," I said. "I shall now use this story to help others to see the point."

"Don't get me wrong," he warned, "don't say I said that laborers were animals."

"No," I replied, "I know you didn't, and I know you are a very humane man. I shall not quote you wrong."

I started to go my way and he half turned to go his.

"Sometime," he said thoughtfully, as we parted, "I'd like to talk more about this."

# NOTES

Mexicans North of the Rio Grande

1. Figures on wages and earnings refer to 1928 or 1929 when I was in the field; in many instances, they doubtless have fallen since that time.

2. Yet the assembly of California had just passed and sent to the senate a bill permitting racial segregation of Mexican children who were of Indian blood.

Documentary History of the Strike of the Cotton Pickers in California 1933

1. See "Agricultural Strikes of 1933" in *Hearings before the House Committee on Labor*, 74 Cong., 1 Sess., H.R. 6288, pp. 342-67.

2. Growers protested against this headline.

3. American Civil Liberties Union, "A Strike is Criminal Syndicalism in California, March 1931." In April 1930, a series of raids, netting 103 arrests, was made "in anticipation of the coming opening of the cantaloupe season. A number of meetings have been held, with a view to organizing for increased wages and to formulate demands as to working conditions." (*Brawley News*, April 15, 1930)

4. Chronology of principal strikes, or attempted strikes, in which Cannery and Agricultural Workers' Industrial Union representatives were active during 1932, 1933, and early 1934: (a) in California, June 1932, San Mateo pear pickers; July, Brentwood fruit pickers; December, Vacaville orchard pruners; January 1933, continuation of Vacaville strike; April, Monterey lettuce workers, San Jose and Alameda County pea pickers; May, pea pickers' strike continued, San Diego and El Monte strawberry harvesters, Watsonville pea and lettuce workers; June, San Leandro pea pickers, San Jose cherry pickers, San Gabriel Valley berry pickers; July, San Gabriel Valley berry pickers' strike continued, Contra Costa apricot workers, Modesto apricot pickers; August, Salinas sugar beet workers, Sacramento and Fairfield pear pickers, Bakersfield grape pickers, San Diego tomato and chile harvesters, Chico peach cutters, Salinas lettuce pickers, San Jose pear pickers, Tagus ranch and Fresno region peach pickers; September, Gridley peach cutters, Oxnard beet workers, Fresno grape pickers; October, Lodi grape pickers, southern San Joaquin Valley cotton pickers; November, Imperial Valley pea pickers; December, Imperial Valley lettuce workers; January 1934, lettuce workers strike continued; February, Imperial Valley pea pickers; April, Alameda County pea pickers, and Florin berry pickers; (b) in other states of the western district: June 1933, New

Mexico cotton choppers, Oregon strawberry pickers; July, Arizona melon workers; August, Oregon pear pickers; September, Oregon hop pickers; October, Salt River Valley, Arizona, cotton pickers.

5. The transition in emphasis which came in early winter, 1932, shows clearly in the trend of the headlines of the *Western Worker:* Hunger march 'Frisco Jan. 11 (January 1, 1932); Open winter relief fight (August 15); Many counties preparing for hunger marches (September 1); 3,000 mass at Alameda Hall of Records for jobless relief (October 24); 400 ranch workers strike at Vacaville (November 28); Jobless to march on Sacramento (December 5); Fight for cash relief (February 4, 1933); Rally to Mooney meet (March 20); Strike ties up Cal. pea fields (April 24); 1,500 strike in So. Cal. fields (June 12); Cherry pickers heroic stand against terror (June 26); Workers answer "Recovery Act" with strikes (July 17); Strikes sweep California fields (August 21).

6. Located at Fresno, Dinuba, Earlimart, Reedley, Visalia, Farmersville, Woodville, Exeter, Tulare, Tipton, Pixley, Delano, McFarland, Wasco, Shafter, Bakersfield, Arvin, Corcoran, and Hanford.

7. The growers reasoned a public defense for this wage rate.

8. See pp. 144-53

9. Receipt of federal money from the California State Emergency Relief Administration by local governmental relief organizations was dependent upon the willingness of the local bodies to extend aid to all needy persons whether residents or not. Some California counties preferred to forego federal assistance rather than accede to the requirement.

Field Reports to Social Security Board on Employment in Agriculture

1. "The farmers don't like relief (for the laborers), but they can't expect them to roll up in a cocoon for the winter."

Migratory Agricultural Workers on the Pacific Coast

1. Julius T. Wendzel, "Distribution of Hired Farm Laborers in the United States," *Monthly Labor Review,* September 1937.

2. Anita E. Faverman, "A Study of the Health of 1000 Children of Migratory Agricultural Laborers in California," *California State Board of Health,* 1937.

3. Bertha S. Underhill, "A Study of 132 Families in California Cotton Camps," *California Department of Social Welfare,* 1937.

4. "Workers on Relief in the United States," *Works Progress Administration, March 1935.*

## Labor Refugee Migration to California, 1937

1. See *Monthly Labor Review,* March (p. 595) and April (p. 852) 1938. Farm-tractor sales for use in the United States reached the record volume of $171,000,000 in 1936. In 1937 a new record of $214,000,000 was established. Between 1937 and 1938 farm tractors in use in the United States increased 10.5 percent. In the ten southern cotton states they increased 13.3 percent. In 1930 the proportion of all farm tractors which was found in the cotton states was only 12.2 percent. By 1937 it had advanced to 15.2 percent (incorrectly given as 18.5 percent in *Monthly Labor Review* for April 1938, p. 865), and in 1938 it rose again to 15.6 percent. Between 1930 and 1937, the number of farm tractors in the United States rose only 50.3 percent (incorrectly given as 23.7 percent), as compared with an increase of 80.7 percent in the cotton states.

2. See *Monthly Labor Review,* March (p. 595) and April (p. 852) 1938.

3. Pierce Williams, "Hard-Core Unemployment; the Challenge of Permanently Depressed Areas," *Survey Graphics,* June 1938, p. 350.

4. Type of farming area No. 248. Counties: (Okla.) Atoka, Latimer, Leflore, McCurtain; (Ark.) Logan, Sebastian, Yell.

# BIBLIOGRAPHY: OTHER WRITINGS BY PAUL TAYLOR ON THIS PERIOD

*Mexican Labor in the United States*
*Imperial Valley*
*Valley of the South Platte, Colorado*
Migration Statistics, I, II, III, IV
Racial School Statistics, 1927
Dimmit County, Winter Garden District, South Texas
Bethlehem, Pennsylvania
Chicago and the Calumet Region
A Spanish-Mexican Peasant Community, Arandas in Jalisco, Mexico, 1933
"More Bars Against Mexicans," *Survey Graphic*, April 1931
"Whither Self-Help?" *Survey Graphic*, July 1934
"Some Problems of Agricultural Labor in California," Conference Bulletin, California Conference of Social Work, August 1936
"Historical Background of California Farm Labor" (with Tom Vasey), *Rural Sociology*, September 1936
"Contemporary Background of California Farm Labor" (with Tom Vasey), *Rural Sociology*, December 1936
"Migratory Farm Labor in the United States," *Monthly Labor Review*, March 1937
"Power Farming and Labor Displacement in the Cotton Belt, 1937," *Monthly Labor Review*, March-April 1938
"The Place of Agricultural Labor in Society," Proceedings of Western Farm Economic Association, 1939
*An American Exodus: A Record of Human Erosion*, with Dorothea Lange; Reynal and Hitchcock, 1939; 2nd ed., Yale University Press, 1960
"Factors Underlying the Insecurity of Farm People in the Corn Belt" (with William W. Allan, *Interstate Migration*, Hearings Before Select Committee to Investigate the Interstate Migration of Destitute Citizens, 76th Congress, 3rd Session, Part 10, pp. 3245-3267
Testimony before Senate Committee Investigating *Violations of Free Speech and Rights of Labor*, 76th Congress, 2nd Session, Part 47, December 6, 1939, pp. 17311-17242, 17266-17286; Documentation and photographs, 17379-17394; Part 50, December 18, 1939, pp. 18198-18202
Hearings Before Temporary National Economic Committee, 76th Congress, 3rd Session, *Technology and Concentration of Economic Power*, April 24, 1940, pp. 17040-17078
*Forces that Jeopardize the Security of Farm People*, Hearings Before House Select Committee to Investigate Interstate Migration of Destitute Citizens, 76th Congress, 3rd Session, Part 10, pp.of 3245-3267

# INDEX

AAA, 196
Abel, Edson, 45, 100, 102-104,
107-108, 110
Abel, Stanley (supervisor, Kern
County Board of Supervisors),
31
Adams, R.L. (U.C. professor), 102
Adobe Cafe, 89
AF of L. *See* American Federation
of Labor
Agricultural Labor Bureau, 103
Agricultural Protective
Association, 39-40
Agriculture, California State
Board of. *See* California State
Board of Agriculture
Agriculture, College of, 134
Agriculture, Department of, x
Allen Ranch, John (Kern County),
47
Amana (Iowa), 239-240
American Civil Liberties Union,
25, 144
American Exodus, xii
American Federation of Labor
(AF of L), 27-28, 93, 123, 152,
161, 168
Arvin (Kern County), 38, 97
Arvin strike riot, 21, 25, 33, 36,
47, 78, 82, 86, 88-89, 97, 105,
120
Associated Farmers of California,
135, 220
"Aviso Oficial," 72
Aztec Circus, 61-62

Bakersfield, 5, 47, 217 illus.
Bakersfield Chamber of
Commerce, 40
Bakke, E. Wight, vii
Beet workers' union, 12
Black Wax Prairie, 197, 204
Blaisdell, Thomas C. (Social
Security), xi, 195, 197, 199
Bonnen, C.A. (professor), 200
Borstadt, A.J. (federal
immigration inspector), 54
Bosque Farms, 186
Bowen, J.H. (striker), 46
Bradley, Louis (striker), 78-79
Branion, R.C. (director, CERA),
93-95, 101, 111-112, 128-129,
140
Bravo, Enrique (Mexican consul),
21-22, 43, 54, 58, 69-72,
100-101, 106, 132
Brawley, 25, 217 illus.
Brite, Perry (chairman, Kern
County Board of Supervisors),
31, 93
Buckner, Van (sheriff, Kings
County), 24, 64, 67-68, 74,
76-78, 91-92, 95-96, 113, 132
Buford-Trenton tract (North
Dakota), 171
bull pens, 49, 52-53, 69
Burke County (North Dakota),
169
Burlington (North Dakota), 171
Burr, C.W. (CERA), 96

California Cotton Cooperative
Association, 140
California Emergency Relief
Administration (CERA), xi, 62,
92-93, 95, 112, 183, 242
California Farm Bureau
Federation, 19, 108, 110, 112,
134, 167-168
California Federation of Labor,
189
California Grange, 189
California Packing Corporation,
195
California State Board of
Agriculture, 167
California State Highway Patrol,
67, 74, 91-92, 110, 129, 166-167
California, University of. *See*
University of California
Calles, Elias (President of
Mexico), 54, 72-73
C&AWIU. *See* Cannery and
Agricultural Workers'
Industrial Union
Cannery and Agricultural
Workers' Industrial Union
(C&AWIU), 19, 26-27, 29-31,
59, 71, 104, 112-114, 120,
122-123, 141, 150, 153-158,
161, 241
Carter, T.J. (undersheriff), 88-89
Cato, E. Raymond (highway
patrol), 67, 91, 117
Caviness, Lee W., 199
Central Utah Dry Land
Adjustment Project, 187